Mavericks

Mystics,

and

Misfits

AMERICANS AGAINST THE GRAIN

—◆—

Arthur Hoyle

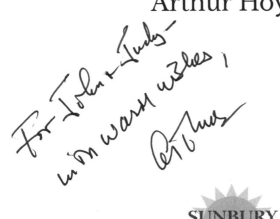

SUNBURY
PRESS

Mechanicsburg, PA USA

Published by Sunbury Press, Inc.
Mechanicsburg, Pennsylvania

www.sunburypress.com

For information about special discounts for bulk purchases, please contact Sunbury Press Orders Dept. at (855) 338-8359 or orders@sunburypress.com.

To request one of our authors for speaking engagements or book signings, please contact Sunbury Press Publicity Dept. at publicity@sunburypress.com.

FIRST SUNBURY PRESS EDITION: March 2020

Set in Adobe Garamond. Interior design by Crystal Devine | Cover by Lawrence Knorr. Edited by Lawrence Knorr.

Publisher's Cataloging-in-Publication Data
Names: Hoyle, Author, author.
Title: Mavericks, mystics, and misfits: Americans against the grain / Arthur Hoyle.
Description: First trade paperback edition. | Mechanicsburg, PA : Sunbury Press, 2020.
Summary: Arthur Hoyle recounts brief biographies of impactful American personalities from colonial times to present.
Identifiers: ISBN 978-1-620062-41-8 (softcover).
Subjects: BIOGRAPHY & AUTOBIOGRAPHY / Historical | BIOGRAPHY & AUTOBIOGRAPHY / Adventurers & Explorers | BIOGRAPHY & AUTOBIOGRAPHY / Famous | BIOGRAPHY & AUTOBIOGRAPHY / Social Activists | HISTORY / United States / General.

Product of the United States of America
0 1 1 2 3 5 8 13 21 34 55

Continue the Enlightenment!

Also by Arthur Hoyle

The Unknown Henry Miller: A Seeker in Big Sur

For Mimi, whose first gift to me was a pen

And in gratitude to Robert Archer

Americans have lost the sense, being made up as we are, that what we are has its origins in what *the nation* in the past has been; that there is a source in AMERICA for everything we think or do.

—William Carlos Williams, *In the American Grain*

Contents

Introduction

This book profiles exemplary American men and women whose lives collectively span the history of our country from the period of the first Puritan settlements to the present time. These individuals have been chosen because their life stories, though often at variance with the direction of the mainstream society around them, exhibit certain enduring qualities of the American character that persist despite the changing circumstances of time and place.

The traits that have come to be associated with a distinctly American character emerged during the early years of the country's settlement. They were formed as the Old World habits, customs, and attitudes that the first immigrants from Europe brought with them were confronted with the environmental conditions of a continent whose native inhabitants lived as a part of the wilderness around them, not separate from it in any kind of "civilization." The challenge for these first immigrants was to adapt their European traditions and modes of survival to the physical realities of the New World. This adaptation produced a new kind of man, the American.

The first immigrants to the New World had come primarily for two reasons. Some, like the Puritans who settled in New England, and the Quakers who later settled in Pennsylvania, were religious dissenters seeking freedom to practice their chosen forms of worship, practices that had marginalized them, and made them subject to persecution in their native England. Others, notably the Dutch, Swedes, and Germans who settled in New Netherland and the Delaware Valley, came primarily in search of greater economic opportunity—the chance to own the land on which they labored for survival and so to become independent, released from the age-old constraints of class that had limited their future prospects in the Old World. Still others came seeking both religious freedom and greater economic opportunity.

The circumstances that provoked these first migrants to leave the familiarity and comforts of their native lands, and the conditions that awaited them in the New World, called out a remarkable set of character traits. To leave their homeland, they had to be both dissatisfied and ambitious, as well as courageous, undeterred by venturing into the unknown and unfamiliar. To endure the long and dangerous passage across the sea, they had to be hardy of body and strong of mind. Once landed on the American continent, they had to be hard-working, resourceful, inventive, practical, able to function independently. And they had to cooperate to get along because they all faced the same physical challenges to survival. Both the political and the physical realities of life in the New World quickly erased class lines. All men were equal when facing the implacable demands of the wilderness. The traits that evolved as the European migrants adapted to conditions in the New World crystallized for the American imagination in iconic figures such as Daniel Boone, Davy Crockett, and James Fenimore Cooper's Natty Bumpo: men who could live off the land like the Indians, but who were not "savages."

The two seemingly contradictory traits that enabled survival in the New World—independence and cooperation—have unfolded in a dynamic tension across American history. Independence required the development of individualism and self-sufficiency. The need for cooperation required the recognition of each man's equality; it also encouraged conformity. A man must pursue his own interests and serve his own needs, but he must do this in a way that does not disturb the collective effort, or interfere with someone else's right to pursue a different interest. From these two imperatives sprang the basic values that were codified in America's Declaration of Independence from England: liberty (personal freedom), and equality (personal freedom for all). These two values have become the bedrock of the American character.

But a third value also took root in the New World, transplanted here by the Puritan and Quaker settlers: the value of dissent. These religious groups insisted on the right of individual conscience, a right that transcends the authority of public opinion and even the authority of law. The right of dissent is the supreme affirmation of individual rights—the right to whistle your own tune and to dispute the majority when you believe that its attitudes and policies threaten liberty and equality. One can regard the colonists' revolutionary war against the mother country, England, as a grand gesture of dissent that gave birth to America.

Dissent has continued to arise when people feel that one of the country's founding principles is being violated or kept unfulfilled. Some of the main historical causes of dissent have been slavery, Jim Crow laws, segregation, and discrimination against ethnic minorities; unjust treatment of Native American peoples; the subordinate political and economic status of women; and economic inequities between capital and labor. The dissent has been expressed in a variety of forms: speeches, writings, petitions, lawsuits, demonstrations, strikes, boycotts, civil disobedience, riots, and rebellions. Most dissent has been an attempt to address and reform America's failures to adhere to its initial declaration that all men (and women) are created equal and are therefore equally entitled to life, liberty, and the pursuit of happiness.

In that reforming sense, all the men and women profiled in this book are dissenters. In one way or another, they have presented an alternative to some prevailing tendency of their time and place that holds the country back from keeping its promise or realizing its potential, and by their words or deeds, they have pointed the way forward. Though all of them have been—to use Henry Miller's term—"exemplars," not all of them have been recognized as visionaries and drawn adherents. Some were marginalized in their own time and have remained outsiders, though their views of America and their example continue to have relevance. They remind us of Emerson's words, "To be great is to be misunderstood."

In dissenters, one may find the tension inherent in the American character between the interests of the individual and the interests of the group resolved. For dissenters, by acting on their individual vision even though it may be at variance with received wisdom or prevailing custom, even though it may threaten the established order, often serve the common good by opening new vistas and liberating others. We owe them our gratitude.

Roger Williams (Courtesy of the Rhode Island Historical Society.
Ink on paper, F. Halpin, engraver. 1847.)

Roger Williams

Prologue

The Puritan men who obtained the charter for the Massachusetts Bay Colony from the English monarch Charles I, and led the settlement of Boston in 1630, were both strong religious dissenters and determined businessmen. They were members of the gentry—lawyers, ministers, merchants—who brought with them to the New World a closely held religious and economic framework for governing the colony. Though these Puritans were themselves dissenters, the government apparatus they created through the charter left no room for dissent within the new society. Their total control of the religious and civil life in Massachusetts was designed both to enhance their chances of survival by ensuring full cooperation and enforcing a rigid orthodoxy of belief and worship. Though the framework left little room for dissent, its authoritarianism invited challenge.

The colony was barely one year old when a devout young Puritan minister arrived from England with his wife and immediately began to question the colony's underlying premises. His name was Roger Williams. Williams challenged the governing framework of the colony on religious, moral, and legal grounds. He disputed the purity of its Puritanism by insisting on complete separation from the Church of England. He objected to the co-mingling of religious and civil authority. And he questioned the legality and morality of the charter's claim to land that, in his view, belonged to the native inhabitants. For his unyielding insistence on reform of these issues, Williams paid the price of ostracism from the colony. But he carried the principles of his dissent to a new community, and there laid the foundation for the democratic ideas that shaped the Constitution of the United States a century later.

Roger Williams – The First American

Part One: Political and Religious Background

On December 1, 1630, the English ship *Lyon* under the command of William Peirce, departed Bristol carrying about two-dozen passengers and two hundred tons of goods. The ship was bound for Boston in New England, where the previous year, a larger party of emigrants under the leadership of John Winthrop had established the Massachusetts Bay Colony as a refuge for Puritans fleeing religious persecution in England. Food shortages, a harsh winter, and disease had shrunk Winthrop's party from 1,000 to 600 in the first year. Two hundred had died, and another 200 had returned to England. But despite the news of hardship brought back by the returners, Puritans seeking a place to practice their distinct form of Protestantism continued to flee to Massachusetts. The *Lyon* was bringing a small party of new settlers and desperately needed provisions for the struggling colony. Prominent among the passengers were the Puritan Divine Roger Williams, age 27, and his wife, Mary. When Williams set foot on the American continent, he brought with him a vision of the New World that we still realize today.

Like many of the Puritans who came before him and those who would follow, Williams was emigrating to avoid the threat of prosecution by the crown and the Church of England. Under the direction of the monarch King Charles I, William Laud, Bishop of London, was using the ecclesiastical Court of High Commission to harass Protestants who refused to conform to the practices and doctrines of the Church of England. The Court had the power to impose fines and remove ministers from their parishes, and, in cases of repeat offenders, subject them to torture and imprisonment. If charged with sedition or treason in addition to heresy, offenders could be executed.

Puritans were the radical arm of the Protestant Reformation. They insisted on a form of worship that gave them direct access to God through

His Word, as found in Scripture. They rejected the ecclesiastical hierarchy of priests, bishops and the papacy that claimed direct descent from the apostles of Christ during the early days of the church. They wanted a simpler, plainer church, modeled on principles enunciated by Luther. They wanted a clergy chosen by each congregation, not a bureaucratic system whose authority derived from the monarch, a secular leader, rather than from God as He was revealed in the Old and New Testaments. They wanted to strip the Anglican service of its elaborate symbolism and ornamentation by eliminating kneeling and making the sign of the cross, by removing stained glass from the windows and all images and statues of saints, by replacing music and the singing of hymns with recitation of the psalms, and by forbidding priests to wear surplices. They rejected the Book of Common Prayer, which standardized the Anglican service. They wanted to return the church to the time of the apostles and peel away centuries of custom and tradition that were being used to buttress the authority of the monarchy.

Williams was born in 1603, the year that Queen Elizabeth died and was succeeded on the throne of England by her Scottish cousin James VI, who became James I of England. Although James was Protestant, his parents were both Catholics, and he married Anne of Denmark, a suspected Catholic, alarming Protestants, and most especially Puritans, that Catholic influence over the Church of England, which had been in decline under Elizabeth, was returning.

James was engaged in a power struggle with Sir Edmund Coke, Chief Justice of England's Court of Common Pleas, which upheld England's tradition of common law. The struggle was over the question of whether the king, as the Supreme Head of both the Church of England and the civil government, was the source of law or its subject and servant. James claimed the divine right of kings, which asserts that the king is as God to his subjects. To rebel against the king by questioning his actions or policies is to rebel against God. It is both blasphemous and treasonous. James's assertion of this doctrine and his attempts to put it into practice put him in conflict with Coke, who insisted that both English common law and the Magna Carta limited the power of the monarch to protect the individual liberties of Englishmen.

Williams became a first-hand observer of this power struggle when, at the age of 13, his skill with shorthand brought him to the attention of Coke. Through his service as Coke's stenographer, Williams gained access to the highest circles of power in England—the Privy Council, of which Coke was a member, and the King's court. He witnessed Coke's courageous efforts to uphold the principle of individual liberty against the encroachments of a monarch claiming divine sanction for his authority. When Coke used the judicial power of Parliament to check the king's claim to absolute power, James dissolved Parliament and imprisoned Coke briefly in the Tower of London on a charge of treason. The lesson for young Williams in this confrontation was that all men, even the sovereign, are subject to human law. Coke's example would subsequently reverberate through Williams's clashes with the leaders of the Massachusetts Bay Colony over the relationship between God's law and man's law.

In 1621 Williams's father James, a London shopkeeper, died, and Coke took over responsibility for the young man's continuing education. He enrolled Williams in Sutton's Hospital, a part of Charter House, a school in London. From there, in 1623, Williams matriculated to Pembroke College at Cambridge University, where he was granted scholarships for his excellence in Latin, Greek, and Hebrew. In 1627, he graduated from Cambridge as a cleric. He had become a Puritan and was appointed the family chaplain to Sir William Masham in County Essex, a center of the Puritan movement. Masham was a Member of Parliament, active in the Puritan struggle with the monarchy over practices in the Church of England and the right to freedom of worship. On December 15, 1629, Williams married Mary Barnard, a companion to Masham's daughter, after being rebuffed in his suit for the hand of the well-born Jane Whalley, niece of an aristocratic Puritan.

Charles I had succeeded James I as monarch in March 1625 and continued his father's pro-Catholic policies. He married Princess Henrietta Maria of France, a Catholic, in a secret ceremony, despite the opposition of many Members of Parliament. He appointed known Catholics to high positions in his government. When he ordered that the names of all chaplains, even those serving on private estates, be disclosed, Williams feared being summoned before Bishop Laud's Court of High Commission and left England for America.

———— • ————

The society that awaited Roger Williams and his wife on the shores of Massachusetts was, in many ways, more tyrannical and repressive than the society of England they had left behind. In the colony, the power to make and enforce laws was held by a tiny minority who claimed their authority from their membership in the company that had obtained the charter granting them land in Massachusetts. And membership in the company was based on their economic and social standing as investors, as well as their membership in the church. Eligibility for church membership for this group of Puritans was predicated on the doctrines of the Swiss theologian John Calvin, whose theory of predestination irrevocably divided mankind into a small elite of the saved—the elect—and a large majority of the damned.

Since the colony was envisioned by this small group of leaders as a city of God living in obedience to His Word, the laws put into effect in Massachusetts were based on Scripture, especially the Ten Commandments—Mosaic Law. Thus, the behaviors proscribed in Scripture were incorporated in the colony's legal and moral code, and the punishments attached to transgressions of the law, no matter how brutal or cruel (public whippings, mutilations, amputations, executions by hanging), were carried out with a sense of moral righteousness and justice sanctioned by Scripture.

The result was a society in which a small group of Puritan men—no more than a dozen—controlled almost every aspect of the lives of thousands of settlers, including those who were not either members of the church or Puritans. For many of the emigrants from England had left for economic, not religious, reasons—yeoman farmers, artisans, tradespeople, indentured servants—people hoping to own land, build businesses, or earn decent wages. The clergy, men like Roger Williams, held positions of great power in this society. Although they were not eligible to hold positions in the civil government (technically Massachusetts was not a theocracy), their role as interpreters of scripture gave them enormous influence over the decisions and actions of the magistrates who made and enforced laws. The Massachusetts Bay Colony was a theocratic oligarchy in which the absolute power of a tiny religious elect had been substituted for the absolute power of the king. Both of these ruling entities claimed that their authority came from God.

It was into this religious and political environment that Roger and Mary Williams stepped ashore in Boston on February 5, 1631.

Part Two: Banishment

Roger Williams was a Puritan Divine who had been brought up under the tutelage of one of the fiercest defenders of individual liberty of his time, the jurist Sir Edward Coke. He had fled England to escape the tyranny of the Anglican Church under Bishop William Laud. He was seeking a place to practice his worship of God according to the dictates of his conscience and to express his opinions freely and publicly. As he engaged with the leaders of the Massachusetts Bay Colony, he soon found that he had exchanged the tyranny of old England for the tyranny of the New. Through a series of challenges he issued to the religious and civil policies of the colony, Williams antagonized its ministers and magistrates. Acting as instruments for the will of the community, they forced him to choose between adherence to his own beliefs and conformity to theirs. When he refused to conform, they ordered him to leave the colony. Williams thus became the first American to assert the right to freedom of speech and freedom of religion in the New World and to accept ostracism as the penalty for upholding his conscience.

Shortly after his arrival in the colony, Williams was offered the position of teacher in the Boston church, replacing John Wilson, who was about to sail for England on the return voyage of the *Lyon*. The teacher served as an assistant to the pastor of the church, interpreting scripture for the congregation and reinforcing doctrine. The pastor led the congregation in prayer, delivered an hour-long sermon during services, and spoke for the church on ecclesiastical matters. The teacher held a prestigious position in the social hierarchy of the colony and received a secure income from the public taxes collected from every resident. Williams's qualifications for the position were well known since he had participated in the planning for the emigration of Winthrop's party. So it was no great surprise that the elders of the church tendered their offer to Williams. The surprise was that he refused it. This was the first of many rebuffs and doctrinal challenges by Williams that alienated him from the colony's leaders. His grounds for refusal revealed both the extent of his religious purity and his willingness to suffer for it.

Williams declined the position because, as he wrote many years later to John Cotton, Jr., another clergyman in the colony, "I durst not officiate to an unseparated people, as upon Examination and Conference I found them to be." (Letter to John Cotton, Jr. 25 March 1671). Williams's objection was that the Boston church had not fully separated from the Church of England. Although the congregation in Boston had abandoned many of the ceremonies of the Anglican Church and was independent of ecclesiastical control from England, it had not broken completely free. It sought to reform the church from within. Partly this may have been due to political and economic considerations, the fear that an open breach with the mother church might lead to revocation of the colony's charter, and with it the loss of legal title to the lands owned by the members of the Massachusetts Bay Company.

Williams also noted that when members of the Boston congregation visited England, as John Wilson was about to do, they attended Anglican services. Williams saw these compromises with their Puritan principles as leading them away from Christ. He later wrote in this vein to John Winthrop: "I know and am persuaded that your misguidings are great and lamentable, and as the further they pass in your way, the further you wander, and have further to come back, and the end of one vexation will be but the beginning of another, till Conscience be permitted (though Erroneous) to be free amongst you." (Letter to John Winthrop, 21 July 1637). This letter also expresses Williams's belief that freedom of conscience must be extended even to beliefs considered "Erroneous" by ecclesiastical authorities. He is saying that there is no such thing as heresy.

Williams also had strong personal reasons for insisting on complete separation from the Church of England. As he wrote many years later to the daughter of Sir Edward Coke, "It was as bitter as Death to me when Bishop Laud pursued me out of [England], and my Conscience was persuaded against the National Church and Ceremonies and Bishops." (Letter to Mrs. Anne Sadleir, April 1652, from London).

Williams gave a second reason for his refusal of the teacher position: that the magistrates claimed the authority to punish breaches of the Sabbath by the colony's residents. Church attendance in the colony was mandatory, and violations of the Sabbath, which could be as harmless as taking a walk in the woods or kissing a spouse, were subject to civil censures. Williams disputed that the magistrates had authority under Scripture to mete out punishments for spiritual offenses. He distinguished between the two tables of Mosaic Law. The first four commandments defined man's duties to God. The remaining six commandments defined man's duties to his fellow man. Williams held that only the second table could be enforced by civil authorities. The first table was the province of the church and the conscience of the individual. This distinction was an early sign of Williams's belief in the necessity for separation of church and state. Many years later, he elaborated this principle in a famous analogy, the Ship of State.

> It hath fallen out sometimes that both Papists and Protestants, Jews and Turks, may be embarqued into one ship . . . All the Liberty of Conscience that I ever pleaded for turns upon these two hinges, that none of the Papists, Protestants, Jews, or Turks be forced to come to the Ship's Prayers or worship, if they practice any. I further add, that I never denied not-withstanding this Liberty, the Commander of this Ship ought to command the Ship's course; yea and also to command that Justice, Peace, and Sobriety be kept and practiced, both among the Seamen and all the Passengers . . . (To the Town of Providence, January 1655).

Several weeks after his refusal of the position in the Boston church, Williams was invited by the congregation of the Salem church to become its teacher, assisting the pastor Samuel Skelton. As the Salem church had been established on Separatist principles, Williams accepted the offer and moved to Salem with his wife. However, in April, the General Court sent a letter to John Endicott, the Governor of the Salem settlement, warning him about Williams's positions and calling for a conference between the Salem church and the Boston church to review the appointment. Bowing to this pressure, the Salem church withdrew its offer. Williams decided to move again, this time to Plymouth, where the Pilgrims from the *Mayflower* had established a Separatist colony in 1620.

Williams was welcomed into the Plymouth colony by Governor William Bradford and admitted as a member of the church, where he became assistant to the pastor Ralph Smith. He supported himself by farming and teaching in the church.

During his two-year stay in Plymouth, Williams had extensive contacts with the neighboring tribes of Indians, the Pokanokets, and the Narragansetts. He studied their habits, customs, religious beliefs, and agricultural practices, and he learned their language. He developed personal relationships with the tribes' chiefs or sachems, Massasoit of the Pokanokets and Canonicus of the Narragansetts. He grew to admire their skill at resource management and to value their friendliness and hospitality to him.

One of the rationales for colonization of the New World by the English was the need, the duty, to convert the heathen populations to Christianity. They believed that the promise of the second coming of Christ could not be fulfilled until Christianity became the religion of everyone on earth. The charters to land in the New World granted by the English kings included this imperative to proselytize the native population. And the English monarchs used their status as Christian kings to claim the right to assign the title of native lands to their subjects.

But despite his extensive intercourse with the native tribes surrounding Plymouth, Williams made no effort to convert them. He was fearful of bringing them to a false conversion by merely teaching them the forms and doctrines of Christian worship. He believed that they must, like all men, come to an experience of the Christian God through the use of their reason and the instruction of experience. They must, like all men, come to a belief in the Christian God "because it agrees with their own Conscience," and not because of any external coercion. He believed that it was his first obligation to understand Indians and their religious beliefs, to learn their language so that he might begin a conversation "to open matters of salvation to them."

As a result of his interactions with the Pokanokets and the Narragansetts, Williams concluded that the Indians owned the land on which they lived, hunted, foraged, and grew crops, and that the English had no right to take their land without compensating them for it. He submitted to the authorities in Plymouth a treatise arguing that the land patents granted by the crown were "a sin of unjust usurpation of others' possessions" and calling on the colonists to reject their royal charter and return it to England. He denied that "Christian Kings (so-called) are invested with Right by virtue of their Christianity to take and give away the Lands and Countries of other men." He called King James I a liar for declaring himself the first Christian prince to discover New England. The treatise also applied several demonizing quotations from the Book of Revelations to King Charles I, a slander that the king might have considered treasonous had he read it.

The treatise quickly terminated Williams's welcome in Plymouth. Bradford now regarded him as a renegade and a disturbance. Williams asked to leave membership in the church, a request that was granted. In August 1633, he left Plymouth for Salem, where he had been reappointed assistant to Samuel Skelton, though the position was unofficial and unpaid. Shortly before he left, his first child, a daughter named Mary, was born.

But Williams was not able to leave the issue of native land rights behind him in Plymouth. Bradford wrote to Winthrop describing Williams's positions, and the General Court of Boston summoned him to appear. The Court rebuked Williams for his insults to King Charles. Williams, perhaps realizing he had been needlessly inflammatory in his attacks on the crown, offered to burn the treatise, which had not been made public. He also promised not to question the legality of the charter. Thus the crisis was defused. But by now it seemed that Williams's devotion to his conscience, and his belief in the rights of all men regardless of their religious creed, were making him an iconoclast in New England, a disturber of the peace. In fact, Williams was the purest of the Puritans. It was the co-mingling of the secular and the sacred that Williams opposed, because the secular profaned the sacred, degraded it. Thus he would condemn his king for claiming Christianity as a justification for taking land from Indians, and he would challenge Massachusetts's magistrates for using their civil authority to enforce church precepts. He was a man of rigid principle, but his principle was not tyrannical, it was the insistence on the right of all men to follow the dictates of their consciences.

Why did Williams value his conscience above the authority of other clergymen and the social norms of the colony? It was through his conscience that Williams maintained union with Christ. In *The Bloody Tenent*, a work he wrote to argue against persecution, he declared (quoting from *Acts* 9.4.), "It is not lawful to persecute any for Conscience sake Rightly informed; for in persecuting such, Christ himself is persecuted in them." For Williams to contravene his conscience, "Rightly informed" as he believed it was, would have been tantamount to abandoning Christ.

Once back in Salem, Williams's troubles with the Boston authorities continued through a series of confrontations, some trivial, some serious, that brought him to trial before the General Court. Through it all, Williams maintained his firm adherence to the principles that set him apart from the majority of his fellow colonists.

In November, the Boston church convened a meeting of all the clergymen in the colony. Williams and Skelton attended this meeting to voice their objections to it as implying a central authority or presbytery of the clergy that could threaten the independence of individual churches. This threat had already become a reality when the Boston church discouraged Williams's appointment as a teacher in the Salem church. The Bay clergymen dismissed their concerns as misrepresenting the intent of the conference, but the complaint was an irritant because it reminded Boston of Salem's Separatist policies.

In March 1634, Williams provoked an argument between Salem's Governor John Endicott and the recently appointed teacher of the Boston church, John Cotton, a highly respected Divine who had arrived from England in September. Williams was insisting that women wear veils in public. This requirement stemmed from the Separatist view that all women had inherited the sin of Eve's failure to resist temptation. Endicott supported Williams's position, quoting Scripture, while Cotton, also quoting Scripture, opposed it. Winthrop snuffed out the debate for the sake of amity between the two towns, but Williams was resented for fostering Separatist views that caused tension between Salem and Boston.

Williams's opinions had support from the Salem congregation, which resisted interference in the town's affairs by Boston officials. Notwithstanding his position on women's veils, Williams was popular with women for allowing them to speak in the church, a practice the Boston church forbade. He also encouraged lay preaching. The liberality behind these policies was consistent with Williams's emphasis on freedom of conscience and freedom of speech. In August 1634, when Samuel Skelton died, the congregation chose Williams as their minister, again over the objections of the Boston clergy.

In November 1634, a more serious issue resurfaced when the General Court learned that Williams, despite his promise to them, was continuing to speak out against the legality of the royal charter. Williams had taken the step of drafting a letter to King Charles I asking him to acknowledge his error. John Cotton defended Williams on the grounds of his conscience and suggested intercession by the ministers of the colony to persuade Williams of his errors. But Williams stood firm. He called the patent a "National sin" and declared that the colony was under a "National duty" to renounce it. Williams's intransigence on this issue hardened the attitude of distrust towards him from the General Court, whose very existence rested on the legality of the charter.

Over the next year, the clashes between Williams and the Court rapidly escalated. In April 1635, Williams was summoned to Boston by the Court to respond to charges that he had preached against a law enacted by the magistrates in March requiring all male residents of the colony to swear an oath of loyalty to the government of Massachusetts Bay. This law had been passed in response to a similar loyalty oath required of subjects in England by the crown. The magistrates and the governor wanted to ensure that the colonists' first loyalty was to them. But these political considerations carried no weight with Williams. He believed that, according to Scripture, an oath was a form of worship, and that the magistrates had no authority to compel a man to worship. He further objected that as the oath would be administered to all residents, including non-church members considered "unregenerate," submitting to it would force people to take the name of God in vain. For the same reasons, he voiced objection to the colony's policy of mandatory church attendance. Williams was striking at the nexus of church-state control of the colony.

Williams was allowed to present his arguments to the Court. Ministers from the colony were then given time to refute them. At this point in the power struggle, the Salem congregation's support began to weaken. Endicott, who had initially supported Williams's position, now turned against him. The previous year, the Court had removed Endicott from office for a year for defacing the British flag by cutting from it the red cross that Puritans regarded as a symbol of the Papacy. His turnabout may have been a gesture of reconciliation to the Court.

In July, Williams appeared again before the Court and was charged with holding "erroneous and dangerous opinions" for teaching that magistrates cannot enforce the first four commandments or require oaths. He was told that he would be admonished by the other churches in the colony. The ministers called on the Salem congregation to remove him as their minister and recommended that Williams be banished.

When the Salem church refused to discharge Williams, the Court retaliated by refusing to grant the town's petition for the title to land on Marblehead Neck that it sought for expansion. In response, the Salem congregation sent a letter to all the churches in the colony, accusing the magistrates of a "heinous sin." The letters were never read to the churches' congregations. The magistrates reacted by refusing to seat Salem's deputies at its next meeting, which would decide Williams's fate.

Williams had become ill under the stress of the situation and unable to preach. John Cotton took this as a sign of God's disapproval of Williams's teaching. In August, Williams asked his congregation to withdraw from communion with the other churches in the colony. When it refused to take this drastic step, Williams withdrew from the Salem church and declared he could no longer hold communion with its members. A few of his dwindling followers left the church with him.

In October, the General Court convened again and ordered Williams to appear. It added to its previous charges defamation of the magistrates in the letters from the Salem church urging dissension. He was asked to retract his errors or face sentencing. Another minister, Thomas Hooker, who later removed his congregation to Connecticut, disputed with him, but Williams would not yield. The next morning the court banished him, ordering him to leave its jurisdiction within six weeks, and forbidding him to voice his opinions while he remained in the colony. Three weeks after the trial, Mary Williams gave birth to their second child, a daughter they named Freeborne.

Williams was shocked by the sentence. He believed he had broken no civil law, but merely exercised his right of free speech. But there was no right of free speech in the Massachusetts Bay Colony. He returned to Salem but continued to hold private meetings in the homes of his remaining supporters. The Salem church sent a letter of submission to the Court, dissociating itself from Williams's errors. The Court, in consideration of Williams's illness and the approach of winter, postponed his banishment until spring, perhaps hoping that he would change his mind and recant. Winthrop corresponded with him and suggested that he relocate with his followers in Narragansett Bay, to the south. Williams sold his house and land in Salem to raise the money he would need to support himself in the new settlement.

But when the magistrates learned of this plan, they became alarmed that a new settlement based on Williams's extreme Separatist principles might be located near the churches of the Massachusetts Bay Colony. They decided to forcibly deport him to England, where he was certain to face harsh persecution from William Laud, now the Archbishop of

Canterbury. They summoned him to Boston on January 11, 1636. When he refused to come, citing his illness, they sent a small ship to Salem with orders to Captain John Underhill to apprehend him and carry him off to England. Winthrop warned him of this plan, and Williams fled from Salem into the wilderness, leaving behind his wife and children. Several months later, the General Court approved Salem's petition for the grant of land on Marblehead Neck.

Part Three: Providence

Williams fled south, traveling by canoe on the sea and rivers, heading for the Indian village of Massasoit, chief sachem of the Pokanokets, whom he had befriended during his stay in Plymouth five years earlier. Along the way, he was fed and sheltered by natives. He settled initially on the east bank of the Seekonk River near Narragansett Bay, on land under the jurisdiction of the Plymouth colony. He was joined there in the spring by several followers from Salem. But Plymouth, under pressure from the Massachusetts Bay Colony not to harbor Williams, ordered him to relocate. He moved his tiny settlement across the river into wilderness country inhabited by the Narragansett Indians and negotiated a gift of land from their chief sachem, Canonicus, another friend from his previous stay in Plymouth. He called his new settlement Providence.

Many years later, trying to resolve a jurisdictional dispute with the leaders of the neighboring Connecticut colony, Williams wrote a letter describing his flight and its outcome.

> First when I was unkindly and unchristianly (as I believe) driven from my house and land, and wife and children (in the midst of New England winter now about 35 years past) at Salem: that ever honored Governor Mr. Winthrop privately wrote to me to steer my course to the Narragansett Bay and Indians, for many high and heavenly public ends, encouraging me from the freeness of the place from any English claims or patents. I took his prudent motion as a hint and voice from God, and (waving all other thoughts and motions) I steered my course from Salem (though in winter snow which

I feel yet) unto these parts, wherein I may say that I have seen the face of God. (Letter to Major Mason, June 22, 1670).

The absence of English control over Williams's new settlement owing to "the freeness of the place" turned out to be both a blessing and a curse. It meant that Williams could design a community along the lines of his own religious and political beliefs (liberty of conscience, separation of church and state, democratic government, respect for the rights of Indians), but it also meant that the community would be open to settlers with a wide range of religious inclinations and economic motives. And it would make the settlement vulnerable to jurisdictional challenges from other colonies, such as Massachusetts and Connecticut, whose ambitions collided with Williams's vision and whose royal charters gave them recourse to the power England's rulers. Roger Williams was a deeply private and spiritual man who founded Providence as a place where he could exercise his devotion to Jesus Christ according to his own conscience. But as it played out, Williams's experiment required him to remain actively involved in the governance of Providence for the remainder of his life. To protect and preserve the principles behind his central life quest, a more perfect union with the spirit of his savior, Williams was forced to adopt the role of statesman.

Williams's survival during the first winter of his banishment depended upon his good relations with Indians, so it was no small irony that in the summer of 1636 the Massachusetts authorities called on him to intervene in the Pequot War that broke out shortly after his wife Mary and their two children joined him in Providence. The request came from Sir Henry Vane, an English nobleman who had arrived in Boston during the month of Williams's trial. Vane was sympathetic to Williams's views, and the two men became friends. In May, Vane had been elected governor of the Massachusetts Bay Colony.

The Pequot War erupted in July when a band of Niantic Indians assaulted and killed an English trader, John Oldham, on Block Island off the coast of Narragansett country. The motives behind the murder and the colonists' response to it reveal the complex rivalries among the

Indians of New England and the way the English settlers played off those rivalries to serve their interests. Land and trading rights were the prizes sought by all the parties.

The Pequots, the Narragansetts, the Niantics, and the Mohegans were contending with one another for land dominance and a favorable trading relationship with the English. Oldham had been killed by the Niantics to discourage English trading with their rivals, the Pequots. But an English militia under the command of John Endicott, after burning the Niantic villages on Block Island, sailed up the coast to a Pequot village and demanded compensation for the death of Oldham. When the Pequots refused and fled into the woods, Endicott burned their village, setting off a wave of reprisals against English settlements. The Pequots called a war council with the Narragansetts, their traditional enemy, to discuss an alliance against the English. Williams learned of this council and made his way to it at great personal risk to dissuade the Narragansetts from joining the Pequots. Canonicus, the chief sachem of the Narragansetts, admitted Williams to the council and allowed him to speak

The Pequot sachem Sassacus argued that eventually, the English would take away all Indian lands unless they were driven out. He advocated a prolonged war of attrition against them, raiding their settlements, killing their animals, and destroying their crops.

Williams warned the Indians against the power of the English. He appealed to the Narragansetts' traditional rivalry with the Pequots, promising them that an alliance with the English would bring far greater long-term benefits than a war against them. Canonicus was persuaded and sent his nephew Miantonomo to Boston with a party of Indians to sign a treaty with Vane. The Mohegans, under Uncas their sachem, had also allied with the English against the Pequots. The English promised to give the Narragansetts hunting rights in Pequot country after the war. But they reneged on this promise and gave the rights instead to the Mohegans, seeding the Narragansetts' resentment and distrust and intensifying their rivalry with the Mohegans.

In May 1637, a force of Connecticut militia under Major John Mason joined by Mohegan, and Narragansett warriors attacked and burned the Pequot fort at Mystic, killing nearly all the inhabitants and destroying the Pequot nation. The few survivors were divided between the Mohegans and the Narragansetts. The Narragansetts, shocked by the brutality of the assault, retreated to their home country. Williams wrote a letter to Winthrop objecting to the cruelty shown by the English and reminding him of their mission to save Indians' souls. A year later, at Hartford, Uncas and Miantonomo signed a treaty forfeiting all rights of possession to Pequot lands, which were claimed by Connecticut as a right of conquest. The sachems also agreed to pay Connecticut annual tribute for their Pequot captives. Roger Williams took custody of a captive Pequot boy and named him Will.

Thus was the prediction of Sassacus fulfilled, with Indian complicity. The Pequot War set a pattern for relations between New England Indians and the English settlers, a pattern marked by the steady encroachment of Indian lands, duplicity by the English and by opportunistic Indian leaders, and growing mutual distrust. Williams, through his knowledge of Indian languages and ways, and his access to their leaders, continued to play the role of mediator for the remainder of his life. Though he was sympathetic to Indian rights, his first loyalty was always to his tribe, the English.

In recognition of Williams's service to the colony during the Pequot War, John Winthrop urged the magistrates of Massachusetts to rescind his banishment, but the magistrates refused.

———•———

The struggle for control and use of land in New England was not confined to the contest between Indians and English settlers. The settlers squabbled among themselves over land rights. Disputes arose between individual landholders with conflicting claims, as well as between colonial governments jousting for jurisdictional control. Because Williams's Providence settlement was unchartered—that is, not based on a legal document issued by the government of England that provided a framework for maintaining order in the colony—the inhabitants had to write their own rules and agree to abide by them. But not all the residents of

Providence had come there with as devout a purpose as Roger Williams. Some were motivated more by a lust for land than a passion for God. And among the godly, there were wide disparities of religious belief that held the potential for disunity. Providence was also in a weak position relative to the chartered colonies of Connecticut and Massachusetts who might, for religious or political reasons, have designs on its territory. The challenges facing Williams to hold his settlement together were formidable.

Williams had established Providence on land he purchased from the Narragansett sachem Canonicus using money from the sale of his property in Salem. The transaction was not documented or recorded in any form that followed English law, although two years later, Williams did draw up a written deed that was filed with the town. The boundaries of the property were defined by rivers and natural landmarks. Williams sold parcels of the land to settlers who had followed him in the summer of 1636 until he had recovered his initial investment. He then donated the remainder of the land to the town, which sold lots to new arrivals, thus accumulating a fund. Williams described the purpose of the settlement as follows: "I desired it might be for a shelter for persons distressed for conscience. I then considering the condition of divers of my distressed countrymen, I communicated my said purchase unto my loving friends, who then desired to take shelter with me."

As more refugees from the repressive atmosphere in England and Massachusetts began to arrive, Williams drafted a compact that articulated their method of self-government in the absence of any legal charter. It is the first enunciation of democratic principles of government in the New World.

> We whose names are hereunder written, being desirous to inhabit in the town of Providence, do promise to submit ourselves, in active or passive obedience, to all such orders or agreements as shall be made for public good of the body, in an orderly way, by the major consent of the present inhabitants, masters of families incorporated together into a township, and such others whom they shall admit unto the same, *only in civil things.*

The compact was signed by thirteen freemen of the town, not all of whom turned out to be "loving friends."

It was not long before Williams's policies of liberality and tolerance bred discord and disunity that disturbed the tranquility of Providence and threatened its integrity by attracting interference from Massachusetts, which regarded Williams's experiment as an affront to its form of government and wanted it to fail.

In the spring of 1638, William Hutchinson arrived in Providence from Boston, seeking a place to settle himself and his family. Hutchinson's wife Anne had been banished from Massachusetts and excommunicated by her Boston church on account of her doctrinal challenges to the teachings of the Boston clergy. Anne was a follower of the Puritan divine John Cotton, who had been instrumental in bringing the sentence of banishment on Roger Williams. Anne, with Cotton's approval, had been holding weekly meetings at her home during which she parsed the sermons and teachings of the Boston clergymen. She accused them of departing from orthodox Calvinistic doctrine by preaching a "covenant of works" under which an individual could earn salvation through righteous behavior. According to Calvin, since the fall of man, only God's grace, bestowed through Christ on a small minority of pre-destined elect, could bring people to salvation. Confronted by the ministers of the Massachusetts Bay Colony with her "errors," Anne had not only refused to recant, she had called down God's curses on them, an act of blasphemy. While Anne, pregnant, awaited her church trial, Will had set off from Boston to Providence to "take shelter" with Roger Williams.

Williams arranged a meeting between Hutchinson and Canonicus, who gave Hutchinson land on Aquidneck Island in Narragansett Bay. A few weeks later, Anne left Boston with her family and several followers. They walked to Aquidneck in six days. They named their settlement Portsmouth. Among her followers was William Coddington, a magistrate of Massachusetts Bay and the treasurer of the colony. He had supported her through her trial and thus had lost favor with the Massachusetts authorities.

A year later, a disturbing force arrived in Narragansett Bay in the form of Samuel Gorton. Gorton roiled the community and prompted a series of legal maneuvers that sent Roger Williams to England in search of a charter from the English government.

Gorton was a bluff, unruly man with strong anti-clerical views and an anti-authoritarian attitude. He had arrived in Boston in 1636 with his second wife and children. After a short stay, he moved to Plymouth, from which he was banished on charges of heresy and refusing to obey a court order. He moved to Portsmouth, where he allied himself with the Hutchinson faction, which had broken with Coddington. Espousing an Evangelical form of Christianity, Gorton attracted followers who joined with the Hutchinson group to vote Coddington out of office. Coddington and eight followers left Portsmouth to found the town of Newport on the southern end of Aquidneck Island. A year later, he succeeded in uniting the two towns, and he moved against Gorton. Gorton had been brought before the court because one of his servants had assaulted an old woman. When Gorton refused to recognize the authority of Coddington's newly formed government, the court sentenced him to a whipping and banished him. He moved to Providence.

There, his reputation preceding him, the town officials refused to admit him as a citizen, but he was allowed to remain as a "sojourner." He quickly became embroiled in ongoing land disputes involving two of Williams's followers from Salem, William Harris and William Arnold.

Harris and Arnold had alienated Williams by obtaining land grants from Indian sachems that exceeded the original grant made to Williams by Canonicus. They had settled a community outside Providence they called Pawtuxet after the river that bordered it and were using various schemes, some fraudulent, to extend their landholdings. Williams lacked the authority to stop them. Gorton complicated this imbroglio when he purchased from townspeople in Providence two parcels that Arnold contested. Arnold appealed to the Massachusetts Bay Colony for relief and offered to submit Pawtuxet to its jurisdiction. In September 1642, Massachusetts welcomed the Pawtuxet secessionists under its government, and Arnold was made a justice of the peace. Gorton had now fragmented two communities. When he failed to appear in Providence court as ordered, he was arrested and taken to Boston, where he was jailed and sentenced to hard labor. Upon his release, he went to England to have his land holdings confirmed.

The Providence townspeople, seeing in this sequence of events the steady unraveling of their community, voted to send Williams to England to obtain a charter that would give them legal parity with the other New England colonies. In the spring of 1643, Williams left for England. He was forced to sail from New Amsterdam because Massachusetts would not allow him entry to Boston. Massachusetts was sending agents to England to petition the Committee on Foreign Plantations to allow the colony to annex Providence, Portsmouth, Newport, and all the territory around Narragansett Bay.

Williams was in New Amsterdam at the time when Anne Hutchinson, who had moved there with her family after the death of her husband, was murdered in an Indian raid that killed all her children save a nine-year-old daughter who was taken captive. Williams mediated a truce between the Indians and the Dutch before departing. While he was at sea, Massachusetts, Connecticut, and New Haven formed a military alliance named The United Colonies and excluded Providence when it applied for admission, further increasing the importance of Williams's mission.

He arrived in England to find the country embroiled in the civil war that brought down the monarchy. Charles I had retreated from London to Oxford with his army, and the country was being governed by the Long Parliament, dominated by Puritans. Fortunately for Williams, his friend Sir Henry Vane was now a powerful Member of Parliament, allied with Oliver Cromwell. With Vane's help, Williams, after a year of waiting during which he wrote treatises in support of freedom of religion and separation of church and state, was granted a charter for Providence Plantations signed by the Earl of Warwick, the governor of the Committee on Foreign Plantations. The charter covered Providence, Portsmouth, Newport, and included the disputed lands in Pawtuxet and Shawomet, Gorton's holdings. The charter allowed the inhabitants to be self-governing, so long as their laws did not contravene English law. Decisions about religion were left to the majority. Civil laws could not enforce religious preferences.

In September 1644, Williams returned to Providence, a hero. When he arrived in Narragansett Bay, he was greeted by a flotilla of townspeople in fourteen canoes. He had brought back a charter that made Providence Plantations the most democratic state, not only in New England but the world. At the new colony's first meeting, Williams was elected chief officer. However, it was not time to celebrate. During his absence, another Indian war was brewing. Following the Hartford Treaty, tensions grew between the Mohegans under Uncas and the Narragansetts under Miantonomo. The Mohegans captured Miantonomo, who had been leading raids against the English. When the English authorized Uncas to execute Miantonomo, the Narragansetts paid the Mohegans a ransom for his life. Uncas accepted the ransom, then slew Miantonomo. But despite these betrayals, Williams was able to persuade the Narragansetts that war against the English would only bring about the destruction of their nation. Narragansett sachems met with the commissioners of the United Colonies and confirmed the terms of the Hartford Treaty. They were further humiliated by having to pay a large fine, return Mohegan captives, and make reparations to Uncas. The Narragansetts were never able to swallow these conditions, and their rancor against the English festered.

For Williams, the pattern of his life in Providence continued along the same path after he returned from England with the charter. The land disputes over Pawutxet persisted, some lasting until 1712, long after his death. The jurisdictional quarrels were occasionally renewed, religious differences sometimes became contentious, and all the while Indian resentment of the spread of English settlements simmered. Williams was asked to return to England again in 1651 to confirm the charter for Providence Plantations after Charles I was beheaded, and the monarchy was replaced by Cromwell's Council of State. Coddington had gone before him to secure a commission that would establish Aquidneck Island as a separate legal entity with him as governor for life. Williams sold his beloved trading post at Cocumscussoc along the coast to raise funds for his trip. He stayed in London as the guest of Sir Henry Vane, through whom he gained direct access to Cromwell. He obtained confirmation of the Providence charter from Cromwell and foiled Coddington's attempt at secession from the colony. After his return in 1654, the townspeople elected Williams President of the colony, placing in him their hopes of repairing their fractured community.

The great tragedy of Williams's life was undoubtedly King Philip's War, which broke out in 1675 when Metacom, who had succeeded Massasoit as chief sachem of the Pokanokets, launched a war of depredation against the English that brought down their wrath against both Metacom and the Narragansetts. When Indians threatened Providence, Williams joined the militia as a captain to defend his town against the people who had enabled him to found it. While he parlayed with some of the attackers outside the town, other Indians set fire to eighteen houses, including his own. During a second attack, all but twenty of the 123 houses in Providence were destroyed. The war ended in August 1676 when Metacom was assassinated. Connecticut took control of the Narragansett country and prohibited Indians from living there. Williams and his family, now poverty-stricken, moved in with his son Daniel and his wife.

Roger Williams died in Providence sometime during the winter of 1683. Nearly a century later, the principles around which he had built Providence Plantations were incorporated in the Constitution of the United States of America and its Bill of Rights.

CHAPTER 2

Anne Bradstreet

Prologue

Outwardly a conforming, dutiful Puritan housewife, Anne Bradstreet revealed through her poetry a rich and independent inner life that belied accepted and approved gender roles for women in the Massachusetts Bay Colony, as well as in the mother country, England. She was a silent, unintended dissenter who publicly downplayed her achievements and relied on her husband and other male allies to promote her work and validate her gifts as a writer. But her major poems, epic in scope, confounded prevailing notions of the limited intelligence and capabilities of women that were used to justify patriarchal control of society, property, and family. Anne Bradstreet was, in effect, an early American feminist who, while accepting her assigned place of subordination, unpretentiously rose above it.

Anne Bradstreet – The First American Poet

Anne Bradstreet was a contemporary of Roger Williams. If she did not know him personally—they lived in different New England towns and attended different churches—she certainly knew of him, for her father Thomas Dudley, in his capacity as Governor of the Massachusetts Bay Colony, was one of Williams's chief prosecutors at his trial and banishment. She had come to New England with her husband Simon and her parents' family in 1630, when she was eighteen years old, as a member of the Puritan emigration party led by John Winthrop. She remained in New England for the rest of her life, giving birth to eight children,

Anne Bradstreet (Courtesy of Boston Public Library.)

becoming a highly competent frontier housewife, and writing thousands of lines of poetry that earned respect and admiration of readers in both old England and New. Her story is remarkable not, as was the case with Anne Hutchinson and Williams, for any dramatic confrontation with the ruling authorities of the colony, but for the way her literary artistry enabled her to transcend the gender role imposed upon her by her Puritan upbringing and community. Anne managed to maintain a respected status as a pious, obedient, and god-fearing Puritan mistress while crossing the boundaries of expected achievement by women in seventeenth-century New England. She did this by writing poetry of unimpeachable Puritan orthodoxy that simultaneously revealed the emotional and spiritual struggles of a Puritan pilgrim whose faith in her God was often sorely tested. If the story of Roger Williams gives us a window onto the external tensions and conflicts shaping the masculine world of Puritan politics and religion, Anne's story affords us an intimate glimpse into the internal world of a devout and sensitive Puritan woman—the first woman, or man, to give poetic voice to the Puritans' experience of the New World.

Anne was born in 1612 in Northamptonshire, in the heart of Puritan country. Her parents, Thomas and Dorothy, were members of the gentry, well educated, and passionately religious. From an early age, Anne was inoculated with Puritan doctrine and so grew up with a sense of her inherent sinfulness as a descendant of the fallen Adam and Eve. For the Puritans, education was the antidote to ignorant sinfulness, so Anne, like all Puritan children, was taught to read so that she could learn directly from scripture the difference between godly and ungodly behavior. But Thomas, who was himself highly literate, familiar not only with scripture but with many of the leading secular writers of his day such as Francis Bacon, Robert Burton, and Edmund Spenser, taught Anne to write as well as read, and introduced her to the technical requirements for writing verse—rhyme, meter, figurative language, and classical allusions. And from her mother, Anne saw modeled the accepted and approved role for a Puritan woman as the helpmate and supporter of her husband. So from an early age, the two influences that would define her intellectual life—Puritan orthodoxy and a highly developed literacy and respect for learning—were flowing from her father and mother.

When Anne was born, Thomas served as a clerk to a prominent lawyer, an experience that would come into play in New England, where he was elected to government positions and served as a magistrate. When Anne was eight, her father was appointed a steward to the fourth Earl of Lincoln, a young nobleman with extensive landholdings burdened by debt from his father's profligacy. Thomas moved his family into the earl's country estate, Sempringham Manor, eighteen miles from Boston in Lincolnshire. In this nobleman's household Anne was exposed to the high fashions and sophisticated culture of a prominent English aristocrat. Given that Thomas found favor with the earl for his skilled management that brought the estate out of debt, it is likely that Anne's education was deepened from instruction by the tutor employed to educate the earl's children.

When Anne was ten years old, her father hired Simon Bradstreet to assist him in managing the earl's estate. Simon was twenty years old, recently graduated from Cambridge, a man without a family. His friendliness and warmth made him a welcome guest in the Dudley household, often taking meals with them, and he and Anne became close. As Anne matured, her attraction to Simon deepened and awakened her sensuality, troubling her with thoughts of sin. Some of her poems, written at a later stage of her life, express her early struggle to come to terms with her carnality.

In 1624 Dudley moved his family to Boston, England, where he remained in the service of the earl, who had property there. Simon took over the responsibilities of steward at Sempringham Manor. He left this position in 1627 to become a steward at another estate in Warwick. These changes reduced the opportunities for Anne and Simon to share each other's company but did not sever their connection.

When Anne was sixteen, she contracted smallpox, the first of several illnesses that, over time, would give her a sense of the fragility and impermanence of human life. Smallpox in the seventeenth century was fatal to one out of four of its victims. As a Puritan who believed that God had a direct hand in everything that occurs on Earth, Anne viewed her illness as a punishment for her carnal attraction to a man not her husband.

When she recovered, Simon proposed marriage to her, and her father gave his consent. Anne moved from Boston to the Warwick estate to take up her life as Simon's wife.

Puritan wives were expected to conform to a strictly defined gender role modeled on the relationship between Adam and Eve, the bride born from Adam's rib. The role entailed obedience, support, and fertility. Women were considered the intellectual inferiors of men, their brains incapable of mastering the complexities of science, art, and religion that men had devised. A Puritan woman's primary role was the procreation of children who would perpetuate the race and the community of the godly. In furtherance of that role, the center of the woman's life and its boundary was the household, where she would raise her children, give them religious instruction, manage the domestic affairs of her family, and assist neighboring women in doing the same. Her skills were cooking, cleaning, sewing, weaving, and care of domestic animals, or if a member of the gentry as Anne was, supervising servants who would perform these tasks. Anne, by virtue of her upbringing, was well suited for her role as mistress.

Although husbands held authority over their wives and owned all property, much as God held authority over mortals and owned the Earth, they were expected to treat their wives charitably and with kindness. For Puritans, genuine love between a husband and a wife was considered a moral duty, and healthy sexual relations producing offspring were an important part of their spiritual union. In the Massachusetts Bay Colony, a man or woman who withheld sexual relations from a spouse could be punished by the General Court.

As her life unfolded in New England, Anne showed herself to be extremely competent in her role as mistress of the Bradstreet household. And the poems she addressed to her husband suggest that theirs was a happy and passionate marriage.

———•———

Anne's father was one of the core members of the Massachusetts Bay Company that had been formed in 1629 for the purpose of founding a Puritan colony in New England. In April 1630, the Dudleys and the

Bradstreets sailed from Southhampton on the *Arbella*, a large privateer named for the sister of the Earl of Lincoln, whose husband Isaac Johnson was a major financier of the expedition. The *Arbella* was leading a fleet of eleven ships carrying seven hundred passengers, livestock, furniture, household goods, provisions, and thousands of gallons of beer. Dudley was Deputy Governor of the Company, and Simon was its Secretary. So from the outset, Anne belonged to the most elite group of Puritan emigrants.

But her status gave her small comfort on the expedition. Conditions on the ship were unhealthy and dangerous. Seasickness fouled their cramped living quarters, food was poor (no citrus to prevent scurvy), and the sailors were, by Puritan standards, brutish and ungodly. Before they had long been at sea, hostile ships were sighted, and the crew threw most of the passengers' furnishings and goods overboard to minimize the risk of fire during the expected battle. The threat evaporated when the approaching ships turned out to be friendly. During the crossing, most of the livestock and some of the passengers perished. When the *Arbella* finally anchored in the harbor off Salem on June 12, Anne and the other passengers were shocked at the condition of the settlement.

The Massachusetts Bay Company had sent John Endicott to New England the previous year with a smaller group of emigrants to establish a settlement that could accommodate the larger party being led by John Winthrop. The new arrivals found the Salem settlement distressed and demoralized, its inhabitants malnourished, poorly housed, slovenly dressed, and given to drink. This was a far cry from the "city on a hill" that Winthrop had envisioned in his inspirational talk to the departing Puritans in Southhampton. For Anne, used to the splendor of Sempringham Manor and Warwick, the contrast must have been dispiriting.

The new immigrants soon began dying from malnutrition and disease. Some immediately went back to England on the returning ships. In August, Lady Arbella died from a fever, and a month later, her husband Isaac also succumbed. The Puritans viewed these events darkly, as warnings from God that their mission was tainted. Winthrop and Dudley convened a meeting of the settlers to restore morale and extract their consent to continue the enterprise. Miscreants whose behavior was thought to be the cause of their misfortunes were sought out and punished. These early experiences of jeopardy to their mission strengthened the leaders' resolve to maintain Puritan forms of discipline in daily life as a way of ensuring the survival of the community.

Not long after this rededication to their mission, the Winthrop party split into two groups. First, the entire party moved to the more hospitable environs of Charlestown, where Endicott had set up a satellite settlement. In September, Winthrop and a group of his followers moved to Shawmut, which had a better water supply, and renamed it Boston. The Dudleys and the Bradstreets remained in Charlestown through the winter, whose harsh conditions took the lives of two hundred settlers and drove another two hundred back to England. In February, the vessel *Lyon* arrived, bringing Roger Williams and desperately needed provisions. Dudley made plans to start a new settlement to be called Newtowne (later named Cambridge), and in 1631 the Dudleys and the Bradstreets moved there.

Anne was in distress because, after three years of marriage, she had failed to conceive a child. She interpreted her fallowness as a sign of God's displeasure with her. In January 1632, she fell ill with a lingering sickness that she also attributed to God's disfavor. During her convalescence, she wrote the first poem that survives from her life in New England, "Upon a Fit of Sickness." It was written in the approved ballad form of the colony's Bay Psalm Book, which the Puritans used in place of the Anglican Book of Common Prayer. The poem shows Anne's facility with rhyme and meter and her conventional Puritan attitudes about illness and death. She is twenty years old and anticipating a death that the conditions of her life in New England may have caused her to wish for:

> Twice ten years old not fully told
>   since nature gave me breath,
> My race is run, my thread is spun,
>   lo, here is fatal death.
>   . . . .

For what's this life but care and strife
   since first we came from womb?
Our strength doth waste, our time doth haste,
   and then we go to th' tomb.

Her fatalism is tempered by her conviction that the trials of her life are, in fact, evidence of God's concern for her ultimate salvation.

Bestow much cost there's nothing lost,
   to make salvation sure,
O great's the gain, though got with pain,
   comes with profession pure.

Not long after completing this poem, Anne became pregnant with her first child, a coincidence that she took as a sign of God's approval of her verse. God had rewarded her creativity with fertility.

After the birth of her first child Samuel in 1633, Anne's outward life fell into the pattern typical of Puritan wives in New England. She bore children, managed her ever-growing household, and assisted her husband, who was often absent from home on colony business, in conducting her family's financial affairs, acting as Simon's "deputy husband." When Samuel was two years old, the Bradstreets and the Dudleys moved to Ipswich, a frontier settlement forty miles north of Boston that had been started by the son of John Winthrop. The following year a daughter Dorothy was born, then in quick succession Sarah in 1638, Simon in 1640, Hannah in 1642. But in spite of the heavy demands of child-rearing and household supervision, and the added challenges of frequently starting over in new settlements, Anne made time to continue writing verse.

In 1643 she wrote an elegy to the English Tudor Queen Elizabeth that placed this revered monarch high in the pantheon of the world's historical and legendary rulers. The poem, approximately one hundred and twenty-five lines written in rhymed couplets of iambic pentameter—the noblest poetic line, favored by Shakespeare and Milton for its solemn rhythm—gave Anne a vehicle to argue, decorously, that women might be the intellectual equals of men. Because her subject was a deceased queen who had presided over the most glorious period of English history, Anne was fortified against the charge of over-reaching her claims of feminine eminence in men's worldly affairs.

In Anne's view, Elizabeth ". . . was so good, so just, so learn'd, so wise,/ From all the kings on earth she won the prize." Through Elizabeth's many accomplishments (was Anne here thinking of her achievements and those of her neighboring Puritan housewives?) "She has wiped off th' aspersion of her sex,/ That women wisdom lack to play the rex." Anne describes Elizabeth's victory over the Spanish, her taming of the French king, her sponsorship of the explorer Francis Drake and asks, "Was ever people better ruled than hers?/ Was ever land more happy freed from stirs?/ Did ever wealth in England more abound?/ Her victories in foreign coasts resound." These lines suggest a comparison between Elizabeth's rule and the reign of the current English monarch Charles I, whose struggles with the Puritan dominated Parliament had just plunged England into a civil war.

After extolling Elizabeth's virtues and placing her fame above both Dido and Cleopatra, Anne brings her poem to a close with an ironic rhetorical question:

> Now say, have women worth? or have they none?
> Or had they some, but with our queen is't gone?
> Nay masculines, you have thus taxed us long,
> But she, though dead, will vindicate our wrong.
> Let such as say our sex is void of reason,
> Know 'tis a slander now but once was treason.

Her elegy to Queen Elizabeth reveals many traits of Anne Bradstreet's character and intellect. It displays her skill with verse and her knowledge of both English and world history. It shows her pride in her gender and her rejection of the conventional view of masculine superiority. But if Anne is asserting feminism in seventeenth-century Puritan New

England, she is doing it discreetly, not confrontationally, as was the case with Anne Hutchinson. She uses Queen Elizabeth to shield her from any implication that she is challenging male prerogatives in the colony. She is only asking that women's talents and contributions be recognized and honored. Anne, as the daughter of a prominent New England magistrate and the wife of another, was in no position to question male supremacy in the colony. But just as clearly, she chafes at the notion that her intellect is in any way inferior to that of men. That she succeeded in this delicate balancing act is evident from the fact that leading men of the colony were instrumental in bringing her verses before the reading publics in old England and New.

———— •·• ————

What launched her was *The Quaternions*, an epic poem she wrote between 1645 and 1647. In 1645 Simon Bradstreet decided to move his family again, this time to a settlement called Andover fifteen miles west of Ipswich. Andover had been founded in 1641 by minister John Woodbridge, Anne's brother-in-law, and a strong supporter of her poetry. Simon began construction of a grand house located on twenty acres of land while Anne and the children remained in Ipswich. The house was completed in 1646, and Anne moved there with her children and domestic servants, joining twenty-two other settlers. She remained in Andover until her death in 1672.

While waiting in Ipswich for her new home to be completed, Anne began work on *The Quaternions*. The poem runs to eighteen hundred lines written in heroic couplets. It is in four parts; each part subdivided into four sections. Anne took for her subject the accepted state of knowledge about the universe and humanity's place in it. The content is based on the Ptolemaic conception of the universe, the Aristotelian theory of the four elements thought to comprise it, and scripture. It is a showcase of Anne's knowledge of both classical and Hebraic texts. (Although Copernicus had published his theory of the solar system one hundred years earlier, it had not yet gained wide acceptance, especially among Puritans, who had difficulty reconciling their theology with a universe in which the Earth was only one of several planets orbiting the Sun.)

The first part of *The Quaternions* was called "The Four Elements." It was based on a cosmology devised by ancient Greek philosophers that still had currency in the English Renaissance. The plays of Shakespeare are laden with imagery derived from this system. According to the Greeks, everything in the universe—living things and all matter—is composed of four elements: Fire, Air, Earth, and Water. Anne treated each of the elements in a separate section. Fancifully and somewhat humorously, she imagined them as quarreling sisters vying for dominance, each claiming superior powers and importance. A brief prologue sets up the situation:

> The Fire, Air, Earth, and Water did contest
> Which was strongest, noblest, and the best,
> Who was of greatest use and might'est force;
> In placid terms they thought now to discourse,
> That in due order each her turn should speak;
> But enmity this amity did break.
> All would be chief, and all scorned to be under,
> Whence issued winds and rains, lightning and thunder;
> The quaking earth did groan, the sky looked black,
> The fire, the forced air, in sunder crack;
> The sea did threat the heavens, the heavens the earth,
> All looked like a chaos or new birth.

Just from these few lines, the reader can feel the force of Anne's personality: her sense of humor, her wit, her compassion, her confidence in herself. The lines are relaxed and self-assured, the rhymes natural. Her ironic positioning of the speaker as overseeing squabbling children (she undoubtedly had good material to draw from in her household) mirrors her maternal role. The peacemaker in the poem, who speaks last and most briefly, modestly, is Air, the most spiritual of the elements. "I am the breath of every living soul," she declares. Was Anne thinking of herself when she wrote after Air's speech:

I have said less than did my sisters three,
But what's their worth or force, the same's in me.
To add to all I've said was my intent,
But dare not go beyond my element.

The second part of *The Quaternions*—"Of the Four Humours in Man's Constitution"—deals with human physiology and the functioning of the physical organism. The four humours were considered to be microcosmic equivalents of the four elements. According to the Bradstreet scholar Ann Stanford, Anne drew from the work of Helkiah Crooke for the content of this poem. Crooke was the physician to King James I and had published in 1615 a large volume on anatomy. This book would have been in one of the large libraries kept by colonists like Dudley, Winthrop, and Nathaniel Ward, the minister in Ipswich with whom Anne frequently conversed. According to Crooke's theory, all food is composed of the four elements. It passes from the stomach to the liver, which converts it into four liquid substances, the humours: Choler, Blood, Melancholy, and Phlegm. Each of the humours rules a particular organ of the body and influences temperament, personality, character, and health. Anne again sets up the poem as a debate among four disputatious sisters. "Mild Phlegm," who speaks last, brings harmony to the contentious humours through her "loving counsel"—another reference to the maternal peacemaking role in the Puritan household.

In the third part of *The Quaternions*, Anne profiles the four ages of man. She correlates these stages to the four elements and the four humours, in keeping with the renaissance belief that the microcosm perfectly reflects the macrocosm in the expression of God's divine architecture. Typically, she describes this relationship using metaphors taken from the family:

Lo now four act upon the stage,
Childhood and Youth, the Manly and Old Age;
The first son unto phlegm, grand-child to water,
Unstable, supple, cold, and moist his nature.

The second, frolic, claims his pedigree
From blood and air, for hot and moist is he.
The third of fire and choler is composed
Vindicative and quarrelsome disposed.
The last of earth, and heavy melancholy,
Solid, hating all lightness and folly.

She also ties this quaternion to the one that follows on the four seasons by likening childhood to spring, youth to summer, manly to autumn, and old age to winter. This metaphoric frame of mind places Anne's poem firmly in the sixteenth and seventeenth-century poetic tradition in finding imaginative correspondences between disparate aspects of life. All of the human life stages are personified as males.

Childhood was clothed in white and green to show
His spring was intermixed with some snow:
Upon his head nature a garland set
Of primrose, daisy and the violet.
Such cold mean flowers the spring puts forth betime
Before the sun hath thoroughly heat the clime.

The poem adheres to the Puritan doctrine of man's sinfulness and redemption through grace but also divulges Anne's anguish over humanity's dark fate and guilt. Childhood is speaking:

Ah me! Conceived in sin and born with sorrow,
A nothing, here today and gone tomorrow,
Whose mean beginning blushing can't reveal,
But night and darkness must with shame conceal.
My mother's breeding sickness I will spare,
Her nine months weary burthen not declare.

Surely here, Anne is letting men know what women endure to bring their children into the world.

Youth parades vanity, a sin Puritans loathed because of its association with the excessive opulence and display of Catholic rituals and cathedrals. Anne allows Youth to puff himself up. Then she deflates him:

> My wit, my bounty, and my courtesy
> Make all to place their future hopes on me.
> This is my best; but Youth is known, alas!
> To be as wild as is the snuffing ass:
> As vain as froth, or vanity can be,
> Those who would see vain man, may look on me.

The section on Middle Age reviews the various roles performed by adult males and their social obligations: husband, nobleman, soldier, pastor, farmer, merchant. She concludes this portrait with a gloomy catalog—lightened by traces of humor—of the ills and ailments that portend the onset of old age.

> The vexing stone in bladder and in reins,
> The strangury torments me with sore pains.
> The windy colic oft my bowels rend,
> To break the darksome prison where it's penned.
> The cramp and gout doth sadly torture me,
> And the restraining, lame sciatica.
> The asthma, megrim, palsy, lethargy,
> The quartan ague, dropsy, lunacy:
> Subject to all distempers, that's the truth,
> Though some more incident to Age or Youth
> And to conclude, I may not tedious be,
> Man at his best estate is vanity.

Anne uses Old Age to review the political upheavals that have roiled England and the continent since the death of Queen Elizabeth. She lays the blame for the turmoil on the Roman Catholic Church—"bloody,

Popish, hellish miscreants." Old Age then goes on to describe the failure of his senses and physical vigor.

> My grinders now are few, my sight doth fail,
> My skin is wrinkled, and my cheeks are pale,
> No more rejoice at music's pleasing noise,
> But waking glad to her the cock's shrill voice:
> I cannot scent savours of pleasant meat,
> Nor sapors find in what I drink or eat:
> My arms and hands once strong have lost their might;
> I cannot labour, much less can I fight.

In closing this poem, Anne returns to the theme of earthly and human vanity that pervades Puritan doctrine. But her references to the sensory pleasures of life that diminish and fade sound like a lament for the passing of it. Old Age exits with the lines, "Triumph I shall o'er sin, o'er death, o'er hell,/ And in that hope I bid you all farewell." It is a hope, not a conviction.

———•———

> Another four I've left yet to bring on,
> Of four times four the last quaternion,
> The Winter, Summer, Autumn and the Spring,
> In season all these seasons I shall bring:
> Sweet Spring like man in his minority,
> At present claimed, and had priority.

So begins the last quaternion of Anne's epic, "The Four Seasons of the Year." She speaks to us in her voice, celebrating the Earth's life cycle and describing, from her observation, the human activities and natural events that the seasons dictate. She structures the poem around the passage of the Sun through the astrological zodiac, noting the changes that the Sun's annual journey brings to the natural world. Her embrace of

life, her delight in its sensuous pleasures, is evident. Here are lines from
Autumn's September, when all is ripeness:

> The vintage now is ripe, the grapes are pressed,
> Whose lively liquor oft is cursed and blest;
> For nought so good, but it may be abused,
> But it's a precious juice when well it's used.
> The raisins now in clusters dried be,
> The orange, lemon, dangle on the tree:
> The pomegranate, the fig are ripe also,
> And apples now their yellow sides do show.
> Of almonds, quinces, wardens, and of peach,
> The season's now at hand of all and each.
> Sure at this time, time first of all began,
> And in this month was made apostate Man.

The Quaternions were a major poetic achievement for Anne Bradstreet,
especially considering the circumstances of their composition. Anne was
living at the edge of a frontier settlement in North America, far from the
literary resources of London, Oxford, or Cambridge, dependent on the
personal libraries of her father and her neighbors. Yet she wrote a poem
that offered her readers encyclopedic knowledge of their physical world,
their history, their theology, their experience as seventeenth-century
English men and women. What these poems reveal about Anne is her
extensive learning, her literary skill, and the fullness of her engagement
with the world she inhabited. But Anne, with typical womanly modesty,
downplayed her remarkable accomplishment. She concludes the section
on Winter with the following apologetic lines:

> My subject's bare, my brain is bad
> Or better lines you should have had:
> The first fell in so naturally,
> I knew not how to pass it by;

The last, though bad, I could not mend,
Accept therefore of what is penned,
And all the faults that you shall spy
Shall at your feet for pardon cry.

After moving to Andover, Anne began work on another quaternion that she titled "The Four Monarchies." Perhaps her most ambitious undertaking, running to over thirty-five hundred lines, the poem was intended to encompass ancient human history down to the coming of Christ to demonstrate the working out of God's plan for mankind. Anne relied on Sir Walter Raleigh's *History of the World* (1628) as her primary source. The poem treated the Assyrian, Persian, Greek, and Roman empires, organized around their most prominent rulers. The scope of the poem, given the constraints of Anne's circumstances, is astonishing. Anne abandoned the poem in 1647 before completing the section on the Roman Empire, and ended it with "An Apology."

To finish what's begun was my intent,
My thoughts and my endeavours thereto bent;
Essays I many made but still gave out,
The more I mused, the more I was in doubt;
The subject large, my mind and body weak,
With many more discouragements did speak.

Anne took up the poem again after a hiatus from writing, but never completed it. Perhaps she was wary of bringing her narrative into the Christian era and risking rebuke from the male guardians of Puritan theology who had put Anne Hutchinson in her place.

In 1647 Anne lost two of her intellectual counterparts and literary supporters when Nathaniel Ward, a minister in Ipswich, whose library she had used, and her brother-in-law John Woodbridge left for England to assist with the Puritan revolution underway there. Woodbridge carried with him a manuscript of Anne's poems. He obtained testimonials to Anne's verse from several respected men in England, including Ward, who gave the manuscript to his publisher, Stephen Botwell. Botwell issued her poetry on July 1, 1650, under the title *The Tenth Muse, Lately Sprung Up In America*. Her poems were prefaced by short tributary verses written by Woodbridge, Ward, John Rogers, and others that cloaked them in the mantle of male approval. The book became a best seller in England as well as New England, where nearly every literate Puritan home held a copy. Anne was a celebrity.

There followed a period of artistic fallowness in Anne's life during which she wrote sparingly, in prose, in her notebook, about her spiritual struggles brought on by a prolonged illness. In 1660 she recovered her health and soon was writing verses again, but now in a more lyrical and meditative vein. In 1661 Simon left for England to seek renewal of the charter for the Massachusetts Bay Company from the restored monarch Charles II. A poem she addressed to him during one of his frequent absences expresses the tenderness of her longing for him in fanciful comparisons to loving pairs of creatures.

> Return my dear, my joy, my only love,
> Unto thy hind, thy mullet, and thy dove,
> Who neither joys in pasture, house, nor streams,
> The substance gone, O me, these are but dreams.
> Together at one tree, oh let us browse,
> And like two turtles roost within one house,
> And like the mullets in one river glide,
> Let's still remain but one, till death divide.
> Thy loving love and dearest dear,
> At home, abroad, and everywhere.

In August 1665 a series of tragedies began cascading into Anne's life that seemed to break her spirit and destroy her enjoyment of life. It began with the death of her granddaughter Elizabeth, the daughter of her son Samuel and his wife, Mercy. Elizabeth died at age one-and-a-half. The following year the Bradstreets' home burned down in a fire started by a servant who dropped a lit candle. Anne lost all her furniture, household goods, her library, and her papers. Simon built them a new home, but the experience reinforced Anne's growing sense of the vanity of earthly things. Three years later her granddaughter Anne, another child of Samuel and Mercy, died of a fever. Five months later her grandson Simon, a one-month-old infant, died. Thereupon Samuel decided to move his family to Jamaica and left his pregnant wife, Mercy, with Anne while he established a new home for them. In September 1670, both Mercy and the new baby, also named Anne, died while Samuel was away.

Anne wrote elegies for each of these losses. In 1671 her health broke again when she came down with consumption. Sensing that she was approaching the end of her life, she wrote "As Weary Pilgrim," her farewell to life.

> A pilgrim I, on earth perplexed
>   With sins, with cares and sorrows vext,
> By age and pains brought to decay,
>   And my clay house mold'ring away.
> Oh, how I long to be at rest
>   And soar on high among the blest.
> This body shall in silence sleep,
>   Mine eyes no more shall ever weep,
> No fainting fits shall me assail
>   Nor grinding pains my body frail,
> With cares and fears ne'er cumb'red be
>   Nor losses know, nor sorrows see.

Anne Bradstreet died on September 16, 1672. Although the location of her burial plot is unknown, the Bradstreet Gate at Harvard Yard in Cambridge, Massachusetts, commemorates her, and she is depicted in a stained glass window in St. Botolph's Church in Boston, Lincolnshire, where she and her family worshipped before coming to New England. Anne left us a powerful example of an orthodox Puritan wife and mother who, pushing tactfully but insistently against conventional concepts of the feminine role, expanded the boundaries of expectations and accomplishments for her gender in a world tightly controlled by men.

Thomas Paine (Courtesy of Smithsonian Institution, National Portrait Gallery.)

CHAPTER 3

Thomas Paine

Prologue

Throughout the colonial period, stresses between the American colonists and the British governing authorities began accumulating and eventually led to a breakdown in trust and mutual amity. In part, these stresses came from the colonists' land hunger, which put them in frequent conflict with Indians, taxing England's capacity to protect its subjects. But they were also caused by the colonists' increasingly resentful involvement in Britain's global power struggles with her rivals France and Spain, who had their designs on the North American continent and traded on Indians' loyalty to further them. These resentments came to a head after the French and Indian War. Parliament passed a series of acts seeking taxation revenue from the colonies to help defray England's war debts and simultaneously issued a proclamation limiting the colonists' westward expansion to reduce conflict with Indian tribes. Many Americans, as they began to call themselves, felt that their interests and the interests of the mother country were at odds. Positions on both sides of the Atlantic had begun to harden around the time that the English writer and provocateur Thomas Paine arrived in America, following the collapse of his life in England.

Widely known in England as an agitator for change and a fierce foe of the monarchy, Paine came to America as the country teetered on the edge of revolution. Although the colonists had provoked England to impose martial law in Massachusetts in response to the Boston Tea Party, and although they were forming militias, opinion was strongly divided on the best means of redress. Loyalists advocated rapprochement with England through diplomatic efforts; patriots and firebrands like Samuel Adams called for complete separation; a third group was either undecided or had no opinion. At the time of Paine's arrival, even George Washington, who became commander of the Continental Army, was unsure that revolution was the necessary and proper course.

Into this maelstrom, Paine hurled his anti-monarchical pamphlet *Common Sense*, which tipped the balance of public opinion in favor of revolution. That done, Paine returned to Europe hoping to aid in the overthrow of the monarchy in France and in England itself. He was a tireless foe of absolute authority and the system of privilege it engendered and carried his assault even into the hallowed sanctuary of religion, which he regarded as the ultimate source of fraudulent claims of authority. He was the archetypal maverick, unafraid to question, in provocative and uncompromising terms, even the most fundamental and widely accepted assumptions of society. For this, he paid a heavy price.

Thomas Paine – The Voice of Revolution

On November 30, 1774, the *London Packet*, a British ship out of Dover, docked at Philadelphia, Pennsylvania, and deposited on American soil an Englishman whose pen would change the course of world history. His name was Thomas Paine. Within two years of his arrival, his political writings would push the wavering American colonies towards independence, rally the spirits of America's military leaders and soldiers during the Revolutionary War, and lay out a vision of a constitutional government for a new federal republic. Thirty-five years later, impoverished and largely forgotten, he would die in a New York rooming house and be refused burial in a Quaker cemetery.

Tom Paine had left England a failure—bankrupt in business, divorced from his second wife, in disrepute with the government, a man with no money and no prospects. He was born in Thetford, Norfolk, on January 29, 1737, into an artisan family. His father, Joseph, a Quaker, earned his living as a maker of stays for women's corsets. His mother, Frances Cocke, an Anglican, was the daughter of a local attorney with connections to Norfolk's ruling family, the Graftons, who owned vast tracts of land and dispensed patronage throughout the county. The Paines lived in a cottage on the edge of town, under the shadow of a bleak and windswept hill known as the Wilderness, where executions of criminals convicted of capital offenses were carried out. As a youth, Tom Paine could witness the death by hanging of men convicted of crimes no more serious than the theft of twenty shillings (the equivalent of $140 US today). The extreme disparities of class and wealth that defined eighteenth-century English society were visible to Tom in the privileged connections of his maternal grandfather, and the cruel justice meted out to men driven by poverty into crime.

Although baptized in the Anglican Church of his mother, Tom attended Quaker meetings with his father. He did not join the Society of Friends, but he remained throughout his life sympathetic to the Quaker view of man's relationship to God and his fellow man. Quakers rejected the hierarchical organization of the Anglican Church, scorned the pretensions of social rank and class, and refused to pay tithes to the clergy. From Quakers, Tom absorbed the values of an egalitarian community undivided by artificial distinctions, and a readiness to question the established organization of society.

At age seven, Tom entered Thetford Grammar School, which dated from the twelfth century. He was a bright student, proficient in mathematics and language. However, he was grouped with the less advanced students because his father forbade him to receive instruction in Latin, a language Joseph Paine believed was used by priests and rulers to conceal their appetite for control of the people.

Tom's formal education ended at age thirteen. Following the custom of the time for a person of his class, he became apprenticed to a trade—his father's staymaking trade. His prospects for success in this trade were slight, as changing women's fashions were reducing the demand for corsets. After a brief stint as a journeyman staymaker at a shop in London, Paine, at age twenty, enlisted as a seaman on the English privateer *King of Prussia*.

Abe-bodied seamen—Paine was only 5'8"—were putting life and limb at risk on privateers in the hope of sharing in sea bounty. The English government commissioned the vessels in time of war to prey upon enemy ships. In 1757 England was in the second year of its Seven Years War with France. Paine went to sea over the objections of his Quaker father and received a taste of how the ambitions and intrigues of monarchs affected ordinary Englishmen swept up in their contests for supremacy. Fortunately for Paine, the *King of Prussia* enjoyed a successful six-month tour, capturing several French vessels and returning to port with plentiful bounty. Paine's share came to thirty pounds, a small fortune for a young man in his station.

This windfall enabled Paine to live in London for several months as a man of leisure. He used the opportunity to pursue his interest in scientific knowledge, then undergoing a historical transformation from the astronomical theories of Isaac Newton. Paine attended public lectures given by Benjamin Martin, a mathematician, and James Ferguson, a Scottish astronomer, who explicated Newton's theories for lay audiences. Paine was joined at these lectures by other men and women from the artisan class interested in self-improvement. Ferguson also taught Paine the art of globe making.

From these lectures, Paine came away with the understanding that the universe—the cosmos—was operating according to physical laws that could be comprehended and explained by man's reason. Paine subsequently applied this understanding to the realms of social organization and politics. He concluded that these provinces of human life should also be subjected to the scrutiny of reason, divorced from prejudice, tradition, and established law.

In the spring of 1758, his privateering booty spent, Paine left London for employment with a staymaker in Dover. There, he attended Methodist meetings and began preaching to the congregation. The humanistic message of Methodism's outreach to the poor and disenfranchised in English society—including its criminals—struck a responsive chord in Paine. A year later, with funds loaned by his Dover employer, Paine moved to Sandwich, in Kent, and established his staymaking shop. He continued his preaching. The egalitarian premise of Methodism—that all men are equal in the sight of God—and its certainty that men are capable of self-government, had a lasting effect on Paine's conception of the ideal form of social organization as expressed in his future political writings.

While in Sandwich, Paine met Mary Lambert, an attractive young woman employed as a waiting-woman to Maria Solly, the wife of the town draper. On September 29, 1759, they were married. Mary was soon pregnant, and when Paine's business failed, they moved to Margate in East Kent. Both Mary and the infant died during childbirth. Paine moved back to Sandwich and lived with the Sollys while recovering from his losses of both trade and family.

He then considered seeking government employment as an excise officer—a collector of the duties imposed on goods imported into England. It was unpopular and dangerous work. Merchants resented the government's reach into their lives, and smugglers avoiding the tax were made desperate by the threat of capital punishment. Paine wrote his father for advice and receiving encouragement returned to Thetford in the spring of 1761. While living with his parents, he was guided through the steps to excise service by a family friend. After his screening, he was required to swear an oath of loyalty to King George III. In December 1762, Paine was appointed to a position in Grantham, Lincolnshire, gauging brewers casks.

His service as an exciseman brought Paine into the world of government control. He became an agent of the government, but before long, its critic. In August 1764, he was promoted to a better paying but more dangerous posting at Alford, Lincolnshire, where he came into conflict with his supervisor, who accused him of stamping. Stamping was the term applied to the filing of false reports of customs inspections that had never taken place. Because it spared smugglers and merchants from government intrusion, and excise men—who were bribed—from hostile reprisals, it was a common practice. Stamping represented a form of government corruption that Paine came to despise as exploitative of all the parties to it. Paine knew that it was his supervisor who had disguised his stamping as Paine's. Paine was dismissed from the service, returned to Thetford, and again found work as a staymaker in the neighboring town of Diss.

Dissatisfied, Paine decided to seek reinstatement with the excise service. While he waited for the outcome of his appeal, he moved to London,
where he found employment as an English teacher at an academy for the
children of artisans. His annual salary of twenty-five pounds, half his earnings as an exciseman, made him poor. He renewed his connection with
James Ferguson and met Dr. John Bevis, another well-known astronomer.

Through the influence of Henry Cocksredge, the man in Thetford
who had guided him into the excise service, the Excise Board reinstated
Paine after he submitted a groveling letter of apology. In February 1768,
he was given an excise post in Lewes, Sussex, a town twice the size of
Thetford with a vibrant social and cultural life. He found rooms above
Samuel Ollive's tobacconist shop and soon was mingling with the town's
political radicals at the White Hart Tavern, where local artisans who
belonged to the Headstrong Club debated national and international issues. Ollive brought Paine into the Society of Twelve, a group of activists
that met twice a year to discuss town issues. Paine also attended meetings
of the Vestry, a church body that used local parish taxes to assist the poor.
All of these involvements can be seen as the seedbed of Paine's catalytic
role in Revolutionary America.

In spring 1771, Paine remarried, to Elizabeth Ollive, Samuel's daughter. He moved into the Ollive family quarters and assisted in the operation of its grocery and tobacco business. But he also continued his excise
employment and in 1772 was asked by activists in the service to bring
grievances about their salary and working conditions to Parliament. To
carry out this mission, Paine wrote his first political polemic, *Case of the
Officers of Excise*.

In this essay, we can hear, for the first time, Paine's voice raised in
protest against social and economic injustice. He argues that the salary
paid to an excise officer—fifty pounds per year—is, after taxes and necessary expenses such as the maintenance of a horse have been deducted,
insufficient to support him and his family while he performs a service
vital to the economic health of his country. His poverty then makes him
vulnerable to corruption and fraud, to his moral detriment, and the
detriment of the revenue on which the government depends. He points

out that what the government loses through corruption and collusion between excise officers and traders is far greater than the additional salary required to pay the officers a living wage. Paine's argument reveals a man both compassionate and reasonable. He begins with sympathy for the difficult choices facing the underpaid excise officer: be honest and starve, or be dishonest to survive but betray the trust placed in him by his government. He insists that poverty is not the result of moral failure but its cause, and cites Scripture—"Lest I be poor and steal" (Proverbs 30: 9)—for authority. But, keeping in mind that the audience for his appeal is Parliament, he stresses the harm that the poverty of the excise officers brings to "the revenue" and, therefore, to the government. He tries to show that the existing policy for salary harms both the individual and the collective. His argument is reasonable and sensible and points to a solution that will benefit all parties:

> With an addition of salary, the excise would wear a new aspect, and recover its former constitution. Languor and neglect would give place to care and cheerfulness. Men of reputation and abilities would seek after it, and finding a comfortable maintenance, would stick to it. The unworthy and the incapable would be rejected; the power of superiors be re-established, and laws and instruction receive new force. The officers would be secured from the temptations of poverty, and the revenue from the evils of it; the cure would be as extensive as the complaint, and new health out-root the present corruptions.

These plain words were written by a man whose formal education ended at age thirteen. They give us a glimpse of the power of his mind, his skill in argument, and the compassion in his heart.

Paine spent the winter of 1772-1773 in London carrying his essay and a petition signed by three thousand excise officers to Parliament. He survived on a stipend the officers raised to cover his living expenses while he represented their cause. But despite support from a commissioner of the Excise Board, Parliament ignored the appeal, and Paine, disappointed and disaffected, returned to Lewes in the spring. Soon he received an official letter from the Excise Commissioners discharging him from the service for being absent from his post without leave. A year later, the Ollive grocery business went into bankruptcy, sold its inventory to pay creditors, and Paine's marriage to Elizabeth collapsed. He was, to our knowledge, never again romantically involved with a woman. For the remainder of his life, he was wedded to revolution.

Paine returned to London with a thirty-five-pound settlement from his marriage. Through his contacts in the scientific community, he managed to secure an appointment with Benjamin Franklin, America's colonial representative. His meeting with Franklin convinced Paine that his future lay in America. With the funds from his marriage settlement, Paine purchased a first-class ticket on the *London Packet* and departed for America at the end of September. He was carrying with him his best hope of a prospect in America, a letter of introduction to Franklin's son-in-law Richard Bache.

———— · ————

The America that awaited Thomas Paine when the *London Packet* arrived in Philadelphia had experienced dramatic growth in the century since the deaths of Anne Bradstreet and Roger Williams. The number of colonies had grown from seven to thirteen. The population had increased twelve-fold, from 200,000 to 2,400,000 (including slaves, indentured servants, and natives living among colonials). Immigration had slowed, most of the population growth coming from a high birth rate and low infant mortality, both signs of health in the new land. The colonists were still predominantly English, loyal to England and its traditions. German and Dutch settlers, concentrated in New York, Delaware, and New Jersey, accounted for about fifteen percent of the population. Most of the white males who held voting rights were farmers, but a prosperous merchant class, benefiting from favorable trade relations with the mother country, clustered along the eastern seaboard and constituted a political and economic elite.

England maintained control of the colonies through its system of royal governors, but each colony had its assembly to manage internal affairs. Parliament dictated foreign policy. Royal governors executed it in the colonies. The vast majority of the colonists thought of themselves as Englishmen and were loyal to the mother country, which protected them from England's rivals France and Spain and gave them favorable trading conditions.

Relations between England and the colonies were upset when Parliament in 1765 passed the Stamp Act to raise revenue to pay the debts from its Seven Years War with France (1756-1763). The act imposed a tax on all documents and publications issued in the colonies. The colonies' united resistance to this act led to its repeal in 1766, but a year later, Parliament passed the Townshend Act, which imposed duties on English goods entering America, including the East India Company's tea. Paine, as an excise officer, no doubt, was aware of these revenue seeking measures, as well as the motives behind them.

This act produced the first confrontation between armed colonists and British troops. It was instigated by Samuel Adams, a radical who advocated independence. Merchants responded to the act by establishing boycotts of British goods, and the colonists gave up drinking imported tea, substituting teas brewed from local herbs. In 1770 Parliament rescinded all the provisions of the Townshend Act except the duty on tea, and the merchants lifted their boycott. Adams, fearing that the colonists were more disposed to reconciliation with England than independence from it, organized the Boston Tea Party. On December 16, 1773, a mob disguised as Indians and blacks boarded a ship in Boston harbor and threw hundreds of chests of tea overboard.

Parliament responded to this defiance in the spring of 1774 with a series of acts that tightened Britain's military grip on the colonies. The acts sent the Royal Navy to blockade Boston harbor, authorized the royal governors to quarter English soldiers in private houses, and rebuked the colonial government of Massachusetts.

These Coercive Acts, as they became known, had the effect of uniting the colonies. Relief flowed into Massachusetts to offset the consequences of the blockade. Political activists, working through Committees of Correspondence in all the colonies, called for a Continental Congress to address the crisis. Congress met in Philadelphia in October 1774, a month before Paine's arrival.

Congress sought reconciliation. It issued a Declaration of Rights asserting that colonists are Englishmen entitled to all legal rights of Englishmen. It listed Parliament's violations of those rights. It also agreed to exclude all imports from Britain after December 1, 1774, if the Coercive Acts were not repealed. Paine arrived in Philadelphia one day before this deadline.

He was seriously ill with "sea fever," most likely typhus contracted from the unsanitary conditions of a two-month ocean crossing. He was helped ashore by a doctor and carried to the home of the brother and sister-in-law of the ship's captain to convalesce. When he had recovered, he found lodgings in the center of the city and began to learn about his new surroundings. He read at the Library Company of Philadelphia—founded by Benjamin Franklin—and browsed in a bookstore owned by Robert Aitken next to his rented room. A conversation between the two men led to Aitken's suggestion that Paine serve as the editor of a journal Aitken was about to launch called the *Pennsylvania Magazine*. It was intended to be a general interest magazine devoted to a wide range of topics on politics, commerce, literature, and religion. Paine was offered a salary of fifty pounds per year. This appointment gave Paine an immediate presence in Pennsylvania's intellectual community and a forum for his challenging societal views. And it gave him space to experiment with his prose style to reach the widest possible audience. He wrote on a broad range of subjects, including an early denunciation of slavery. Before long, Paine had made *Pennsylvania Magazine* the biggest selling periodical in America. The voice of the revolution had arrived.

When Paine landed in America, public opinion favored reconciliation with England, not independence from her. While the colonists had grievances over the Coercive Acts, they felt bonded to the British nation and sought relief through diplomatic and legal channels. Paine himself initially thought reconciliation the preferable course. But during the next year, attitudes on both sides of the Atlantic hardened as England escalated its punitive measures against the colony and refused to address its complaints. Voices of moderation and conciliation in England were shouted down, and radicals in America, like Samuel Adams, gained credibility and influence.

In March 1775, Parliament passed the New England Restraining Act that forbade the four colonies of New England to trade with any part of the world except Great Britain and Ireland. The Act also denied their fishermen access to the rich fishing banks off of Newfoundland and Novia Scotia. In April, General Thomas Gage, Governor, and Captain-General of Massachusetts Bay dispatched soldiers to Concord to destroy a reported militia munitions site. Paul Revere and other riders warned the countryside and mustered out the Minute Men, who confronted the British troops at Lexington, where "the shot heard 'round the world" was fired. Eight Minutemen were killed before the colonials withdrew. The British troops marched on to Concord, where they were routed by a larger force of American militia. During their disorganized retreat, the Redcoats killed non-combatants and looted property, actions that turned public opinion against them in both England and America.

The colonies responded by calling a Second Continental Congress that met in Philadelphia in May. Congress created a provincial army and sent diplomatic agents to Europe. At this point, Loyalists held a majority in Congress. New York, New Jersey, Pennsylvania, and Maryland instructed their delegates to oppose independence. Following a second military engagement at Bunker Hill, which the British won at the cost of over one thousand men, Congress issued the Olive Branch Petition asking King George III to repeal the Coercive Acts and end the war. The king refused to accept the petition, proclaimed the colonies in rebellion, and ordered it suppressed. In December, Parliament passed an act forbidding all trade and commerce with the colonies. By the time news of this act reached America, colonials were reading Tom Paine's pamphlet *Common Sense.*

The Battle of Lexington changed Paine's mind about America's relationship with England. The atrocities committed by British troops during their retreat inflamed him and made him doubt that the liberties sought by the colonists could be obtained by peaceful means. In July

1775, he wrote an essay for *Pennsylvania Magazine* titled "Thoughts on Defensive War" that justified taking arms against the mother country. "Whoever considers the unprincipled enemy we have to cope with, will not hesitate to declare that nothing but arms or miracles can reduce them to reason and moderation. They have lost sight of the limits of humanity. The portrait of a parent red with the blood of her children is a picture fit only for the galleries of the infernals." In respect of his Quaker origins, Paine signed the article "A Lover of Peace." He was then in the midst of a falling out with his publisher Robert Aitken, not over editorial policy, but the terms of his contract. The magazine was flourishing under his guidance, and he wanted to share in the spoils of its success. When Aitken refused to agree to an arbitration on his demands, Paine began to employ his pen on another project.

Paine had met Dr. Benjamin Rush at Aitken's bookshop. Rush was a leading figure of the Enlightenment in America, a scientist and humanitarian who opposed slavery and advocated for public education. Conversations between the two men in the bookshop led to a friendship, and in the summer of 1775 Rush encouraged Paine to express his views on the crisis between America and England. The result was the pamphlet *Common Sense*, a title Rush suggested. Rush cautioned Paine not to argue for independence or a republican form of government, as Rush believed public opinion did not support such a radical change. Paine ignored this advice, and his pamphlet became the means of altering public opinion.

Paine's grand object in writing the pamphlet, which runs to about forty pages, was to build an argument for establishing on the American continent a new nation based on the principle of a representative government chartered and chosen by the governed. He regarded independence as the means to the creation of a federal union of all thirteen colonies. He unfolded a vision of a republic devoted to granting and protecting the freedoms of its citizens, in contradistinction to the British government that in Paine's view imposed on its subjects the will of the monarch. Though revolutionary in intent, it was moderate and reasonable in tone, except when exposing the evils of England's monarchical system.

Paine begins his argument by distinguishing between society and government. Society encompasses people's interactions through commerce, worship, education, and recreation. It exists to promote happiness. The government regulates these social interactions. It exists to restrict wickedness. Government is a necessary evil, necessary because people lack adequate moral virtue to be governed by it alone. But the function of government is to serve the interests of society, not to impose them. Paine was an advocate of limited government. He writes: "Wherefore security being the true design and end of government, it unanswerably follows that whatever form thereof appears most likely to ensure it to us, with the least expense and the greatest benefit, is preferable to all others."

Paine next examines the government of England. He finds there tyranny entrenched in the hereditary monarchy and House of Lords and the House of Commons, an impotent republican partner, created to check the power of the king but in reality, incapable of doing so. He calls the monarchical tradition in England unnatural because based on distinctions between the person of the king and his numerous subjects that are entirely artificial. The only distinction Paine recognizes is the natural one between man and woman.

Paine traces hereditary monarchy to its roots in heathen societies in which might ruled. "Could we take off the dark covering of antiquity and trace them [kings] to their first rise, we should find the first of them nothing better than the principal ruffian of some restless gang." Such a one was William the Conqueror, who started England's line of kings: "A French bastard landing with an armed banditti and establishing himself King of England against the consent of the natives, is in plain terms a very paltry rascally original." Aiming an arrow at the collusion between rulers and priests, Paine adds, "Original sin and hereditary succession are parallels." He points out that because monarchs rule their subjects instead of serving them, their main occupations are dispensing patronage to supporters and initiating wars with rival monarchs that impoverish the people.

Paine then considers the current state of affairs between England and America. He knows that he is writing to an audience that favors reconciliation over independence. The wealthiest and most powerful colonials have strong ties to England and see independence as a threat to their privileged position. The majority of colonials are yeoman farmers whose strongest grievances are against the colonial elite, not the British. Paine weighs the advantages and disadvantages of continued dependence on England. He focuses on commerce and argues that as an independent nation, America will be free to engage in commerce on its own terms, rather than on terms dictated by England. Free of English control, America can trade with England's enemies France and Spain, even in times of war. This argument played effectively on colonial resentment of England's heavy-handed restrictions on American trade.

Paine anticipated that his readers would wonder about the form of government that would replace the monarchy. Under the system prevailing at the time he wrote *Common Sense*, each colony had its representative assembly that managed internal affairs. Royal governors appointed by the king carried out England's broad policies for America. Foreign relations were controlled from London. The colonies were separate and distinct, sometimes with competing interests that were resolved through appeals to the crown. Paine saw that what was needed to replace imperial control was a federal union, and he sketched one that foreshadowed many, but not all, of the features contained in the Articles of Confederation.

Paine also addressed the question of whether America had the military capability to win a war of independence from England. He provided a detailed inventory of America's physical and social resources to support his contention that the time to fight for independence had arrived. America's chief advantages were its distance from the mother country, its unity of purpose, and the vast extent of the continent that England would have to subdue and control.

He concluded his polemic with a stirring vision of a future for America as an independent nation: "We have it in our power to begin the world over again. A situation similar to the present, hath not happened since the days of Noah until now. The birthday of a new world is at hand, and a race of men, perhaps as numerous as all Europe contains, are to receive their portion of freedom from the events of a few months."

————•————

The impact of Paine's pamphlet on public opinion in America was immediate and widespread. Editions, some unauthorized, flowed from publisher Robert Bell's press and made Paine, when it became known that he, not Franklin, was the anonymous author, famous throughout the colonies and Europe. Paine estimated that over 150,000 copies of *Common Sense* were sold in America. He donated his profits to the war effort. George Washington was converted to the cause of independence, and Congress, recognizing the shift that had taken place in the colonists' attitude towards England, created a five-man committee chaired by Thomas Jefferson to draft a Declaration of Independence. Paine was actively involved in the movement that pressured Congress to take this step. The language of the Declaration adopted by Congress echoes the arguments Paine made in *Common Sense* about the proper relationship between a government and the members of society.

> We hold these truths to be self-evident, that all men are created equal, that they are endowed by their Creator with certain inalienable Rights, that among these are Life, Liberty and the pursuit of Happiness. – That to secure these rights, governments are instituted among Men, deriving their just powers from the consent of the governed. – That whenever any Form of Government becomes destructive of these ends, it is the Right of the People to alter or to abolish it, and to institute new government, laying its foundation on such principles and organizing its powers in such form, as to them shall seem most likely to effect their Safety and Happiness.

The premise of equality, the assertion of "inalienable rights," the subordination of government to the will of the governed are all concepts around which Paine based his argument for America's separation from England, where government issued not from the people but from a monarch of doubtful legitimacy and predatory intent.

Shortly after Congress issued the Declaration, Paine joined a Pennsylvania militia unit called the Associators as secretary to General Daniel Roberdeau and marched to Amboy, New Jersey, where the British were preparing to invade New York. He witnessed the build-up of British forces as ships carrying soldiers and munitions filled up Raritan Bay. In September, he traveled to Fort Lee, an encampment above the Hudson River across from New York City, to serve as the aide-de-camp to General Nathanael Greene. Washington had tasked Greene with keeping the British from occupying the Hudson Valley and so cutting off New York from the New England colonies. Paine sent war reports from the region to the Philadelphia press.

In November, British forces captured Fort Washington across the Hudson from Fort Lee, and Greene was forced to retreat. Recognizing that the war was not going in America's favor, Paine decided to write a series of propaganda pamphlets designed to bolster the morale of America's troops and address the colonists' fear of British military superiority. He titled the series *The American Crisis* and wrote thirteen essays, one for each colony, issued between December 1776 and April 1783, when Washington declared victory.

Paine returned to Philadelphia to find the city in a state of panic. Congress had relocated to Baltimore, and people were fleeing in anticipation of an attack by British forces massed north of the city on the Delaware River in Trenton, New Jersey. Washington had retreated through New Jersey with the Continental Army to prevent the British from capturing Pennsylvania, considered the "keystone" in the colonists' war for independence. Paine published the first *Crisis* on December 19, 1776. He signed it "Common Sense." On Christmas Eve, Washington read the eight-page pamphlet to his troops as they prepared to launch a surprise night attack against the British.

The essay begins with legendary words calling forth America's resolve: "These are the times that try men's souls. The summer soldier and the sunshine patriot will, in this crisis, shrink from the service of their country; but he that stands it *now* deserves the love and thanks of man and woman. Tyranny, like hell, is not easily conquered; yet we have this consolation with us, that the harder the conflict, the more glorious the triumph."

Paine writes to remind Americans of their high purpose in fighting the British, to reassure them about the direction of the war and its outcome, and to express confidence in Washington's leadership. Washington's retreat through New Jersey had raised concerns about the possible loss of Philadelphia and provoked questions about his competence. Paine, who accompanied Washington, describes the retreat as tactical and orderly, and dismisses the loss of Philadelphia, should it occur, as of no lasting consequence. He insists that Britain's ultimate defeat is certain because she must fight on too many fronts at once. Speaking with the confidence of a victor, he diminishes King George III by comparing him to a highway robber. He warns the colonists not to hearken to British offers of peace and mercy that are meant to divide the colonies and weaken their determination. He also attacks the Tories for their loyalty to the crown and urges Congress to appropriate their land and property once the British are defeated.

He concludes with a stirring call for unified support of the war effort:

> I call not upon a few, but upon all: not on *this* state or *that* state, but on *every* state: up and help us; lay your shoulders to the wheel; better to have too much force than too little when so great an object is at stake. Let it be told to the future world that in the depth of winter when nothing but hope and virtue could survive, that the city and the country, alarmed at one common danger, came forth to meet and to repulse it. Say not that thousands are gone, turn out your tens of thousands, throw not the burden of the day upon Providence, but *"show your faith by your works,"* that God may bless you.

After reading Paine's words to his troops, Washington crossed the Delaware River in the dead of night and attacked the sleeping British army, still groggy from Christmas Eve celebrations. His troops captured Trenton with only four wounded, taking over nine hundred prisoners, most of them Hessian mercenaries, as well as twelve hundred small arms and six brass cannon. This triumph was followed by victories at Princeton, Hackensack, Elizabethtown, and Newark. Washington's success in New Jersey during this winter campaign was a turning point in the war. Colonial morale revived, enlistments rose, and confidence in Washington was restored.

The war dragged on for six more years. Over its course, Paine continued his role as the voice of the revolution, sending forth new issues of *Crisis* at decisive moments. He stoked American resolve when it faltered, diminished British successes, often with mockery, and delivered provocative and demoralizing messages to the British people and especially their leaders. He spoke as one who never for a moment doubted that America would win the war and obtain her independence from England. He held out a vision of freedom for the colonists and never wavered from it.

The war unfolded in seesaw fashion, with American victories in one colony offset by British victories in another. Britain had military superiority but was fighting on numerous fronts far from her sources of provisions and munitions, which had to be continually replaced by ship. Her army might capture ground in a battle but then would have difficulty holding it. Britain sought to capitalize on its military successes by making offers of reconciliation that fell short of granting independence. Paine saw these offers as signs of England's uneasiness about the outcome of the war and seized on them to rally his readers with the prospect of ultimate victory.

Paine issued his second *Crisis* in January 1777 as a letter to Lord Richard Howe, the vice-admiral of the British fleet, who had come to America seeking to negotiate with Congress, which rebuffed him. Paine addressed him in a condescending tone, employing sarcasm and insult to debunk England's military capability and its intentions towards America. Howe returned to England after being refused a meeting with George Washington for failing to address him as General. In March, Congress returned to Philadelphia, and Paine, on a recommendation from John Adams, was chosen as Secretary to the newly created Committee for Foreign Affairs.

Later in the year, Howe's brother General Sir William Howe, commander in chief of the British forces, defeated Washington's troops at the Battle of Brandywine Creek outside Philadelphia and captured the city on September 26. Washington's counter-attack at Germantown two weeks later was repelled, and he retreated to Valley Forge, where the Continental Army spent a grim winter, poorly sheltered, clothed, and fed. Paine responded to the loss of Philadelphia with his fourth *Crisis*, in which he impudently declared that the British victory was actually a defeat: "Look back at the events of last winter, and the present year, there you will find that the enemy's successes always contributed to reduce them. What they have gained in ground, they paid so dearly for in numbers, that their victories have in the end accounted to defeats." This assessment glides over the fact that American casualties (killed, wounded, captured) totaled 2,411 as compared with 1,120 British losses—more than double. "And such a brush," he writes, "notwithstanding we lost the ground, would by still reducing the enemy, put them in a condition to be afterwards totally defeated."

In the winter of 1778, morale in the colonies reached low ebb. The contrast between the miserable circumstances of Washington's army at Valley Forge and the comfort of Howe's army quartered in Philadelphia disturbed the entire country. Paine sought to boost America's morale in his fifth *Crisis*, which he addressed to Howe. Again he adopted the pose of the conqueror, speculating facetiously on the best method of disposing of Howe's remains. "It, fortunately, happens that the simple genius of America has discovered the art of preserving bodies, and embellishing them too, with much greater frugality than the ancients. In balmage, sir, of humble tar, you will be as secure as Pharaoh, and in a hieroglyphic of feathers, rival in finery all the mummies of Egypt." Paine's cheekiness and crude humor in picturing the English general departing America tarred and feathered must have brought chuckles from Paine's dispirited readers.

While Washington and his men shivered at Valley Forge, Benjamin Franklin was in France negotiating an alliance that would tip the balance of power in the war and be the first step in making America and France sisters in revolt. Franklin also successfully petitioned King Charles III of Spain for assistance. These diplomatic moves so alarmed England that Parliament passed a measure giving Americans everything they wanted except independence: repeal of the Coercive Acts, a full pardon to the rebels, and assurance of no further levies. Parliament sent five commissioners to treat with Congress, which held out for independence and sent them back to England empty-handed. In desperation, Parliament in October issued a Manifesto and Proclamation calling on Americans to overthrow Congress and accept its terms. Paine published his sixth *Crisis* to deflect any appeal that the Proclamation might have for wavering colonists and to defend the alliance between America and France. Paine was undoubtedly elated by this treaty, which brought America closer to nationhood, the fact that underlay England's alarm.

The war slogged on, inconclusively, at times, degenerating into punitive raids rather than strategic battles. The British waged a successful campaign in the south, capturing Georgia in the spring of 1779 and Charleston, South Carolina, in May 1780. Paine responded to these losses with his usual aplomb, seeing opportunity in defeat by blaming the loss of Charleston on "the want of a sufficient supply of provisions" and using it to leverage a voluntary subscription fund that raised three hundred thousand pounds. The funds formed capital for establishing the first bank in America, the Bank of Philadelphia, and were used to supply the army. Paine donated his entire salary of $500 as a clerk of the Pennsylvania Assembly to the fund, but it was returned to him.

England's southern campaign then aimed at North Carolina and Virginia but was stopped on October 7, 1780, by an American victory at King's Mountain, where a local militia raised from the countryside defeated a force of 1,400 Loyalists led by a Scottish Major. In December, Washington put Nathanael Greene, Paine's old commander, in charge of the Southern Army. Greene succeeded in pushing England's forces under General Charles Cornwallis back into Charleston. There, Cornwallis reassessed England's position in the war and proposed consolidating her forces in Virginia, a suggestion not followed by his superior, General Sir Henry Clinton, who commanded the British army in New York. Instead,

Clinton remained in New York with his army and ordered Cornwallis to establish a deep-water port at Yorktown, Virginia. There Britain suffered a military defeat that effectively ended the war, although negotiations for peace dragged on for another year and a half.

The American victory could not have been accomplished without the aid of France. As a combined force of 8,000 French soldiers and 8,000 Americans approached Yorktown by land, a fleet of French warships under the command of Rear-Admiral the Count de Grasse defeated the British navy at the Battle of Chesapeake Bay and blockaded the harbor, cutting off Cornwallis's escape route to the sea. Trapped and outnumbered, Cornwallis surrendered on October 19, 1781. Over 7,000 of his troops were taken prisoner. French and American casualties totaled fifty-eight killed and 301 wounded.

Despite this catastrophic military setback, King George III a month later delivered a bellicose speech to Parliament vowing to continue the war, and Parliament voted to do this. Paine replied to the king's speech with *Crisis* number ten, issued on March 5, 1782. In a tone of lofty superiority, Paine regards the speech as worthy of no more than America's curiosity. "It was inquired after with a smile, read with a laugh, and dismissed with disdain." He gloats over the desperation behind England's decision to prolong a war she has clearly lost. "The British king and ministry are constantly holding up the vast importance which America is of to England, in order to allure the nation to carry on the war: now, whatever ground there is for this idea, it ought to have operated as a reason for not beginning it, and, therefore, they support their present measures to their own disgrace, because the arguments which they now use, are a direct reflection of their former policy."

Although the war continued for another year and a half, it was confined to the west, where England had formed alliances with Indian tribes. The last land battle took place on November 10, 1782, in Ohio, when George Rogers Clark routed Shawnee warriors. As England was at war not only with America and France but also with Spain and the Netherlands, peace negotiations took place in Paris under French supervision. Benjamin Franklin, John Jay, and John Adams comprised America's peace commission. Recognized by England as "Commissioners of the Thirteen United States," they obtained for the new country all land west to the Mississippi, north to Canada, and south to the Floridas. The treaty was signed on February 3, 1783. Two months later, after news of the armistice reached America, Washington announced the end of the war. Paine issued his final *Crisis* on the same day. " 'The times that tried men's souls' are over—and the greatest and completest revolution the world ever knew, gloriously and happily accomplished," it begins. Paine urges on his countrymen a union of the United States to preserve the freedoms they have won. He concludes with a personal statement of the revolution's significance for him:

> It was the cause of America that made me an author. The force with which it struck my mind, and the dangerous condition the country appeared to me in, by courting an impossible and an unnatural reconciliation with those who were determined to reduce her, instead of striking out into the only line that could cement and save her, a DECLARATION OF INDEPENDENCE, made it impossible for me, feeling as I did, to be silent: and if, in the course of more than seven years, I have rendered her any service, I have likewise added something to the reputation of literature, by freely and disinterestedly employing it in the great cause of mankind, and showing that there may be genius without prostitution.

On November 25, 1783, Paine rode proudly with George Washington at the head of a parade in New York that celebrated the city's recovery from the British.

———•—

Though Paine had indeed "rendered service in the great cause of mankind," he found himself politically marginalized after the war, with few prospects for participation in the structuring of the new country. Partly this was due to his role in a scandal that had earned him enemies in Congress, and partly it was due to his revolutionary nature. From his early years as an excise officer to his numerous roles in the American war of independence, Paine had shown himself to be an agitator, an agent of change, a provocateur. Now that the war was won, Americans faced the challenge of governing themselves. What was needed for this purpose were consensus builders who could forge coalitions out of America's diverse population, not provocateurs skilled, as was Paine, at polarizing issues and inflaming passions. Given Paine's character, it is not surprising that after struggling to find a place for himself in the new America, he returned to Europe to participate in the French Revolution.

Paine's fall from favor in America began with the Silas Deane affair. In the build-up to the Franco-American alliance, Congress sent one of its members, Silas Deane, on a mission to France to obtain military supplies. His compensation was to be a five percent commission on the war materials that he purchased. Deane left for France in the spring of 1776 and returned in July 1778 after arranging for shipments of guns, ammunition, and other military goods. Paine became involved in the business when he learned from Arthur Lee, a witness to the transactions in France, that the material Deane claimed to have purchased, and on which he received a substantial commission, had actually been a gift. In his position as Secretary to the Committee for Foreign Affairs, Paine had access to government documents that showed Lee's allegations to be true. Paine publicized what he had discovered, and in a series of letters addressed to Deane, accused him of betraying the revolution for personal profit. Deane's allies in Congress came to his defense, and Paine was forced to resign his position as Secretary when the French government complained that the scandal was jeopardizing negotiations for the alliance. The affair ended Paine's official relations with the Congress. To support himself, he was forced to take a humble position as clerk to a Quaker merchant who supplied the American army with grain.

In November 1779, Paine returned to politics when the Pennsylvania Assembly appointed him clerk. But his dissatisfaction with America's treatment of him persisted. During the summer of 1780, he made plans to leave America for England to promote revolution there. He resigned his position with the Assembly but was dissuaded from leaving for England by his friend Nathanael Greene, who convinced him that England would try and execute him for treason. Later that year, Paine was asked by Colonel John Laurens, an aide to George Washington, to accompany him as secretary on a fundraising trip to France. When Congress refused to approve Paine for the position, he joined the mission at his own expense. After successful negotiations for aid that included arms, clothing, supplies for the army, and 2.5 million silver Livres, Paine contemplated remaining in France. Laurens insisted that he return. Their ship arrived in Boston on August 26, 1781, just as Washington was preparing his assault on Cornwallis at Yorktown.

Paine's role in securing this assistance from France went unacknowledged. Unemployed, broke from having spent his own funds on the trip to France, he wrote to Washington asking for help. Through Washington's advocacy, Paine was given a position writing tracts for Robert Morris, the newly appointed Superintendent of Finance, who was pursuing greater taxation to support the war effort and the operations of government. This position came to an end early in 1783 when Morris, discouraged by the refusal of some states to agree to higher taxation, resigned as Superintendent. Paine retreated to Bordentown, New Jersey, where he stayed as the guest of Joseph and Mary Kirkbride, his closest American friends, on their farm. From there, he sent out appeals to various government agencies seeking compensation for his services to America during the revolutionary war. He reminded his audience that he had sacrificed his welfare to the cause of independence, donating proceeds of his writing to the war effort.

Gradually, he was rewarded. In November 1783, while staying at George Washington's estate before their triumphant entry into New York, Paine received an honorarium of twenty-four hundred livres from the French envoy Chevalier de la Luzerne. Paine used this gift to purchase a small property in Bordentown and a horse. In April of the following year, New York granted him a three hundred acre farm in New Rochelle that had been confiscated from a Loyalist who had fled to Canada. A year later, the Pennsylvania Assembly, acting on Washington's recommendation, awarded Paine five hundred pounds. And on October 3, 1785,

Congress voted him an award of $3,000. Paine used these funds to pay off creditors and rented his farm to secure an income stream.

Paine then withdrew from political life in America to work on the design of a single span bridge. During his travels around America, he had noticed that bridges supported by pilings were susceptible to damage from winter ice. He hired as his assistant a skilled artisan newly arrived from England, John Hall, and together they worked on a model of the bridge at the Kirkbrides' farm. They built an iron model thirteen feet high and sent it to Philadelphia for Franklin's inspection. But failing to find either financial or political support for the project, Paine decided to take it to Europe. He sailed for France from New York on April 26, 1787. As it turned out, the real bridge that Paine was transporting was a revolution. He did not return to America for fifteen years.

———•———

Once in France, Paine showed his model to a committee of the French Academy of Sciences, which issued a complimentary report and recommended the construction of a test span. But the more authoritative Council of Bridges was not receptive, so Paine took the project to England. There, after visiting his widowed mother in Thetford, he found a patron in Peter Whiteside, an American businessman from Philadelphia. In August 1788, he obtained a patent for his design, and he persuaded the owners of an ironworks in Yorkshire to build a demonstration span one hundred and ten feet long and five feet high. This model was displayed in a London park but did not attract support from investors.

While his bridge project languished, Paine returned to Paris and gave his attention to the French Revolution. In January 1790, he wrote a letter to Edmund Burke, the Irish political philosopher and Member of Commons who had hosted him for a week at his house in London. Paine predicted that revolution would spread from France to other nations in Europe, including England. Burke responded with the essay *Reflections on the Revolution* in which he defended the perpetuation of the monarchy and the peerage through the principle of hereditary succession. Paine, now back in England, answered Burke with *The Rights of Man*, a

40,000-word treatise dedicated to George Washington. It was published in March 1791.

In *The Rights of Man*, Paine defends the French Revolution on the same principles that he used to support the American war of independence. He asserts the right of the people to self-government and rejects Burke's acceptance of tradition, arguing that the present should not be bound by the past. Each generation should be free to act for itself. He repeats his belief that man's natural, God-given rights entitle him to create his own form of government through a written constitution. Paine attacks England's government as despotic, lacking sanction from its subjects and making their lives miserable while fostering war with other nations.

The Rights of Man was hugely popular. Fifty thousand copies were sold in England within three months of publication. Translations appeared in France, Holland, and German lands. It became the most widely read book of its time. Although Paine came under attack by the establishment press, the government chose not to prosecute him, fearing to inflame public opinion even more. As he had done with *Common Sense*, Paine refused all personal profit from the book and assigned his share of the proceeds to an English activist group, the Society for Constitutional Information.

Paine returned to France before the release of the book and began work on an anti-monarchical tract that became *The Rights of Man Part Two*. It was issued in February 1792. This work continued his attack on the monarchy and the ruling class in England, declared its government to be illegitimate, and called for a revolution to overthrow the monarchy and establish a government chosen by the people. In response, Prime Minister William Pitt orchestrated a furious campaign of harassment and slander against Paine. A paid hack wrote a defamatory biography of him, Court-organized mobs burned him in effigy, and a royal proclamation banning seditious writings stopped the sale of the book. Paine was formally charged with seditious libel, but the government, not wishing to martyr him, postponed his trial in hopes that he would voluntarily leave England. He departed from Dover in September 1792, never again to return to the country of his birth. He was tried in absentia and sentenced to death for treason.

When Paine arrived in France, he was greeted by enthusiastic crowds, offered French citizenship, and, though he spoke no French, elected as a delegate from Calais to the National Assembly convening in Paris. He was once again in his favorite milieu, the turmoil of revolution. He did not foresee the tyrannical future towards which the French Revolution was moving. When the Assembly took up the fate of Louis XVI in November, Paine argued, through a translator, that the king should be tried and sentenced to exile in America, not executed. Kill the monarchy, but not the monarch, was his plea to the delegates. But by a majority of only one vote, the Convention sentenced Louis to death, and he was beheaded on January 21, 1793.

When the Jacobins seized power later in the year, and Robespierre began the Reign of Terror, imprisoning and executing thousands of "enemies of the people" after secret trials conducted at night, Paine's sympathy for the person of the king, and the threat that he might turn his pen against the conduct of the revolution, placed him under suspicion. He ceased attending sessions of the Assembly, retreated from political involvement, and began writing his third major work, *The Age of Reason*. This book, which traced the roots of political despotism to the enslavement of people's minds by the myths and superstitions of organized religion, was Paine's most radical utterance. It set him apart from other political thinkers of his time and further eroded his reputation among God-fearing Americans when they read it.

In *The Age of Reason,* Paine approached the Bible, the foundation of Christianity, as a rationalist. Seventy years before the appearance of Darwin's *On the Origin of Species*, Paine questioned the reliability of the Bible as a true account of the story of mankind. He viewed it not as the Word of God, but as a collection of myths, legends, and histories transmitted by man. His skeptical dismissal of some of the most important claims of Christianity—Mary's immaculate conception, Jesus' resurrection and divinity—earned him the enmity not only of the clergy, but also the entrenched political class their doctrines helped sustain in power.

Paine begins the book with an exaltation of reason. "The most formidable weapon against errors of every kind is reason," he writes. He then applies this faculty to an examination of the Old and New Testaments, comparing their narratives with the known facts of history. "These books [the OT], beginning with Genesis and ending with Revelation (which by the bye, is a book of riddles that requires a revelation to explain it), are, we are told, the Word of God. It is, therefore, proper for us to know who told us so, that we may know what credit to give to the report. The answer to this question is that nobody can tell, except that we tell one another so." Paine then applies the test of reason to the doctrine of revelation.

> Revelation is a communication of something which the person to whom that thing is revealed did not know before. For if I have done a thing, or seen it done, it needs no revelation to tell me I have done it, or seen it, nor to enable me to tell it or to write it.
>
> Revelation, therefore, cannot be applied to anything done upon earth, of which man himself is the actor or the witness; and consequently all the historical and anecdotal parts of the Bible, which is almost the whole of it, is not within the meaning and compass of the word revelation, and, therefore, is not the Word of God.

But Paine makes it clear that in arguing thus, he is not declaring himself an atheist, which his detractors claimed. He believes in God and believes that God's Word has been revealed to man. "THE WORD OF GOD IS THE CREATION WE BEHOLD, and it is in *this word*, which no human invention can counterfeit or alter, that God speaketh universally to man." This statement expresses Paine's deism, his belief that God is visible in the physical universe, whose perfection and glory man can apprehend through the use of his reason. Paine held that man should worship God, not through fawning submission to clergymen in ritualized behavior that exhibited his deference to authority, but by using the rational faculty bestowed on him by his Creator.

So threatening was Paine's assault on the collusion between religious and political authorities that he was immediately branded an atheist and hanged in effigy in England. The book was suppressed, and its publisher imprisoned. When Paine finally returned to America in 1802, he found that *The Age of Reason* had made him a non-believer in the eyes of his adopted countrymen.

On Christmas Day 1793, Paine was arrested at his hotel in Paris and taken to Luxembourg Prison, where he was confined in a ten-foot by eight-foot cell. The Committee of Public Safety, a kind of secret police, had ordered him arrested as a foreigner disloyal to the Republic. He was considered an Englishman, not an American, and the subject of a country at war with France. The fact that he had been granted French citizenship seems to have been forgotten. His appeals to America's Minister to France, Gouverneur Morris, to intervene for his release were of no avail. Morris, an old political foe from Philadelphia, preferred having Paine in prison so that he could not upset Franco-American relations by writing articles critical of the Republican government. Paine narrowly escaped execution only because his jailers mistakenly marked the wrong side of his cell door with chalk.

When James Monroe replaced Morris in August 1794, Paine wrote to him for help, insisting that he was an American citizen and had been wrongly incarcerated. Paine was released to Monroe's custody and remained with him while recovering from a prison illness. Paine was restored to his seat in the Assembly and paid his back salary, but in October 1795, his service as a deputy was terminated.

While incarcerated in Luxembourg Prison, Paine accumulated bitterness towards George Washington, then serving as the first President of the United States, for failing to intervene on his behalf. In September 1795, he sent a letter to Washington, accusing him of treachery for being complicit in his imprisonment. In the letter, he left the door open for reconciliation should Washington "give me cause to think otherwise." When Washington did not reply, Paine wrote a longer, open letter to him that he sent to Richard Bache in Philadelphia for publication. The letter attacked Washington's character and his military capabilities. Paine was now employing for his agenda the propaganda tactics that he had put in the service of America's cause against England. The letter backfired on Paine. His attack on the hero of America's revolution alienated even Paine's friends and compounded the hostile reception that he would receive on his return to America.

During the last five years of his stay in France, Paine resided at the home of Nicolas de Bonneville, a bookseller and printer he had befriended. He grew increasingly disenchanted with the movement of the French Republic towards a new despotism and abandoned his hope for a worldwide revolution. He wanted to return to America but was reluctant to sail because the war between England and France would put him at risk of capture by the British navy on the open sea. His unyielding egalitarian principles had made him a man without a country. After the Treaty of Amiens temporarily ended hostilities between France and England, Paine took passage, once again, on the *London Packet*, and sailed for America. He was accompanied by the wife and children of Nicolas de Bonneville, who had been imprisoned for comparing Napoleon Bonaparte to Oliver Cromwell. He arrived in Baltimore on October 30, 1802.

He soon found himself a pawn in the bitter partisan struggles between the Federalist and Republican parties. The Federalists exploited Paine's reputation as an atheist and slanderer of Washington to attack their enemy Thomas Jefferson, who had courageously welcomed Paine at the White House. Paine became a pariah, denied lodging at inns, refused transportation on coaches, shunned at social gatherings. He sought refuge at the Kirkbrides' farm in Bordentown, and in December 1803 moved to his New Rochelle farm for the winter. Suffering from gout, he moved temporarily to New York, where he stayed in a hotel. By midsummer, he was back in New Rochelle. He sold sixty acres of his farm to pay creditors. Through all these travails, Paine continued writing, defending his deist views, and seeking to remove the label of atheist from his reputation.

In July 1806, Paine suffered a stroke. He was then living in New York with William Carver, a blacksmith from Lewes, who had taken him in. Depressed by America's neglect of him and his fall from grace, Paine was drinking heavily and neglecting his hygiene. Carver asked him to leave and presented him with a bill for rent that Paine was unable to pay.

Paine's poverty and slide towards a lonely and miserable death continued. His request to Congress for a government stipend was rejected. An appeal to Jefferson went unanswered. In July 1808, friends arranged for him to be lodged with a family in Greenwich, a village on the outskirts of New York. In January 1809, his life forces ebbing, Paine made preparations for his death. He executed his will, making his largest bequest, one hundred acres of his farm, to Mme. de Bonneville to use for the education and upbringing of her children. His request for burial in a Quaker cemetery was refused because he was not a member of the Society of Friends, who feared his notoriety. In May, Paine moved into rooms Mme. de Bonneville had rented in Greenwich, and he died there on June 8, 1809. He was buried on his New Rochelle farm in a ceremony attended by Mme. de Bonneville and a few friends. Ten years later, his bones were dug up and removed to England, where they were lost.

Josiah Gregg (Courtesy of William Elsey Connelley. *Doniphan's Expedition and the Conquest of New Mexico and California*. Kansas City, MO: Bryant & Bryant, 1907.)

CHAPTER 4

Josiah Gregg

Prologue

Josiah Gregg's life coincided with and exemplified America's period of "Manifest Destiny," its reach across the plains to the Pacific Ocean that began with Lewis and Clark's journey up the Missouri River and across the Rockies following the Louisiana Purchase. Gregg embodied the westering impulse in the American character, its propensity for restless wandering in pursuit of the undiscovered and unknown. He witnessed and participated in the major events of America's westward expansion into the southwest and California: the Santa Fé trade, the Mexican-American War, the gold rush.

Gregg also displayed many of the traits of the generalist that were indispensable to survival on the frontier. He was a man of wide interests and varied skills: a surveyor, a land speculator, a botanist, a doctor, a writer, a successful merchant. But in none of these capacities did he find fulfillment. Though a significant player in a major episode of American history, he always remained an outsider—dissatisfied with the company of most men, critical of anyone in authority over him, indifferent to the opinions of his associates. He died unwed and without progeny. Gregg was a paradoxical character, acting out widely shared American tendencies, impulses, and ambitions, but remaining a loner, a misfit, an odd sort of person.

Josiah Gregg – A Wanderer on the Prairie

On May 15, 1831, in Independence, Missouri, a sickly young man in failing health was carried onto a wagon bound for New Mexico on the

Santa Fé Trail. He was heading out onto the prairie on the advice of his physicians, who had recommended a change of climate and scene as a treatment for the chronic dyspepsia and consumption that had kept him confined to his room for months. So began a twenty-year odyssey that would take Josiah Gregg to the far corners of the American west and produce a unique personal record of America's relentless expansion to the Pacific Ocean in fulfillment of its "Manifest Destiny."

The land that Gregg was about to cross had until recently been a province of Spain. It was now occupied largely by Indians, many of whom had been forcibly relocated there from their ancestral lands in the old northwest and south, east of the Mississippi River. Gregg became one of the advance guard of pioneers, fur trappers, and adventurers who opened the West for settlement by Anglo-Americans and eventual inclusion in the federal union.

The story of how these lands came to belong to the United States has a long pedigree. At the time that English colonials in the northeast issued their Declaration of Independence from Great Britain and drew up their Articles of Confederation, Spain controlled two-thirds of the American continent—Florida and most of the territory west of the Mississippi—and this mighty river was regarded as the likely western terminus of the United States. Spanish possession had begun nearly three hundred years earlier, with the arrival of Christopher Columbus in the West Indies in 1492. Columbus, an Italian explorer, sailing under a charter granted by the queen of Spain, made landfall on an island in the Bahamas that he named San Salvador and, believing he had reached the fabled Indies, called the native inhabitants Indians, an appellation that stuck. Columbus initiated over three centuries of Spanish exploration and colonization in North and Central America.

After his initial "discovery," Columbus made two more voyages, bringing colonists to Cuba and Hispaniola (Haiti), where gold was discovered, setting off a Spanish treasure hunt that sent conquistadors into the vast unexplored regions of Central and North America. From their base in the Caribbean, Spanish explorers fanned out in a search for land and treasure that gave them sovereign claims to vast amounts of territory in Florida, Mexico, the southwest, and the Great Plains long before Puritan refugees from England began building the communities in New England that became part of the fledgling United States.

Spain's claims to the enormous extent of land its explorers had passed through were based on "an international legal principle that is known today as the Doctrine of Discovery. The Doctrine is one of the very first international law principles that allegedly authorized European Christian countries to explore and claim the lands and rights of peoples outside of Europe. When European countries set out to exploit new lands in the fifteenth through twentieth centuries and planted their flags and crosses in 'newly discovered' lands, they were undertaking the well-recognized procedures and rituals of Discovery to make claims to these territories and over indigenous peoples. The Doctrine provided that Europeans automatically acquired property rights in native lands and gained governmental, political, and commercial rights over the indigenous inhabitants without their knowledge or consent. This legal principle was created and justified by religious, racial, and ethnocentric ideas of European and Christian superiority over other peoples and religions. The Doctrine is still international and domestic law today, and is being actively applied against indigenous peoples and nations." (Robert J. Miller. *The International Law of Colonialism: A Comparative Analysis.* 15 April 2011, Lewis and Clark Law School. Spring Symposium: The Future of International Law in Indigenous Affairs.) To obtain the highest sanction for exercising their rights under this principle, the Spanish crown had in May 1493 obtained authorization for her discoveries in the New World from Pope Alexander VI.

Spain's extensive holdings in North America were considerably enlarged by the acquisition of French Louisiana under the terms of the Treaty of Paris in 1763 that concluded the Seven Years War between England and France. By 1800, when she reached the zenith of her power in the New World, Spain controlled virtually all of the territory west of the Mississippi River, excluding Oregon, Washington, and Idaho. From this point forward, her holdings rapidly shrank. She secretly receded Louisiana to France in 1800 under pressure from Napoleon, ceded Florida to the United States in 1819, and lost New Spain (Mexico) to independence in 1821. These rapid changes in Spain's standing in North America set the stage for the life and career of Josiah Gregg and thousands of others like him.

Josiah was born on July 19, 1806. He was the middle child in a family that grew to seven children, four sons, and three daughters. His father, Harmon, was a wheelwright who had been raised in Kentucky, then moved to Tennessee. His mother, Suzannah Smelser, came from Pennsylvania. The Greggs' ancestors were Scots who moved to America in the seventeenth century as refugees from the rule of Charles I.

Many of the Americans who had crossed the Appalachian Mountains to settle in Kentucky and Tennessee were restless adventurers who enjoyed the freedom and the hazards of life on the edge of the wilderness. In 1808, Harmon moved to Illinois, and then, in 1812, when war broke out between Great Britain and the United States, and the Indian tribes of Illinois, Indiana, and Ohio fought on the side of the British, he relocated his family to Cooper's Fort in Missouri.

During the War of 1812, the Greggs were not safe inside the stockade at Cooper's Fort. Sometime in 1814, Indians attacked the stockade, killing Josiah's uncle William Gregg and capturing his cousin Patsy Gregg, who was later recovered. When the war ended, Harmon moved his family outside the stockade and took up farming. Josiah began his schooling in a one-room log cabin schoolhouse in Cooper's Fort. He was an apt student with a love of reading and a gift for mathematics. At age twelve he designed and built a quadrant that he used to measure the height of trees, to the amazement of his schoolmates. He tutored other students in math and began keeping notes of his observations of the world and the people around him, a habit that continued for the rest of his life. When he was sixteen, his eyes already on the horizon, he learned to survey, believing it would be a valuable skill for mapping the uncharted country of the far west.

In 1824 Josiah went to Clay County near Liberty, Missouri, and started a school where he taught for one year. In 1825 Harmon moved his family again to the Blue River country in Jackson County, where he remained for the rest of his life. He farmed a site near a settlement that in 1827 became Independence, Missouri, the jumping-off point for trails leading to Santa Fé, California, and Oregon.

Josiah's scientific curiosity led him to apply to Dr. John Sappington of Sabine County, Missouri, for the study of medicine, but Sappington turned him down. Instead, Josiah took up the study of law but found it baffling and soon abandoned it. "Its dry details and old, Saxon, arbitrary forms were suited, neither to his tastes nor his genius," remarked his brother John in a letter to a mutual friend.

Josiah, throughout his youth, had been in frail health, as a consequence of which his parents had spared him the hard physical labor demanded by life on the frontier, and had encouraged his more scholarly and intellectual interests. In 1830 his health broke down under chronic dyspepsia and consumption, and he was confined to his room. All remedies failing, his physician astonished the family by recommending that Josiah join one of the caravans crossing the Great Plains from Independence to Santa Fé. And so on May 15, 1831, Gregg embarked from Independence with a caravan bound for New Mexico. Too ill to ride a horse or even sit upright in a wagon, he began the journey lying on a pallet inside one of the wagons. Within a week, the adventure, the dry clear air, the boundless expanse of the prairie, revived him. He mounted a pony and joined a buffalo hunt. His life as a prairie wanderer had begun.

The Santa Fé Trail had been blazed as early as 1792 by a French explorer named Pedro Vial. But the Spanish, who had closed their American frontier to foreigners, kept his journey a secret. Foreign traders who managed to reach Santa Fé were imprisoned, and their goods confiscated. This exclusionary policy changed when Mexico achieved independence from Spain in August 1821. A month later Hugh Glenn and William Becknell, traveling with four companions, left Franklin, Missouri, reached Santa Fé on November 16 and returned to Franklin in January with their saddlebags bulging with silver dollars. In May 1822, Becknell set out again with twenty-one men and three wagons, the first vehicles to cross the Great Plains. In 1828 a hundred-wagon caravan carrying merchandise worth $150,000 left for Santa Fé from

Independence, which had become the new starting point when Franklin was washed away by flooding from the Missouri River. Another flood in 1844 washed away the landing in Independence, and Westport Landing in what is now Kansas City became the main point of departure.

Caravanning on the Santa Fé Trail was both arduous and dangerous, qualities that over the years he lived as a trader endeared it to Josiah Gregg. The physical hardships entailed managing large numbers of livestock on the open plains, crossing swollen streams and rivers in heavily laden wagons, finding water in dry regions, weathering storms, and coping with illness and injury far from civilization. The danger came from raiding parties of marauding Indians in search of horses, mules, weapons, and trade goods.

Caravans leaving Independence for Santa Fé had first to pass through Indian Territory in what are now Kansas, Oklahoma, and Texas. In 1825, as Indian removal from the country east of the Mississippi continued, Congress approved drawing a line to mark the western limits of white settlement. The line ran north from the Red River in Texas along the border of the Arkansas Territory, Missouri, and northward up the Missouri River. In 1830 the land west of this line was designated as Indian Territory and used to relocate Indians from the northwest and the southeast. Omahas, Pawnees, and Otoes moved onto land that eventually became Nebraska. Delaware, Sauk and Fox, Shawnee, and Potawatomi Indians, among others, were given land in Kansas. To the south, Osages, Cherokees, Creeks, Seminoles, Chickasaws, and Choctaws were relocated to lands in Oklahoma and Texas. Also, in 1825, Congress paid the Osage and Kansas Indians for the right of transit across their lands for the Santa Fé trade.

The western boundary of Indian Territory was the one-hundredth meridian. Beyond it lay unorganized territory where roamed the wild tribes of the western plains—the Sioux, the Cheyenne, and the Arapaho in the north, the Comanche, Apache, and Navajo in the south. The "rules" governing relations between trading parties on the Santa Fé Trail and these Indians were simply the rules of encounter.

Between 1831 and 1840, Josiah Gregg made four round trips on the nine hundred mile Santa Fé Trail, established himself as a successful merchant of the southwest trade, and made many acquaintances in New Mexico and Mexico. He kept detailed notes of his travels and in 1844, transformed them into *Commerce of the Prairies*, a full account of the natural history and human culture he had observed on the Great Plains of America. His book is an open window through which we can absorb the sights, sounds, and smells of the western prairies and witness the acting out of our nation's idea of Manifest Destiny.

———•———

In *Commerce of the Prairies,* we meet three aspects of Josiah Gregg: the pragmatic Santa Fé trader seeking to build a livelihood, the scientific observer and commentator of the western scene, and the peripatetic wanderer who embodies the restless spirit of America.

The caravan Gregg joined on his first trip consisted of two hundred men transporting merchandise valued at $200,000 in nearly one hundred wagons. Gregg was a passenger, not a trader. He hoped the journey would restore his failing health. He wrote:

> My health had been gradually declining under a complication of chronic diseases, which defied every plan of treatment that the sagacity and science of my medical friends could devise . . . In this hopeless condition, my physicians advised me to take a trip across the Prairies, and, in the change of air and habits which such an adventure would involve, to seek that health which their science had failed to bestow.

They left in wagons drawn by mules, eight per wagon, which meant that each night on the trail, the muleteers would have to feed and corral (against Indian depredations) eight hundred mules. Mules were preferred over oxen as draft animals, even though they cost more, because, according to Gregg, they survived better on the prairie. Oxen had tender hooves and were more likely to drown pulling the wagons across the rivers and streams that ran like arteries through the plains. On a caravan as large as the one that Gregg had joined, hundreds of different kinds of merchandise would be loaded onto the wagons. The largest category was household goods—tableware, dishes, cooking utensils, storage boxes, hardware, bottles, and glasses. The inventory also included fabrics, clothing, tools, medicines, books, toys, musical instruments, and religious items. The caravan was also a traveling fort carrying rifles, shotguns, pistols, knives, and two cannon mounted on wagons to deter Indian attacks. Gregg describes "the wild and motley aspect" of the caravan's occupants: "the city-bred merchants in their fashionable fustian frocks, the backwoodsman with his linsey or leather hunting-shirt—the farmer with his blue jean coat—the wagoner with his flannel-sleeve vest—besides an assortment of other costumes which go to fill up the picture."

The wagons loaded, the mules in their traces, the men armed and eager, the caravan departs.

> At last, all are fairly launched upon the broad prairie—the miseries of preparation are over—the thousand anxieties occasioned by wearisome consultations are felt no more. The charioteer, as he smacks his whip, feels a bounding elasticity of soul within him, which he finds it impossible to restrain;—even the mules prick up their ears with a peculiarly conceited air, as if in anticipation of that change of scene which will presently follow. Harmony and good feeling prevail everywhere. The hilarious song, the *bon mot* and the witty repartee, go round in quick succession; and before people have had leisure to take cognizance of the fact, the lively village of Independence with its multitude of associations, is already lost to the eye.

Eleven days out, the wagons rendezvous at Council Grove, so named as the site where the Osage and Kansas Indians met with representatives of the US government to negotiate the right of passage on the Santa Fé Trail. By this time, Gregg is no longer an invalid carried in a wagon but has joined the mounted riders. At Council Grove, the travelers pause to organize their expedition. They choose a captain and agree on rules of governance for the journey—democracy in action. The captain directs the order of travel during the day and selects the camping ground at night. Gregg, who on a subsequent excursion was chosen captain, likens the role to the master of a ship. "Truly, there is not a better school for testing a man's temper, than the command of a promiscuous caravan of independent traders . . . He is expected to keep order while few are disposed to obey . . . For my own part, I can see no reason why the captain of a prairie caravan should not have as much power to call his men to account for disobedience or mutiny as the captain of a ship upon the high seas."

Scouts are chosen to find the best creek and river crossings, and every man is assigned a night watch duty. The wagons are ordered to advance four abreast to minimize delays in case of a breakdown, and also to facilitate forming a square for defense against Indian attack. At night, the wagons form a stockade around a central corral where the animals are secured. The travelers build their campfires outside the stockade and sleep out in the open. "The serene sky of the Prairies affords the most agreeable and wholesome canopy," Gregg notes approvingly.

Council Grove is heavily wooded, the last substantial stand of timber they will encounter until they reach the mountains of New Mexico. The men procure wood for repairs and store it on the undersides of the wagons. Gregg remarks on the fertility of this region and its suitability for settlement in terms that display the white man's sense of entitlement to the land, regardless of promises made to the Indians.

> This stream [Council Grove creek] is bordered by the most fertile
> bottoms and beautiful upland prairies, well adapted to cultivation:
> such indeed is the general character of the country from thence to
> Independence. All who have traversed these delightful regions, look
> forward with anxiety to the day when the Indian title to the land
> shall be extinguished, and flourishing "white" settlements dispel the
> gloom which at present prevails over this uninhabited region. Much
> of this prolific country now belongs to the Shawnees and other In-
> dians of the border, though some portions of it has [sic] never been
> allotted to any tribe.

A few days after leaving Council Grove, the party sights a herd of buffalo, "quietly grazing in the distance." Gregg joins in the hunt that immediately ensued.

> Every horseman was off in a scamper: and some of the wagoners, leaving their teams to take care of themselves, seized their guns and joined the race afoot. Here went one with his rifle or yager—there another with his double-barrelled shotgun—a third with his holster-pistols—a Mexican perhaps with his lance—another with his bow and arrows—and numbers joined without any arms whatever, merely for the "pleasures of the chase"—all helter-skelter . . . The fleetest of the pursuers were soon in the midst of the game, which scattered in all directions, like a flock of birds upon the descent of a hawk.

Later in his career on the prairie, Gregg lamented the "wanton slaughter of [the buffalo] by travelers and hunters, and the still greater havoc made upon them by the Indians," and predicted their eventual extinction. He admitted that he, too, was guilty of slaying buffalo simply for the sport.

After the caravan left Council Grove, it had to cross the plain between the Arkansas and Cimarron rivers—a fifty-mile journey that would take at least two days. Gregg describes the landscape ahead of them: "This tract of country may truly be styled the grand 'prairie ocean'; for not a single landmark is to be seen for more than forty miles—scarcely a visible eminence by which to direct one's course. All is as level as the sea, and the compass was our surest, as well as principal guide." Each wagon carries a five-gallon cask of water for drinking and cooking.

As they approach the Cimarron River, they are met by a party of about eighty Sioux. Though initially apprehensive at the sight of these Indians, the travelers are reassured when one of the Sioux holds aloft an American flag, a friendly form of greeting that indicated their desire to engage in trade. Communicating through sign language, the Sioux inform them that a large party of Comanche and Blackfeet is encamped along the Cimarron River.

The caravan enters the valley of the Cimarron and is immediately confronted by a small band of warriors on horseback, followed closely by a "countless host" coming towards them at full gallop. The panicked traders are unprepared for combat, but quickly form up the wagons into a fortress and take aim at "the intruders," but hold their fire. The Indians are more curious than hostile and surround the caravan in great numbers. A comical scene ensues.

> It was deemed expedient to force them away, so as to resume our march, or at least to take a more advantageous position. Our company was therefore mustered and drawn up in "line of battle"; and, accompanied by the sound of drum and fife, we marched towards the main group of the Indians. The latter seemed far more delighted than frightened with this strange parade and music, a spectacle they had, no doubt, never witnessed before, and perhaps looked upon the whole movement rather as a complimentary salute than a hostile array . . . The principal chief (who was dressed in a long red coat of strouding, or coarse cloth) appeared to have full confidence in the virtues of his calumet; which he lighted, and came boldly forward to meet our warlike corps, serenely smoking the "pipe of peace."

This drama, though amusing, is a telling sign of the misunderstanding and distrust that Anglo-Americans often brought to their encounters with Native Americans as the United States grew. It suggests an underlying animus towards the original occupants of the land.

Gregg's party moves on to the river, where they make camp a few hundred yards below the Indian encampment. From the number of lodges spread out along the river, Gregg estimates an assemblage of two to three thousand Indians, including at least one thousand warriors. The travelers' fear of attack lessens as they realize that the presence of children and squaws makes hostilities unlikely. As a further indication of their friendly intentions, at night, several warriors lead their squaws into the caravan's encampment to render their favors to the traders, who primly turn away this offer of plains hospitality.

The caravan moves on the next day, trailed by crowds of Indian men and women who follow like sea birds in the wake of a fishing vessel, hoping for scraps. The traders soon discover items missing from their wagons. Only when they decide to give presents to several of the chiefs as "ratification" of the peace between them, do the Indians fall back and allow the caravan to continue on its way unmolested.

———•—•———

Sometime in late July, Gregg joined a party of men who rode ahead of the caravan into Santa Fé to make "arrangements" for the admittance and storage of the merchandise that would be offered for sale. The tariffs imposed by the Mexican government were exorbitant—sometimes as much as one-hundred percent. But payoffs to local customs officials, an acceptable alternative, were less onerous. Additionally, the unpopular governor of New Mexico, Manuel Armijo, imposed his tariff of $500 per wagon. Gregg had by now become a valuable member of the trading party. He had been hired as a bookkeeper by the trader Jesse Sutton, and, astonishingly, he had learned to speak Spanish during the ten-week journey, a skill that made him an important negotiator.

Gregg spent several months in Santa Fé before traveling back to Missouri with a return caravan. During this time, and on his subsequent trips to New Mexico over the next nine years, he formed strong opinions about the New Mexican people and their culture. His assessment was, for the most part, unfavorable. He found their culture deficient in many ways, the implication being that perhaps they were not good stewards of the land they occupied.

At the time of Gregg's first visit to New Mexico, the population of the province was approximately forty-five thousand. This number included both "pure" blooded Spanish residents and mestizos, but not the Pueblo Indians, who numbered around ten thousand. Gregg's profile of this population is unflattering. He states that seventy-five percent of the population is illiterate. He attributes this to the lack of educational institutions and the absence of a public press, noting that no newspapers or periodicals are published in New Mexico. He reports that there are no doctors or lawyers in the province because the people are too poor to afford their services. He finds their artisans unskilled, their tools clumsy, their architecture primitive in its imitation of Pueblo buildings. He deplores their unsophistication: "There is no part of the civilized globe, perhaps, where the Arts have been so much neglected, and the progress of Science so successfully impeded as in New Mexico." He blames this backwardness on the government and on the Roman Catholic Church, who have done their best "to keep every avenue of knowledge closed against their subjects of the New World." He also chides the government for a justice system corrupted by bribery, and the church for exploiting the fears and suspicions of the populace for profit by charging exorbitant fees to perform marriages and burials. "In the variety and grossness of popular superstitions, Northern Mexico can probably compete with any civilized country in the world," he writes. "Here, the popular creed seems to be the embodiment of as much that is fantastic and improbable in idolatrous worship, as it is possible to clothe in the garb of a religious faith." He finds the comportment of New Mexicans at their religious services puerile: "These religious exercises, however, partake but seldom of the character of true devotion: for people may be seen chattering or tittering while in the act of crossing themselves, or muttering some formal prayer."

Gregg saves his harshest criticisms for the character of the New Mexicans. They impressed him as vicious people—cruel, cowardly, vain, and addicted to barbarous amusements like cockfighting, bull-baiting, and gambling. "The New Mexicans appear to have inherited much of the cruelty and intolerance of their ancestors [the Spanish], and no small portion of their bigotry and fanaticism . . . They have no stability except in artifice; no profundity except for intrigues: qualities for which they have acquired an unenviable celebrity." Priests are no exception to this pattern of debauched behavior; in fact, they set the example. "The padres themselves are foremost in most of the popular vices of the country: first at the fandango—first at the gaming table—first at the cock-pit—first at the bacchanalian orgies—and by no means last in the contraction of those liaisons which are so emphatically prohibited by their vows." Gregg traces these traits to the founders of New Mexico and to the Spanish charter that sanctioned their rule. "In every part of this singular document," he observes, "there may be traced evidences of that sordid lust for gold and power, which so disgraced all the Spanish conquests in America; and that religious fanaticism—that crusading spirit, which martyrized so many thousands of the aborigines of the New World." Later in his career as a trader, after having visited several cities in Mexico, Gregg would write: "Everything in this benighted country now seems to be on the decline, and the plain honest citizen of the old school is not unfrequently [sic] heard giving vent to the ejaculation 'Oh for the days of the king'."

Towards the Pueblo Indians who inhabit New Mexico, Gregg is more charitable. He admires their agriculture and animal husbandry, and finds them "a remarkably sober and industrious race, conspicuous for morality and honesty, and even very little given to quarreling or dissipation, except when they have had much familiar intercourse with the Hispano-Mexican population." He sympathizes with them on account of their exploitation by the Spanish, who took away their lands and gave them "baptism and the cross in exchange."

If Gregg comes across as severely judgmental and partisan in his condemnation of New Mexican society, we should keep in mind that over the nine-year period of his activity in the Santa Fé trade, tensions between Mexico and the United States were building towards the Mexican-American War that brought Spain's former possessions north of the Rio Grande River under American control. Gregg was an observer and participant in that war, and we shall see that he could be just as acerbic in his criticisms of American conduct of the war and its leaders as he was in his descriptions of New Mexicans. He was throughout his career an iconoclastic, some might say curmudgeonly, commentator on the society around him. He preferred the wilderness to human society.

———•———

Between 1834 and 1840, Gregg made three more round-trips to Santa Fé. On his last trip, he decided to find a shorter route across the plains and moved his starting point south to Van Buren in Arkansas. The more southerly departure enabled him to leave earlier in the year and held the promise that he would arrive in Santa Fé ahead of other caravans and so gain a trading advantage. He departed April 21, 1839, with a party of thirty-four men that included his older brother John, a German peddler, two German wanderers, a Frenchman, two Polish exiles, a Creek, and a Chickasaw, and several Mexicans. They carried merchandise in fourteen wagons, half drawn by teams of eight mules, half drawn by teams of eight oxen. Gregg was armed with a Colt repeating rifle and two pistols.

The party was embarking on five hundred miles of uncharted and previously unexplored territory with only a compass and sextant to guide them. Their route took them across the Arkansas River through Indian lands occupied by the Creeks, the Chickasaws, and the Seminoles. They were escorted by a band of forty dragoons as far as the one-hundredth meridian, the supposed terminus of US territory.

Whatever apprehension the travelers may have felt when the dragoons turned back for the United States was dispelled by several friendly encounters with plains Indians: a lone Kiowa warrior and his squaw camped with them; a solitary Comanche buffalo hunter offered his hand in friendship; a large party of Comanches accepted presents from the traders as a token of friendship; and a Comanche chief named Big Eagle gave them information about the land ahead. These incidents confirmed Gregg's belief that the majority of plains Indians were friendly towards whites and observed a code of hospitality when dealing with them. It was the accumulating brutality of traders and adventurers crossing Indian lands that had led to violence between the races.

As the travelers followed the course of the Canadian River across Texas, Gregg appreciatively described the landscape through which they were passing:

> We made an effort to cross a ridge of timber to the south, which, after considerable labor, proved successful. Here we found a multitude of gravelly, bright-flowing streams, with rich bottoms, lined all along with stately white oak, black walnut, mulberry, and other similar growths, that yielded us excellent materials for wagon repairs,

of which the route from Missouri, after passing Council Grove, is absolutely in want.

Although we found the buffalo extremely scarce westward of Spring Valley, yet there was no lack of game; for every nook and glade swarmed with deer and wild turkeys, partridge and grouse.

Such descriptions would act as a siren call to the land-hungry American pioneers gazing westward from the border of the United States.

Gregg's caravan reached Santa Fé on June 25 after a journey of seventy-four days. Josiah continued into Mexico to trade in Chihuahua, while his brother John, a family man, returned home to Missouri. Of his brother's departure, Josiah remarked pointedly, "Men under such bonds are peculiarly unfitted for the chequered life of a Santa Fé trader."

Gregg spent several months in Chihuahua, a city to which he would return during the Mexican-American War, sold his goods to two English merchants established there, and returned to Santa Fé at the end of October in another caravan. After a scrape with the owner of a hacienda angered by their trespassing, Gregg arrived in Santa Fé in early December. On February 25, 1840, Gregg set out from Santa Fé with a party of forty-seven men, two hundred mules, three hundred sheep and goats, and twenty-eight wagons. They were accompanied by a Comanche who served as a guide along their route south of the Canadian River. They reached Van Buren on April 22, and Gregg's career as a Santa Fé trader was over.

The Santa Fé trade was in its waning days when Gregg retired from it. The volume of merchandise had been declining steadily, though it had spiked in 1843, the year Mexico closed Santa Fé to foreign traders owing to the break-out of hostilities that culminated in the Mexican-American War. From his "home" in Missouri, Gregg looked back on his years of prairie wandering with nostalgia and regret.

Since that time, I have striven in vain to reconcile myself to the even tenor of civilized life in the United States; and have sought in its amusements and its society a substitute for those high excitements which have attracted me so strongly to Prairie life. Yet I am almost ashamed to confess that scarcely a day passes without my experiencing a pang of regret that I am not now roving at large upon those western plains. Nor do I find my taste peculiar, for I have hardly known a man, who has ever become familiar with the kind of life which I have led for so many years, that has not relinquished it with regret.

Gregg now entered upon a period of restless maneuvering and experimenting in "civilization" that left him dispirited and in poor health. His main accomplishment during this period was to write and have published *Commerce of the Prairies*, the account of his life as a trader on the Santa Fé Trail that opened many readers' eyes to the appeal of the plains that lay beyond the western border of the United States. After the book was published, he made another attempt to join a caravan but was instead brought back to the southwest by the Mexican-American War. After the war, he settled in Mexico for a brief time, finding its society more congenial to his tastes and temperament than the society of Americans. From thence, he was drawn to California by the spell of the gold rush, reaching the Pacific Ocean and so completing his American odyssey.

After his return from Santa Fé to Van Buren, Gregg spent a year living in Jackson County, Missouri, with his parents. In June 1841 he returned to Van Buren to join his brother John in a business enterprise. He traveled into Texas, which had broken away from Mexico in 1836 and been recognized by President Andrew Jackson as the Lone Star Republic. Looking for land to buy on speculation, he visited Red River County, Lynchburg, Houston, Galveston, and Austin, traveling on horseback and by steamboat. In Austin, he witnessed the inauguration of Sam Houston for his second term as president of the new republic. Houston stayed at Gregg's hotel, and Josiah wrote about the hero of San Jacinto in the unflattering terms he often used when treating supposedly great men. Gregg faults Houston for the showy costume he wore at his inaugural—"a linsey-wooley hunting shirt, and pantaloons, and an old wide-brimmed fur hat"—imputes "his drunken and dissipated character," and predicts a fall in his popularity. In the course of these extended travels, Gregg, acting as an agent for his brother John and John's business partner George Pickett, purchased six hundred and forty acres of land on Bayou San Miguel near Nacogdoches. Purchase price: fourteen mules and two hundred dollars cash.

In January 1842, Josiah was back in Van Buren, where he became a partner in his brother's business. Drawing on the survey skills he had acquired as a youth, he was hired to re-survey the town of Van Buren, a task that he completed at the end of the year.

Around this time, Gregg began compiling notes for his book about the Santa Fé trade. He may have been encouraged in his writing ambition when in March 1843 the *Arkansas Intelligencer* published an account he had written of sighting a comet. In July, he left Van Buren for Philadelphia, where he intended to complete the manuscript and find a publisher for it. Gregg became ill with influenza on his arrival in Philadelphia and relocated to Camden, New Jersey, where he lodged in a boarding house.

Gregg wrote to his brother John in October that he had completed eighteen chapters of the book. He now intended to go to New York to seek a publisher. He has found the task of becoming an author daunting. "The job is surely ten times more tedious and laborious than I had supposed—had I anticipated it, I would hardly have undertaken—but my motto is 'go ahead.'" From this letter, we also learn that the Gregg family owned slaves. Josiah refers to a slave named Jerry, who had run away to Canada, been recovered, and jailed. Josiah recommends that his father sell Jerry.

Over the coming months, Gregg would struggle to finalize his manuscript and find a suitable publisher. In this effort, he was ably assisted by a young New York lawyer named John Bigelow, who served as editor and arranged a contract with the publisher Henry G. Langley. He left New York at the end of June with one hundred copies of *Commerce of the Prairies*. When he returned to Jackson County in September, after a stopover in Shreveport where John was living, he learned that his father, who had diabetes, had died on August 18.

Commerce of the Prairies, in addition to recounting Gregg's experiences in the Santa Fé trade and celebrating his proclivity for wandering, also offers a portrait of life on the unsettled plains—its geography and geology, its natural history, its human inhabitants. In this, he was a literary pioneer, for at the time that he wrote: "there is scarcely a province in the whole range of Nature's unexplored domains, which is so worthy of study, and yet has been so little studied by the natural philosopher."

In his descriptions of the natural features of the prairie, Gregg is considering the suitability of the country for settlement. What resources does it offer that could sustain "civilization?" Some regions he finds hospitable, others forbidding. He asserts that the country to the immediate west of Missouri, called the Uplands, offers rich soil, ample fresh water, and a healthy climate. As he writes, this is Indian country, occupied by many of the tribes relocated from the old northwest. Tellingly, in describing this region's features and extent, he estimates it "affording territory for two States, respectable in size, and though more scant in timber, yet more fertile, in general, than the two conterminous states of Missouri and Arkansas. But most of this delightful region has been ceded to the different tribes of the Frontier Indians." In other words, the Indians have better lands than Americans. The lands further west, between the Red River and the western sources of the Missouri River now occupied by the hunting tribes of the Great Plains, lack good soil and water, but even these he finds suitable for grazing sheep and cattle since they can support large herds of buffalo.

Another obstacle to settlement and the commerce it depends upon is the lack of navigable rivers on the Great Plains. Except for the Missouri, most of these rivers are too wide and shallow to accommodate transportation. In the hot summer months, many of them are completely dry.

Gregg also admires a region called Cross Timbers that runs north from the Brazos River in Texas to the Arkansas River in Kansas—across lands ceded to the Chickasaws, the Creeks, the Cherokees, and the Osages. His description of this area reads like a land agent's promotional flyer.

> The region of the Cross Timbers is generally well-watered; and is interspersed with romantic and fertile tracts. The bottoms of the tributaries of the Red River, even for some distance west of the Cross

Timbers (perhaps almost to the U.S. boundary), are mostly very fertile and timbered with narrow stripes of elm, hackberry, walnut, hickory, mulberry, bur-oak, and other species.

His favorable estimation of Cross Timbers and the Uplands may explain why Gregg could write, in defense of the United States' Indian relocation policies, "The lands that they at present occupy are, for the most part, of a more favorable character than those which they have left." Gregg believes that these policies have been too benevolent—"a mistaken philanthropy." The annuities granted Indians have made them indolent and ungrateful, and not disposed to take advantage of the available resources to develop manufactures and agriculture. The implication is that this productive land is wasted under their tenancy.

Gregg concludes his inventory of the resources to be found on the Great Plains with a listing of the major species of animals that live there. Lures for hunters and trappers include the buffalo, the mustang, the gray wolf, the coyote, elk and deer, black bears, antelope, and bighorn sheep.

Gregg provides an extensive discussion of the aborigines inhabiting the Great Plains. He notes the features they hold in common—their mythology, religious beliefs, marriage and burial customs, and their shared ethic of hospitality—and those that distinguish them. The differences are in their mode of survival, which is determined by where they live. The frontier Indians who inhabit Indian Territory most resemble white civilization in their way of life. They live in settled villages, practice agriculture, value education, and govern themselves through political systems that are modeled on the US Constitution. He considers the Cherokees, the Choctaws, and the Chickasaws, the most advanced of the tribes, despite their continued practice of polygamy.

The wildest tribes—"those savage hordes which may be considered as the Prairie Indian proper, have made little or no perceptible progress in civilization. They mostly live by plunder and the chase: a few eke out a subsistence by agriculture." Gregg is referring to the tribes of the far west—the Comanches, the Apaches, the Navajos, the Kiowas, the Arapahos, and the Cheyenne—who hunt buffalo, engage in warfare, raid white settlements, and follow a nomadic way of life. In between these two groups of Indians are the intermediate tribes—the Pawnees and the Osages—who live partly by hunting and gathering, partly by agriculture. Of these less civilized tribes, Gregg is most respectful towards the Comanches for their rejection of alcohol (which Gregg also disdained), their horsemanship and skill with bow and arrow, and their courage in battle.

What Gregg accomplished with *Commerce of the Prairies*, apart from commemorating his adventures on the Great Plains, was to portray the vast expanse of land west of the Mississippi River—land heretofore considered suitable for habitation only by Indians—as more of the "promised land" awaiting the fulfillment of America's Manifest Destiny.

In the years following the publication of *Commerce of the Prairies*, Gregg was at loose ends. He missed the life on the plains. After returning in October 1844 from a short trip into Indian Territory looking for wild honey, Gregg wrote to his friend John Bigelow about the salutary effects of this excursion.

> I find that even the little jaunt I took contributed very much to strengthening the tone of my stomach and system generally. But I fear a relapse on my return to the luxuries of civilization; in fact, I am already laboring under a severe cold, contracted since my return, whereas I did not even have the slightest catarrh during the time I was "camping out" . . . My desire to be on the "wild roam" continues to increase; yet, at this time, I have no particular expedition in contemplation.

The success of *Commerce* brought Gregg back to New York in November to assist in bringing out a second edition, for which he wrote a Preface. The New Year found him in Shreveport, Louisiana, staying on his brother John's farm. In August, he was asked to accompany a band of Cherokee Indians who were breaking away from the main nation to start a settlement somewhere in Texas, but he declined the opportunity. Instead, he decided to enroll at the Medical Institute of Louisville to become a physician.

Gregg had more of a scientific than a practical interest in studying medicine. He had read medical books while on the Santa Fé Trail and had gained a reputation as a physician for his ability to serve as a "doctor" to injured or ill travelers in his caravans. He undertook the study of medicine in part to try to understand his chronic illnesses. Though an able student, Gregg struggled in Louisville because ill health made it difficult for him to attend the six hours of daily lectures. He wrote to Bigelow that he was under an "oppression of spirits" and felt he had to get away from human society. "I am therefore bound for a foreign expedition, in some shape or other." He left the Medical Institute in March after receiving an honorary degree of Doctor of Medicine and returned to Independence. The "foreign expedition" he hoped to find turned out to be the Mexican-American War.

In the spring of 1846, Gregg's spirits lifted at the prospect of joining a caravan bound for Santa Fé, which had been reopened to foreigners by President Santa Anna in 1844. He wrote enthusiastically to John Bigelow in May: "The spirit of 'Westward, Ho' is on the wing in all directions. The emigrations this spring to California & Oregon will be immense—but more for the former country, it is believed, than the latter." In June Gregg joined a caravan that had been organized by his friend Colonel Samuel Owens. But the caravan had not gone far from Independence when it was overtaken by a messenger bringing requests from two United States representatives from Arkansas—Congressman Archibald Yell and Senator Samuel Sevier—for Gregg to return to Independence to join the Arkansas Regiment of the United States Army. He was promised an "honorable and profitable situation." On May 11, 1846, Congress had declared war on Mexico after Mexican troops crossed the Rio Grande and inflicted casualties on US dragoons camped there. President James Polk had provoked the war by sending an army under the command of Zachary Taylor to cross the Nueces River into the Mexican state of Tamaulipas and camp on the left bank of the Rio Grande. Mexico regarded this maneuver as an invasion because it considered the Nueces River, not the Rio Grande, as its border with the United States.

Gregg left for Washington in Hempstead County to join the Arkansas Regiment, which then marched to Shreveport to combine forces with volunteers from Kentucky and Tennessee to form a division of between four and five thousand horsemen. The terms of Gregg's service had not been clarified, but he wrote to Bigelow, "I am willing to undergo any privations and labor, which my physical powers can endure, where there is even a remote chance of serving my country." In August, the volunteers left Shreveport for San Antonio, a distance of twelve hundred miles, where they were to rendezvous with an army under the command of General John Wool.

It was not long before Gregg became disillusioned with his appointment and the men under whom he served. He finds Wool "amiable" but "old womanish," his preparations for the advance on Chihuahua sluggish and inept. The "honorable and profitable situation" he had been promised—he had assumed he would be commissioned as an officer—did not materialize. Instead, he is called a government agent and paid the salary of an interpreter, a lowly role looked down upon by the men. He resents that men of inferior abilities and intelligence gain preferment over him by Wool. He doubts the military leadership qualities of the officers on Wool's staff, who include Archibald Yell, holding the rank of Colonel to which Gregg himself aspires. He is critical of what he regards as inadequate military discipline amongst both officers and men. In short, he is a malcontent. The only officer who earns his respect is Lieutenant Colonel William Harney, who, in reckless defiance of orders from his superiors, attacked and captured the Presidio del Rio Grande without having to fire a shot. While waiting for Wool's army to move towards Chihuahua, Gregg made solo excursions into the countryside and recorded his observations about climate, soil, and inhabitants.

By December, American forces were concentrated in Saltillo, where Santa Anna was massing an army estimated at between thirty and forty thousand men. Gregg was with General William Butler, who commanded the American army there. Although Butler had offered him a position as an interpreter at a high salary, Gregg had stubbornly refused it. "The low grade in which interpreters are held, and the low class of people, in fact, generally engaged in such, is one reason why I have refused to accept this office." Instead, he served Butler as a volunteer, which gave him the freedom and independence he valued so highly. In his diary, he continued to question American military strategy and tactics. He was especially critical of Wool, who had retreated from Parris at the reported approach of Santa Anna and abandoned the sick without provisions or protection. Talk of Wool's cowardice circulated among the men.

Reports of an imminent attack by Santa Anna proved to be false. Gregg suspected that Santa Anna was starting rumors to pin down the American army. While the army waited, Gregg shuttled back and forth between Saltillo and Monterrey on errands for Butler. He met General Zachary Taylor, who was occupying Monterrey. He collected botanical specimens and wrote letters to newspapers in Arkansas and Louisville, reporting on the progress of the war.

By February 1847, Santa Anna was on the march towards Saltillo with an army of ten thousand men, badly depleted by desertions and sickness. Taylor brought his forces to Saltillo to join Butler. Gregg went with Colonel Yell to Taylor's camp at Agua Nueva outside Saltillo and remained there. On February 23, Gregg witnessed the Battle of Buena Vista, which took place on mountainous terrain seven miles south of Saltillo. Though Gregg was an observer of the battle, not a participant, he placed himself in the thick of it and rendered a thrilling account of the engagement of the troops.

> I had started toward a commanding point to the right, and in advance, and was some 200 paces in the rear of our combatants when the attack was commenced. A more incessant fire of volley after volley, accompanied by rapid-fire of artillery, could not well be conceived. As the Mexicans shoot too high, almost universally, I was perhaps in more danger than if I had been in the line of battle. Such a whizzing of balls, on either side—before—behind—above—then striking the ground under my horse's feet—could only be compared to a hail-stone in a hurricane! How myself and horse escaped was

difficult to conceive; in fact, I heard one strike upon the blanket of my saddle, but it was too far spent to penetrate. Many of our troops fell by the fire, not half nor quarter as many as would have been expected. They made, in return, great slaughter in the ranks of the enemy. But the great superiority of the numbers of the latter enabled them to force our troops over the hill, yet the enemy soon retreated in turn, and finally fell back under cover of the hills.

During the night, Santa Anna withdrew to Agua Nueva and, after declaring victory, sped to Mexico City to quell a political coup.

Colonel Yell was a casualty of the battle, killed by a lance wound in the breast. Also slain was Henry Clay, Jr. of Kentucky. Gregg visited the battlefield the following day. He reported 264 American dead and four hundred wounded. Mexican casualties he estimated at three thousand. The Battle of Buena Vista was a turning point in the war, ended the campaign in northern Mexico, and made Zachary Taylor a hero. A month later, General Winfield Scott captured Veracruz with an amphibian force and advanced toward Mexico City. On April 18 he defeated Santa Anna at Cerro Gordo and offered him armistice terms, which Santa Anna rejected. Scott captured Mexico City on September 17. Santa Anna abdicated, and on February 2, 1848, representatives of the United States and Mexico signed the Treaty of Guadalupe Hidalgo. Under the terms of the treaty, Mexico ceded Texas to the Rio Grande boundary, New Mexico (including Arizona), and Upper California (including San Diego). The United States paid Mexico fifteen million dollars (the same amount she paid France for Louisiana in 1803) and assumed unpaid claims against Mexico. Polk, ill and worn out, did not run for re-election, and Zachary Taylor became the next US president. Gregg had been a witness to American history and had described his role in it in uncompromising terms.

After the Battle of Buena Vista, Gregg traveled to Chihuahua to recover the belongings he had left behind with Samuel Owens's caravan. Colonel Alexander Doniphan had captured Chihuahua a few days after the Battle of Buena Vista. Gregg found his belongings in good condition but learned that Samuel Owens had been killed during the capture of the town. He returned to Saltillo with his baggage in company with Doniphan, collecting plant specimens along the way to the rude taunts of the untutored soldiers, who also mocked him for using an umbrella as a shield against the hot desert sun.

While in Saltillo, Gregg met the American trader Samuel Magoffin, who proposed a business partnership that Gregg quickly accepted. He left on June 7 for the Gulf of Mexico, sailed to New Orleans, and continued to Philadelphia, where he was authorized to purchase forty thousand dollars worth of merchandise. He reached Philadelphia in July, only to find a telegram from Magoffin canceling their enterprise. He then went to Washington to meet James Polk in hopes of finding government employment—a surprising aspiration given his army experience—and left the White House empty-handed and with a low opinion of the president. "It is remarkable that a man so short of intellect should have been placed in the executive chair," he remarked disapprovingly in his diary. He decided to return to Saltillo to practice medicine.

Gregg remained in Saltillo for just under a year. He arrived there on January 4, a month before the Treaty of Guadalupe Hidalgo was signed. The town's population of ten thousand Mexicans was still swelled with the presence of US soldiers. He offered them free Spanish instruction, but found they preferred to spend their leisure time at "card parties." He wrote contemptuously of the American governor of Saltillo, Colonel John Hamtramck, who pompously paraded himself in the town and acted tyrannically. He started his medical practice and soon was flooded with patients because of his charitable fees. He enjoyed practicing medicine, though it taxed him, and was at ease in the society of Saltillo. He wrote to his brother John in May, giving a picture of his life there.

> My practice continues brisk as usual or a little more so. In fact, I am worried beyond endurance. There is not a day, or come a meal that I get to eat in peace. In the morning before breakfast, they are after me. When I come home to dinner, I rarely fail to find several waiting for me. At least half the nights, I am kept from eating my supper till 9 o'clock when I sup at 7. I often refuse to go and send them to my

night doctors when I can. Though it often happens, when I refuse to go, they will get some one of my friends to come after me, whom I can't refuse. So you see, I have gained some sort of reputation. Though it is difficult to say how; except by my knowledge of the language, customs, etc., and my tact at making myself agreeable among "the natives." I have often thought that if I could make myself as easy in American society, I would be willing to live in the United States.

In June, he formed a medical partnership with an army surgeon named Grayson Prevost. He hoped to gain practical knowledge and companionship from him but was soon disappointed. Grayson had careless professional habits and became distracted by a love affair with a thirteen-year-old Mexican girl. Gregg decided to go to Mexico City and from there up the Pacific Coast to California, where gold had recently been discovered. He left Saltillo on December 14 with a party of about forty distinguished citizens of the town. Along the way, he collected botanical specimens that he intended to ship to St. Louis to Dr. George Engelmann, an eminent scientist with whom he carried on a regular correspondence about botany.

His plant collecting slowed down the party, which soon tired of his delays and tried to ditch him. He made an irritated entry in his diary on January 1, 1849, which indicates how his scientific pursuits had alienated his traveling companions. The party is about to leave from San Miguel de Allende.

> I stopped my baggage wagon to set my barometers, suggesting to Don Antonio Goribar to make a halt, as I would hardly delay 15 minutes: yet, though my stop was only about 12 minutes, the party continued on, and at so brisk (in fact accelerated) a pace that instead of overtaking them, they gained upon me, until they stopped at noon. There was but little (yet acknowledged some) danger of robbers, to be sure; still, the movement was ungenerous and showed me so little regard, as not to leave me in a very good humor again: still I paid no attention to it.

In fact, since coming off the Santa Fé Trail, Gregg had been exhibiting in his diary and letters to intimates such as Bigelow and his brother a growing disenchantment with human society. There are recorded a stream of altercations and confrontations with steamboat captains, baggage handlers, clerks, not to mention his frictions with the men he dealt with in the army. Gregg was unhappy in the company of most human beings. His misanthropy—perhaps "constitutional aversion" is a better way to express it—was revealed in a letter he wrote to Bigelow in April 1845 from Shreveport after his second trip to New York. "I spend my hours (and days and weeks) on my brother's farm, five miles from town—and roving in the 'wild wood' round about; and therefore I see nobody—hear nothing but the singing of the birds, etc. And consequently, have little or no means of acquiring news." His crankiness and obsession with pursuing his scientific interests at all costs would prove to be his undoing.

Gregg arrived in Mexico City on January 8 and remained there until April. He made sightseeing tours in the surroundings, visited Mexican dignitaries, and attended social events, whose frivolity he scorned. He renewed his attacks on the Catholic Church after witnessing the celebration of Easter. "Poor deluded people! They have never read that passage of Scripture which tells of the people's giving food to their heathen gods, and the priests consuming it at night." He calls the priests "sanctified beggars."

He had written to Engelmann in February of his intention to travel up the Pacific Coast to California and perhaps Oregon. In April, he hired two Americans to accompany him, but they turned out to be thieves who robbed him of two mules, bridles, and saddles. He wrote Engelmann that he intended to send him seven hundred species of plants he had collected during his travels in Mexico.

Gregg left Mexico City in a party of seven men and a Mexican servant. Gregg employed five of the men and the servant. They traveled overland to Mazatlan, passing through Morelia, Guadalajara, and Tequila. When they reached the coast, Gregg was exhausted and decided to travel to California by sea rather than overland, as originally planned. From Mazatlan Gregg shipped to Engelmann 1250 species of plants, fifteen fowls, as well as shells, vials of insects, rocks, woods, and seeds—the fruits of years of collecting. Many of these specimens were eventually named after Gregg by botanists. On July 16, Gregg sailed for San Francisco on the steamer *Olga*. Not surprisingly, Gregg questioned the captain's navigational skills during the voyage.

From San Francisco, Gregg went to Big Bar on the south fork of the Trinity River, where a mining camp had been established. He was carrying a government commission to lead an expedition from Big Bar across the Scott Mountains to find a passage to the sea and a harbor that could accommodate commerce to and from the mining camps along the Trinity River. If Gregg kept a diary of this journey, as was his habit, it has never been found. Lewis Keysor Wood, a member of his expedition, wrote the account of Gregg's final wandering.

Gregg was to lead a party of twenty-four men guided by local Indians. They were departing late in the year, at the beginning of November. "No one seemed better qualified to guide and direct an expedition of this kind than he," wrote Wood. Heavy rain and a snowstorm delayed their departure, and the Indian guides dropped out, saying the snow depth would make the trip across the mountains impossible. Even after all but eight of the men in the party backed out, Gregg insisted on going. They set off with only ten days provisions, believing they would reach the Pacific Ocean in eight days. Instead, the trip lasted one month. Wood gave the following summary of the ordeal that they endured:

> Here commenced an expedition, the marked and prominent features
> of which were constant and unmitigated toil, hardship, privation,
> and suffering. Before us, stretching as far as the eye could see, lay
> mountains, high and rugged, deep valleys, and difficult canyons,
> now filled with water by the recent heavy rains.

A week out of Big Bar, their food supplies were exhausted, and their pack animals were starving. Some proposed turning back, but Gregg would not hear of it. They killed some deer and rested in camp to recover their strength. When they encountered a nearly impenetrable redwood forest, Gregg slowed them down by stopping to take measurements of the trees, infuriating his companions. They covered only two miles per day through the forest. They finally reached the coast at the mouth of Little River. The party's dislike for Gregg intensified as he persisted in his scientific observations despite the hardship facing all of them. When two of his mules became mired crossing a stream, no one would aid him. The men survived on seafood provided by the local Indians. One of their party discovered Trinidad Bay (now called Humboldt Bay) while searching for water, accomplishing their mission.

As discipline broke down, the party split into two groups. One group remained with Gregg at Trinidad Bay. The other group moved south, looking for settlements and help. Gregg fell from his horse on February 20, 1850, dead from starvation and exhaustion. He was buried at Clear Lake. A "necrologue" commemorating Gregg's career to be written by Dr. Engelmann and published in the *American Journal of Science* was never written.

Epilogue

Reading the story of Gregg's life as it is revealed in *Commerce of the Prairies* and his diary, I cannot help but wonder if Gregg, reaching California, had also reached the limits of his tolerance for wandering, and, faced with the prospect of a life in civilization, chose to end it in the wilderness doing what he loved, blazing trails and studying the land. The decisions he made on this final expedition seem out of character. He was a skilled outdoorsman who, though unafraid of the unknown, was always prudent and thoughtful in his preparations because he respected nature. Why would a man who had roamed the plains for years and often relied on the guidance of Indians ignore the warnings of the natives who knew the terrain of the Scott Mountains he was about to enter? Why would a man who understood the importance of comradeship and solidarity to survival in the wilderness so antagonize his traveling companions on the Trinity River? Did he feel he had reached the end of his life when he reached the end of the American continent?

CHAPTER 5

William and Ellen Craft

Prologue

It's difficult for those of us living today to imagine the extent to which slavery dominated the national consciousness during the first two hundred years of America's history. Slavery, an established practice during the colonial period, had been sanctioned by the Constitution as a concession to the southern colonies when the nation formed. Seven of the first ten American presidents were slaveholders, including George Washington and Thomas Jefferson, and up to the time of the Civil War, expansion of the United States was conditioned on maintaining a political balance between slave and free states.

Slavery—free labor—was the underpinning of the country's economic prosperity and shaped its political life. As the country grew, the rift between pro and anti-slavery forces widened until it threatened to fragment the Union. Southern slave states were kept in the Union by force, but its citizens and representatives, by and large, refused to accept that African-Americans were entitled to the same personal liberties as whites, and did all in their power to keep blacks in a state of subjugation and inferiority. Racial tensions continue to plague the country today.

Against this backdrop, the story of William and Ellen Craft's escape from slavery and subsequent dedication to liberating their people stands out as a heroic example of rebellion and redemption. Uneducated and illiterate, held in bondage in the Deep South, they outwitted their owners and a gauntlet of slavery's watchdogs with a breathtakingly daring escape plan. Once free, they joined the international abolitionist movement and became two of its star figures. After the Civil War, at great personal risk,

Ellen Craft (*The Illustrated London News*, April 19, 1851)

they returned to the South and put themselves in service to their recently emancipated brethren. Their assertion of their right to "life, liberty, and the pursuit of happiness," made in defiance of the legal and cultural system that sought to oppress them, is a testament to both their courage and the power of righteous dissent.

William and Ellen Craft – Runaways to Freedom

William and Ellen Craft were a slave couple living in America's antebellum South who, in 1848, against very long odds, successfully ran away from their masters to become free. Their daring and improbable escape from Georgia deep in the Lower South to freedom in the North, and ultimately England, made them celebrities in the international abolitionist movement during their lifetimes. The notoriety of their flight throughout the South was a burr to slaveholders and became a factor in Georgia's decision to secede from the Union in 1861. It thus helped precipitate the United States' Civil War. Their return to Georgia during Reconstruction and their efforts to improve the lives of their fellow blacks has made them legendary figures in African-American history. The story and background of their remarkable adventures illuminate the manifold ways in which slavery, and the racism on which it was based, defined American social and political life for over two centuries.

Slavery is America's original sin, a betrayal of the promise of equal rights to life, liberty, and the pursuit of happiness that the New World held out to the Old through the Declaration of Independence. Slavery had a long tradition in Europe going back before the Greeks and Romans. In Roman times, most slaves were captives of war whose lives had been spared and who then became their captors' property. (An exception to this rule were those who sold themselves into slavery to escape destitution or pay off debts.) Slaves were considered socially impotent, having no rights other than those granted by their masters. Roman law provided an elaborate system of regulations for slavery that was followed by the Southern slave codes. Slaves had no standing before the law, which granted owners absolute power over them. But the Romans did not enslave the children of slaves, were liberal with manumission, and did not enslave only blacks. The concept of racial superiority that rationalized slavery was a Southern innovation.

In Europe throughout the Middle Ages and into the Renaissance, slavery was considered a normal part of the social system. Slaves were used as laborers in agriculture, as domestic servants in the homes of the wealthy, and as artisans. Thus, it is no surprise that Columbus brought slavery with him to the New World on his voyage in 1492. Three blacks who may have been slaves sailed with Columbus on the *Santa Maria*. When Columbus made landfall in the Bahamas on an island he called San Salvador (now Haiti), he quickly appraised the slave potential of the friendly natives he encountered and brought captives with him on his return to Spain for display before Queen Isabella. But the queen, who regarded the inhabitants of newly "discovered" San Salvador as royal subjects, forbade the enslavement of natives unless taken captive in a "just war." In 1503 she prohibited the slave trade to the Americas, but her decree barely dented the burgeoning slave trade between the Old World and the New.

Slaveholding was common in most of the early English settlements along the eastern seaboard in both the North and the South. Slave owners were supplied by the Atlantic slave trade, which had been started by the Portuguese in the fifteenth century. Blacks from African agricultural tribes—the Ibo, the Bakonga, and Arada, among others—were captured by more militaristic tribes like the Yoruba, Dahomey, Ashantee, and Hausa and sold to Portuguese traders who shipped them across the Atlantic under horrific conditions. Packed so tightly together in the holds below decks that they could not sit upright, the captives were left to lie for hours in their excrement. Over one-fifth of the slaves perished during the two-month-long Atlantic voyage from either disease or suicide. (Many jumped overboard during infrequent exercise periods.) Others went insane before they reached the shore. Once on land in the New World, the survivors were cleaned up and sold at slave markets. Approximately ten million Africans were brought to the New World in this way between the sixteenth and mid-nineteenth centuries. The majority of these slaves—forty-one percent—went to Brazil to work on sugar plantations. Seven percent came to the American colonies, where most of them labored on tobacco and cotton plantations in the South. By 1825, around the time that William and Ellen were born, there were 1,750,000 slaves in the southern United States.

The first slaves at an English settlement were acquired in 1619 when twenty blacks were either sold or traded for supplies by a Dutch man of war. During the seventeenth century, Holland, Sweden, Denmark, France, Germany, and England joined Portugal in the African slave trade. By the mid-seventeenth century, England had become the dominant slave trader. Slavery spread rapidly throughout the English colonies. By 1670, slavery was legal in Massachusetts, Connecticut, New York, New Jersey, Virginia, and Maryland. New England merchants owned slaves as domestic servants or hired them as artisans, and they also engaged in the slave trade. In 1830, thirty-six thousand blacks were in bondage in the North, mostly in New York and New Jersey.

Many of the signers of the Declaration of Independence, as well as the framers of the United States Constitution, were slave owners. As a result, the institution of slavery, a relic of Old World culture, was embedded in the document that marked the birth of the United States of America. Article I, Section 2, Clause 3, allowed slave owners to count each slave as three-fifths of a person when determining the basis for Congressional representation and direct taxation. This clause created a political incentive to own slaves, since doing so increased one's voting power. As the slave population of the South grew, while that of the North declined, the South gained a disproportionate share of federal power in Congress, the Supreme Court, and the Presidency (five of the first seven presidents were slave owners). This set the stage for a power struggle between North and South over the expansion of slavery into newly acquired territories in North America.

By 1818, slavery had been abolished in all the existing Northern states, creating a national schism between North and South on the issue. The three-fifths clause gave the South political leverage far above its actual citizen base since the slaves counted for electoral purposes had no standing as citizens. The South had succeeded in corrupting the political process from the very inception of the country.

Georgia, the state where William and Ellen were born, was for a time an exception to the colonial pattern of slaveholding. Georgia was the youngest of the original thirteen colonies. It had been chartered in 1663 to eight Lords Proprietors by a grant from Charles II. The charter prohibited slavery. Although the ban was lifted in 1683 after the Lords Proprietor returned the charter to the crown in 1729, a new charter was issued to James Edward Oglethorpe in 1732. Oglethorpe, though himself a slave owner, wanted to build an agricultural society in Georgia composed of small yeoman farmers rather than a planter aristocracy. In 1735, two years after the first settlers began to arrive, Oglethorpe and the other Trustees of the colony persuaded the House of Commons to ban slavery in Georgia. But the ban was immediately resisted by the settlers, who avoided the law by leasing slaves from owners in the Carolinas. In January 1751, the ban on slavery in Georgia was lifted. Then land policies were altered to allow the establishment of large plantations. The slave population rapidly grew. In 1750, there were six hundred blacks in Georgia. By 1773, there were fifteen thousand, comprising forty-five percent of the population. By 1820, three years before William Craft's birth, the slave population of Georgia had reached one hundred and fifty thousand. And by the outbreak of the Civil War, nearly half a million slaves lived in Georgia. They were owned by approximately forty-four thousand adult white men. A small planter elite numbering sixty-five hundred adult white men owned the majority of slaves, controlled the state legislature, and determined the state's political direction.

———◆———

William and Ellen Craft were born slaves in Georgia. Ellen, born in 1826 in Clinton, was the daughter of Major James Smith, a wealthy hotel and plantation owner, and a light-skinned house slave named Maria, whom he took as his concubine when she was seventeen. Ellen was raised as a house slave, like her mother, and suffered cruelty from the tongue and hands of Mrs. Smith, who resented her as evidence of her husband's infidelity. When Ellen was eleven, the Smith's legitimate daughter Eliza, Ellen's half-sister, married Dr. Robert Collins, the owner of the Monroe and Bibb Railroad and Banking Company in Macon. Collins owned more than ten thousand acres of farmland and sixty-two slaves, assets that placed him among the planter elite. Mrs. Smith, to be rid of Ellen, gave her as a wedding present to Eliza. Ellen moved with Eliza into Collins' four-acre estate in Macon. By William's later account, Eliza was a kind mistress to her sister.

Less is known about William's origins. He was the son of field hands owned by Mr. Craft. His grandparents were Africans who had been captured and sold as slaves for transport to America. His grandfather had been a tribal chief. William had two brothers and two sisters. Mr. Craft owned their entire family.

The fate of William's family reveals the cruel economics of the Southern slave system under which human beings were regarded as nothing more than chattel. As William's mother and father aged and became less productive as field hands, Craft sold them to separate owners before they could become valueless to him and an expense to maintain. Subsequently, Craft also sold both of William's brothers and one of his sisters. Then, wishing to raise money to speculate in cotton, Craft mortgaged William and his sister Sarah to Collins' bank in Macon. When Craft became delinquent on his loan payments, the bank took ownership of William and Sarah and sold them at a slave auction. Sarah was sold to a planter from a distant town, and William was sold to Ira Taylor, the cashier of Collins' bank.

William was a clever and industrious slave. Recognizing his talents, Craft had taken him from his fields and apprenticed him to a cabinet-maker in Macon. William thus entered the small and elite artisan class of slaves who were hired out by their owners in exchange for wages. Craft's new owner returned him to the cabinetmaking shop and allowed him to keep a small portion of his wages. William also worked as a waiter at a hotel in Macon in exchange for a room.

Both William and Ellen had comfortable lives, by slave standards. William was permitted considerable freedom, earned his own money, and lived in a hotel among whites. Ellen lived in a wealthy home under the supervision of a sister who was kind to her, although legally, her owner was Robert Collins. The vast majority of slaves in Georgia and throughout the South were field hands who labored on plantations under hot, humid conditions growing cotton, tobacco, rice, indigo, and sugar. They worked from sunrise to sundown in labor gangs controlled by black slave drivers under the supervision of white overseers who had the authority to flog them for breaking tools or working at too slow a pace. In addition to their fieldwork, plantation slaves had other chores—feeding livestock, preparing their meals, cleaning their rude cabins. Because the food given them was often inadequate, many of them hunted and fished in their "free" time to supplement their diets.

Sometime in the year 1844, William and Ellen met in Macon. Perhaps Ellen accompanied Eliza and her husband to the hotel where William worked. Or perhaps William was hired to perform cabinetwork for Collins' home. A courtship ensued, a slave wedding that had no legal standing was performed in front of friends, and William moved into Ellen's cottage on the Collins' estate. William's experience with the destruction of his family made them resolve to remain childless so that their children could not be born into slavery as the property of their owners.

In December 1848, the Crafts decided to run away from their owners and seek freedom. Runaways were a common feature of slavery in the antebellum South. Slaves might run away because they were being mistreated or because they wished to join family members or loved ones who had been sold away from them. Most runaways did not leave the South, and most were sooner or later recovered by their owners. They might live in the hills or woods for a while in maroon communities, or they might make their way to large cities or towns where they could hope to blend in with the black population. But the chances for a successful escape were slim. Slaves were not allowed to wander far from their owners without passes, and under the prevailing slave codes, any white person could challenge a black, demand to see either a pass or proof of manumission and take a suspected runaway into custody. A reward system encouraged whites to be on the lookout for runaways. Additionally, mounted slave patrols were active in the countryside, and slave hunters using trained bloodhounds would be sent in search of fleeing slaves. The penalties when runaways were caught could be severe: floggings, torture, maiming, or sale into an even harsher environment than the runaway had fled.

To escape into the North and achieve freedom was extremely difficult and extremely rare, especially if one was running away from the Deep South. Being illiterate, most slaves did not know Southern geography or transportation systems. Slaves trying to reach the North using the Underground Railroad found their way by following the North Star and might be aided at stations along the way. Using public transportation was out of the question because slaves could not buy tickets, even had they the money for the fare. The Crafts knew all this from talk among other slaves, and from conversations they had overheard among whites at the Collins' home and at the hotel where William worked. They had contemplated making a run for freedom, but the likelihood of being caught and losing their privileged slave status deterred them.

But as Christmas of 1848 approached, William hit upon a bold plan. They would disguise Ellen, who easily passed for white, as a male planter traveling to Philadelphia to seek treatment for severe arthritis in his right arm. William would accompany the planter to be called Mr. Johnson as his personal slave. Using the money they had saved from Ellen's work as a seamstress and William's job in the cabinet shop, they would purchase at Macon shops items for Ellen's disguise as Mr. Johnson. They would obtain passes from their owners, giving them permission to travel away from Macon for a few days. Then they would ride out of the South by train and steamboat.

The plan placed enormous demands on Ellen to successfully impersonate Mr. Johnson under circumstances that could not be foreseen. She doubted her ability to carry it off, and dreaded the consequences should she fail. But William expressed complete confidence in her and added clever distractions to her disguise. To protect her eyes from the gaze of white men, he bought her glasses shaded dark green. To conceal her smooth cheeks, he bound her head in a bulky tourniquet to ease

"Mr. Johnson's toothache." To give Mr. Johnson an excuse not to write his name if asked, his arthritic right arm was bound in a sling. Just before they set off, William cut Ellen's hair and finished off her disguise with a top hat. Thus costumed, Ellen walked out of her cabin before dawn on December 21, heading for the Macon railway station. William, carrying their luggage, followed by a separate path. During the next four days, the Crafts would face daunting challenges and mishaps that tested Ellen's mettle and sometimes brought them to the edge of desperation.

At the railway station, Ellen bought tickets for herself and William, and they boarded the train, Ellen, in a first-class compartment, William, in the Negro car with the luggage. Just before the train departed, William saw through the window the cabinetmaker who employed him running down the platform, obviously looking for him. William quickly ducked down below the window. Fortunately, the train began to move before the man could board his car. Ellen had a fright when she realized she was sitting across from Mr. Cray, whom she had served the evening before at a dinner hosted by Robert Collins. Mr. Cray did not recognize Ellen. When he tried to engage Mr. Johnson in conversation, Ellen pretended to be deaf. Mr. Cray gave up trying to talk to her, and to her great relief, disembarked after a few stops.

After a twelve-hour journey, the Crafts reached Savannah. They rode in a carriage to the waterfront, where Ellen bought tickets on a steamer to Charleston, South Carolina. When they boarded the steamboat, Ellen went immediately to her berth to rest and to avoid contact with other passengers. William spent the night on deck and tried to sleep on some grain sacks. In the morning, Ellen took breakfast at the captain's table. William attended her to cut Mr. Johnson's food. A passenger chided her for being too kind to her slave when she thanked William. The captain warned Ellen that William would likely run away when he reached Philadelphia, at which point another passenger offered to buy William.

At Charleston, they went to a hotel to dine before boarding another steamer. They learned that during the winter months, steamers did not run directly from Charleston to Philadelphia. They must travel in stages, sometimes by boat, sometimes by rail, a process that increased their risk of detection as they passed through multiple checkpoints. Ellen bought tickets through to Philadelphia. A problem arose when Mr. Johnson was asked to register his name and the name of his slave for the passenger list. Ellen tried to excuse herself from signing by pointing to her crippled right arm, but the official was insistent. A delay ensued, irritating the other passengers. Finally, the captain of the steamer from Savannah vouched for Mr. Johnson and signed for him. The narrow escape rattled Ellen.

The Crafts rode the steamer overnight to Wilmington, North Carolina, then took a train to Richmond, Virginia. Ellen was joined in her compartment by a planter and his two daughters, who fancied Mr. Johnson and flirted with him, adding a humorous touch to the Crafts' adventure. To avoid conversation, Ellen lay down on her seat and pretended to sleep. When they changed trains at Richmond, a woman passenger mistook William for her runaway slave Ned and sounded the alarm. But when she saw William close up, she realized her mistake, and once again, the Crafts avoided detection.

At Fredericksburg, Virginia, they boarded a steamboat that conveyed them up the Potomac River to Washington, a Southern city. From there, they traveled by train to Baltimore, Maryland, their final stop in the South. After boarding the train, thinking they were only a few hours from freedom, exhausted from three days of travel with no sleep, Ellen was ordered to disembark from the train to show proof to an official in the station that she owned William. She was told that this requirement applied to all masters taking slaves to the North. Ellen argued with the official, showed her tickets, and garnered enough sympathy from the waiting crowd to cause the official to allow them to leave.

On the ride to Philadelphia, William fell asleep. He failed to leave the luggage car when passengers were ferried across the Susquehanna River to meet another train. Ellen experienced a moment of panic when she could not find William, but they were reunited after he was brought across the river with the luggage, still sleeping. The train pulled into Philadelphia on Christmas morning, and they were free.

The Crafts were now in abolitionist country. On the train, William had met a free black who suspected he was a runaway and gave him the address of a black abolitionist couple who ran a boarding house in Philadelphia. The Crafts took a carriage from the train station to this address after their arrival, then stunned their hosts when Ellen removed her disguise and announced that William was her husband. Their landlord introduced the Crafts to William Stills, a free black who was active in the Pennsylvania Society Promoting the Abolition of Slavery, a vigilance committee that assisted runaway slaves with counsel and if needed, funds. Stills was the son of a slave father who had purchased his freedom and a slave mother who had escaped the South with two of her four children. His parents owned a farm in New Jersey, where he was born on October 7, 1821. He had moved to Philadelphia in 1844 to join the anti-slavery movement and rose to become chairman of the vigilance committee.

Stills interviewed the Crafts to establish the authenticity of their escape and to obtain information about their masters and their treatment that he was compiling for a book about the Underground Railroad that was published after the Civil War. He advised the Crafts that they would not be safe from slave hunters in Philadelphia, and arranged for them to move to safer quarters. They soon relocated to a farm twenty-five miles from Philadelphia on the Delaware River, belonging to Barclay Ivens, a white Quaker, and his family.

The abolitionist movement in both England and the United States had originated with the Quakers, who regarded slavery as a sin that stained personal holiness. Quakers took the lead in calling attention to both the immorality of slavery under Christian doctrine—especially the Golden Rule—and its incompatibility with the political principles of equality on which the United States was founded. At their annual meeting in Philadelphia in 1758, the Quakers voted to ban from membership in the Religious Society of Friends, any person participating in the slave trade. In 1780 Pennsylvania passed an act of gradual emancipation that freed the unborn children of slaves on their twenty-eighth birthday. Other states then followed, and by 1791 abolitionist societies had been organized in all the states except North Carolina, South Carolina, and Georgia. In 1790, Quakers and the Pennsylvania Abolition Society petitioned Congress to abolish the international slave trade, an action it finally took in 1808, though its motives were economic—controlling the supply of slaves—rather than humanitarian. Due to the proslavery majority in Congress, the abolitionist movement failed to gain political support at the federal level, and by 1810 only the abolitionist societies of New York, New Jersey, Delaware, and Pennsylvania were still active.

The abolitionist movement was revived during the 1830s under the impetus of an upwelling of religious fervor known as the Second Great Awakening. Propelled by evangelical preachers in the Methodist and Baptist churches, the Awakening reasserted the moral sinfulness of slavery and brought a flood of petitions, mostly signed by women who could not vote, to a Congress that refused to receive them. But this new crusade steadily gained momentum, found political support from pragmatic secular leaders like John Quincy Adams, Joshua R. Giddings, and Samuel Chase, and brought on the Civil War.

In 1831 the American Anti-Slavery Society was established. Its leaders were Arthur and Lewis Tappan, Theodore Weld, William Lloyd Garrison, publisher of *The Liberator*, and Gerrit Smith, a Presbyterian minister from New York. By 1838 the society had 1,346 auxiliaries with roughly one hundred thousand members. Widespread hostility towards the anti-slavery movement in both the North and the South resulted in mob violence against abolitionists (Garrison was beaten by an angry mob in Boston in 1835), and this, in turn, won to the abolitionist cause sympathizers concerned about bullying tactics that threatened free speech in the North. In 1839 Weld issued a pamphlet titled *American Slavery As It Is: Testimony of a Thousand Witnesses* that refuted the Southern myth of its benevolent institution by shocking readers with thousands of documented cases of cruelty to slaves. It became the most influential anti-slavery tract of the antebellum period, doing for the cause of emancipation what Paine's *Common Sense* had done for the American Revolution—moving public opinion.

In 1840 the abolitionist movement gained a political foothold with the formation of the Liberty Party, which campaigned on the single plank of opposition to slavery. Though it had small electoral success, the party evolved into an anti-slavery coalition within the Republican Party (formed in 1854) that won the White House in 1860 with the election of Abraham Lincoln. By then, moral and political pressures to end the continuation of slavery and its spread into new territories such as Kansas, Nebraska, New Mexico, and Arizona had converged to overwhelm Southern control of the federal government.

———— •◦• ————

The Crafts remained on Ivens' farm for about two weeks. The family gave William and Ellen their first lessons in reading and writing and taught them to sign their names. The kindness of these Quakers enabled Ellen to overcome her fear and distrust of white people.

While in the Philadelphia area, the Crafts were introduced to William Wells Brown, an escaped slave who had become a prominent abolitionist and lecturer. Brown had been born a slave in Lexington, Kentucky, in 1814. Like Ellen, he was an inter-racial child. His father was his master's cousin; his mother, Elizabeth, was one of forty slaves owned by Dr. John Young, a physician and gentleman farmer. As a young man, William was hired out to perform a variety of odd jobs: field hand, physician's assistant, gang boss for a slave trader, steamboat steward. He escaped from slavery on January 1, 1834, when his steamboat docked at Cincinnati, Ohio.

He took the name of Wells Brown, a Quaker who had helped him, and headed north for Canada. He found a job on a Lake Erie steamboat and began to assist other fugitive slaves seeking freedom in Canada from Buffalo, New York, and Detroit, Michigan. He moved to Buffalo in 1836 and made his home there a station in the Underground Railroad. After meeting Frederick Douglass at an anti-slavery lecture in Buffalo in 1843, Brown became a traveling lecturer for the Western New York Anti-Slavery Society. Then at a meeting of the American Anti-Slavery Society in New York City in May 1844, he met Garrison and Wendell Phillips, another leading abolitionist from Boston. Subsequently, Brown was invited to lecture in New England for the Massachusetts Anti-Slavery Society, and he moved to Boston, the hub of the abolitionist movement in the North.

When Brown met the Crafts and heard their story, he immediately recognized in them new ambassadors for the abolitionist cause. They were attractive and intelligent, and their brilliant escape strategy and execution rebutted southern stereotypes of black inferiority and incompetence. Brown wrote a letter to Garrison informing him that the Crafts would be coming with him to Boston and would join him at a series of lectures he had scheduled in Connecticut and Massachusetts. "Their history, especially that of their escape, is replete with interest," he wrote. "They will be at the meeting of the Massachusetts Anti-Slavery Society in Boston, in the latter part of this month, where I know the history of their escape will be listened to with great interest. They are very intelligent. They are young, Ellen 22, and William 24 years of age. Ellen is truly a heroine." Garrison published this letter in the January 12, 1849 issue of *The Liberator,* and news of the Crafts daring run to freedom rapidly spread throughout the North, where they became showcases for the abolitionist movement, and throughout the South, where their embarrassed owners plotted a recovery plan.

Though the Crafts did not know it at the time, their journey had placed them in the path of large historical forces reshaping the United States, and their escape would play a role in intensifying them.

———•———

The Crafts followed Brown to Boston and traveled with him on his New England lecture tour for four months. They drew large crowds eager to hear the story of their escape and see the former slave woman who had fooled the South into believing she was an invalid white planter. Initially, William related their adventures while Ellen was put on display, but after audiences asked to hear from Ellen, she began speaking too, an unusual role for any woman at a public meeting in 1850. Brown rounded out the program with a talk on the evils of slavery and the importance of the anti-slavery movement. Following the program, a collection was taken to support the American Anti-Slavery Society and the Crafts.

After Brown left for New York and then Europe, the Crafts curtailed their lecturing and tried to normalize their lives. They wanted to find employment in Boston, buy a home, and start a family. But William immediately ran into Northern discrimination against blacks. Many

Northerners did not support the anti-slavery movement, believing that it exacerbated tensions between the North and South. And even within the abolitionist movement, some whites accepted the myth of the racial inferiority of blacks. There was also a powerful resistance to equality of black employment opportunity from a surging white immigration population seeking work. As a consequence, William found doors closed to him when he sought to practice his trade as a cabinetmaker. Unable to get work, he opened a second-hand furniture store in the black section of Boston and used his skills for the restoration of furniture.

Ellen fared better. Because she passed for white, the white women of Boston accepted her and helped her find work as a seamstress. She learned to upholster and joined William in his business. The Crafts lived in a boarding house owned by another fugitive slave couple, Lewis and Harriet Hayden. The house also served as an Underground Railroad station.

The Crafts' settled life in Boston was upended in September 1850 when President Millard Fillmore signed into law a series of acts passed by Congress known as the Compromise of 1850. The acts were an attempt to maintain the fragile political equilibrium between the free states of the North and the slave states of the South and prevent the South from seceding from the Union. The Mexican-American War that ended with the Treaty of Guadalupe Hidalgo in 1848 gave the United States vast new territories in the West, including Arizona, New Mexico, Nevada, Utah, parts of Colorado and Wyoming, and California. The South wanted to extend slavery into these new territories, although under Mexican control, it had been banned. The short-lived California Republic had banned slavery at its constitutional convention in 1849 and had applied to Congress in 1850 for admission to the Union as a free state. The Compromise of 1850 admitted California as a free state and banned the slave trade (but not slavery) in the District of Columbia. To further placate the South, Congress enacted the Fugitive Slave Law, which gave slave owners the power to use the federal government to recover fugitive slaves from the North. The law empowered any white to claim as property any black alleged by oral affidavit to be a fugitive. It denied blacks due process of law. Federal marshals were authorized to form citizen posses to recover runaways, and citizens who obstructed slave catchers were liable to large fines and imprisonment. The law meant that even blacks born free could be taken as slaves on the word of a white. The law had the long-term effect of driving many blacks further north into Canada (approximately twenty thousand emigrated between 1850 and 1860) and pushing the United States closer to civil war. Some Northern states passed legislation nullifying the Fugitive Slave Law, and many local communities resisted recovery attempts in defiance of federal authorities. Northern hostility to the law was rooted more in resistance to the South's political over-reaching than in sympathy for fugitive slaves.

One short-term effect of the law was to drive William and Ellen away from America to England. Their owners, Robert Collins and Ira Taylor, immediately sent slave catchers to Boston to recover them. But the anti-slavery forces in Boston were ready for them. Three weeks after the Fugitive Slave Law was signed by President Fillmore, blacks in Boston organized a Meeting of Fugitives. They voted to form a League of Freedom to resist the law and protect fugitives. Lewis Hayden was elected President, William Craft, a vice-president. On October 13, the Crafts were featured guests at a rally at Faneuil Hall addressed by Wendell Phillips and Frederick Douglass. At this rally, a Committee of Safety and Vigilance was established, with Reverend Theodore Parker, another fervent abolitionist, as its chairman.

The following week slave catchers sent to the North by Collins and Taylor appeared in Boston. William Knight, an employee of the cabinet-maker's shop where William Craft had worked, visited William's furniture store on the pretext of paying a social call. He asked Craft to show him the sights of Boston, and when Craft declined, he invited him to tea at his hotel. He suggested that Craft bring his wife with him to pass along messages for her mother, Maria, that he would carry back to Georgia.

The Crafts learned that Knight was accompanied by Willis Hughes, the Macon town jailer. When their ruse did not work, Knight and Hughes sought to obtain a warrant for the Crafts' arrest from a federal judge. After a three-week search, they found a judge willing to issue the warrant.

Parker led the vigilance committee in a campaign of harassment against Knight and Hughes. They were arrested numerous times on flimsy charges but always found slavery sympathizers in Boston willing to post their bail. When Hughes was nearly assassinated by an enraged black man after his release from jail, Parker went to the United States Hotel, where Knight and Hughes were staying and told them that they were risking their lives by remaining in Boston. The frightened slave hunters left the city immediately for New York.

Learning of this, Robert Collins wrote to President Fillmore, demanding that he enforce the Fugitive Slave Law. Fillmore ordered six hundred federal troops to Boston tasked with recovering the Crafts. Although the Crafts had resolved not to run from slave hunters, they feared that their cause would result in bloodshed for the members of the vigilance committee who had vowed to protect them. They decided to leave the United States. A British abolitionist visiting Boston urged them to go to England, where they would receive a warmer welcome than in Canada. Before they departed, Theodore Parker came to the Haydens' boarding house to marry William and Ellen. He made William promise to defend Ellen from slave hunters, using force if necessary. To underline this message, he gave William a bowie knife as a wedding present.

The Crafts traveled overland to Halifax, Nova Scotia, where they planned to board a steamer for Liverpool. The Reverend Samuel May accompanied them as far as Portland, Maine, and gave them a letter of introduction to Dr. John B. Estlin, a physician in Bristol, England. They avoided Boston harbor from fear that federal troops would be stationed there to look for them. After they left, Parker wrote a letter to a pastor in Liverpool, Reverend James Martineau, telling him the Crafts' story and the reasons for their flight to England. He called the Fugitive Slave Law, "one of the most atrocious acts ever passed since the first persecution of the Christians by Nero." He urged Martineau to spread the word in England about the Crafts' persecution by the US government to bring international pressure on the United States to end slavery. "I thank God that Old England, with all her sins and shames, allows no slave hunter to set foot on her soil."

The Crafts reached Halifax after a harrowing journey beset by mishaps and accidents that left Ellen ill with pneumonia following a seven-mile walk in pouring rain after their carriage broke down. They missed their connection to the steamer because of this delay and were forced to layover in Halifax for two weeks. Because they experienced prejudice against blacks from Canadians at the inn in Halifax, they took lodgings with a black couple. At the last moment, they needed the help of a white abolitionist to obtain steamship tickets from a clerk who refused to sell to William. In late November, they left North America onboard the S.S. *Cambria*. Ellen was ill throughout the voyage, and William feared she would die. But she recovered as they came in sight of land. They arrived in Liverpool in mid-December 1850, almost exactly two years after their flight from Georgia.

———•———

Upon their arrival in Liverpool, the Crafts stayed briefly in a hotel, then accepted an invitation to lodge with a local minister, Reverend Francis Bishop, and his wife. When Ellen had recovered from her arduous journey, William Wells Brown shepherded them on a lecture tour of Scotland. They were quickly taken up by the abolitionist movement in England and exhibited before astonished audiences as specimens of the "peculiar institution" in the American South.

The British anti-slavery movement had started in 1787, and like the anti-slavery movement in America, it had been initiated by Quakers who found slavery morally repugnant. The Quakers made alliances with the Methodists and the evangelical arm of the Anglican Church to build a powerful grassroots movement that employed mass meetings and petitions to Parliament to sway opinion. In 1807 Parliament passed a bill ending Britain's participation in the slave trade. The anti-slavery movement then pushed for the emancipation of slaves throughout the British Empire. In 1823 The London Anti-Slavery Committee was formed again with the support of Quakers, Methodists, and Anglicans. The movement also found allies among the British aristocracy who regarded the anti-slavery cause as part of a broader effort to increase individual liberty in the conduct of human affairs. In 1834 England passed an Emancipation Act that freed all slaves in the British Empire in stages and provided compensation to slave owners for the loss of their property. British abolitionists then turned their attention to slavery in the United States. They sent speakers to America, raised funds from British citizens, and used the British foreign office to bring pressure on the American government. At the time of the Crafts' arrival in England, Prince Albert, husband of Queen Victoria, was head of the British Anti-Slavery Society.

In tow with Brown, the Crafts attended meetings at grand country homes and kept company with prominent British aristocrats, including Alfred, Lord Tennyson, and Lady Noel Byron. Ellen was put on display in her planter disguise while William spoke about their experiences as slaves and fugitives (women were not permitted to speak in public in Victorian England). The letter of introduction from the Reverend Samuel May of Boston brought the Crafts to the home of Dr. John B. Estlin and his daughter Mary Ann in Bristol, where they remained for several months. In the spring, they attended the Great Exhibition at London's Crystal Palace in company with Estlin, Brown, and other prominent British abolitionists. It is possible that they were introduced to Queen Victoria and Prince Albert as they toured the exhibition hall. A picture of Ellen in her escape disguise had been published in *The Illustrated London News*, making her an instant celebrity.

Plans were made to provide William and Ellen with a formal education so that they could become fully literate. Estlin and Lady Byron raised funds to enable them to attend Ockham School in a small village twenty miles from London. The school had been founded by Lady Lovelace, daughter of Lady Byron, to provide industrial education as well as instruction in letters and science. The Crafts were also employed there as teachers in carpentry and sewing. They moved to Ockham in the Fall of 1851 and settled into a small cottage on the grounds of nearby Ockham Park, an estate owned by Stephen Lushington, a prominent barrister and anti-slavery advocate. At the beginning of the New Year, Ellen became pregnant, and a son named Charles Estlin Phillips Craft was born in October 1852.

The Crafts were offered positions as Superintendent and Matron at the Ockham School, but turned them down, to the dismay of their patrons. They wanted to strike out on their own and had decided to open a boarding house in London, as the Haydens had done in Boston. Estlin tried to dissuade them, believing that the enterprise was doomed to failure because Craft was undercapitalized, but he was determined to become independent. They moved to London in 1853, and though the boarding house soon failed, as Estlin had predicted, William started another business selling rain gear made from the newly developed vulcanized rubber that supported them. William Jr. was born in 1855 and Brougham two years later. In 1860 William had published *Running a Thousand Miles For Freedom*, his account of their escape to the North. The book launched him on another speaking tour. A daughter named Ellen was born in 1861.

The Crafts were prospering enough to buy a cottage in the London suburb Hammersmith. William was then hired by a group of merchants and philanthropists to undertake a dual mission to the Kingdom of Dahomey on Africa's west coast. The merchants wanted him to trade merchandise for palm oil, and the philanthropists wanted William to persuade the King of Dahomey to discontinue his trading in slaves. The King promised William to consider his request, then gave William a gift of three African boys in a gesture of friendship. Upon his return to England, William and Ellen adopted the boys into their family and freed them. William also purchased his mother and sister Sarah from their owners and attempted to purchase Ellen's mother, Maria, but her owner Major Smith refused the sale. Maria was emancipated at the end of the Civil War and took up residence with another black family in Macon.

In 1864 William undertook another trading mission to Dahomey that yielded disappointing results. Not only did the King of Dahomey dismiss William's pleas to end the slave trade, but he also paid William for his merchandise with sixty slaves rather than the palm oil sought by his backers. William took the slaves to a British colony in Africa and freed them, returning to England empty-handed and with the loss of his commission for three years work.

During William's absence, Ellen's mother had come to England. With the help of her American friends in the North, Ellen had located Maria in Macon and sent her the funds for the journey to England. She arrived in London in November 1865. Ellen had also become active in British efforts to assist freed American slaves in the South. She formed a ladies auxiliary of the British and Foreign Freedmen's Aid Society and engaged in fundraising activities. The Society's work complemented the work of the Freedmen's Bureau in America, which had been set up by Congress in March 1865 to assist blacks in building new lives as free people. Ellen now moved confidently in England's aristocratic anti-slavery circles and spoke out forcefully in defense of her race.

About a year after William's return from his second trip to Africa, the Crafts received a letter from their old friend Lewis Hayden in Boston. Hayden had received an appointment to the Massachusetts State House, placing him among the first blacks to achieve positions of political influence. He wrote the Crafts describing the urgent need for experienced and skilled blacks to assist the freed slaves in the American South. The Crafts decided to return to America to help their people. In the summer of 1869, they sold their home in Hammersmith and traveled back to Liverpool, where they boarded a steamer for Boston, accompanied by Maria and three of their children, including the infant Alfred. Their sons William Jr., now fourteen, and Brougham, age twelve, wanted to remain in England to complete their educations, so the Crafts arranged for them to live with friends. The three African adoptees also remained in England, though eventually they returned to Africa as teachers.

———•◆•———

When the Crafts arrived in Boston after their Atlantic crossing, they stayed with Lewis Hayden and his wife for seven months. At the time of their arrival, the Fifteenth Amendment giving blacks the right to vote was in the process of being ratified by the states. This amendment was the culmination of efforts by the North to bring black people, most of whom had been shipped to the United States from Africa in bondage, into a condition of full citizenship with other Americans. The Civil War, fought to preserve the Union when Southern states seceded over the slavery issue and formed the Confederacy, became during its course the path to freedom for America's nearly four million slaves. The Confederacy's military defeat and surrender to the North at Appomattox in April 1865 set in motion a series of laws, acts, and constitutional amendments that removed the legal and political shackles holding blacks in servitude. But Southern resistance to these progressive moves undermined them and left most Southern blacks in circumstances that differed only slightly from their lives under slavery.

In January 1863, Lincoln had issued the Emancipation Proclamation, freeing all black people. This did not have the full effect of a law passed by Congress; it was a military order from the Commander-in-Chief of the Union Army made during the war. But it shifted the political priorities of the war from preservation of the Union to the human rights of black people and thus elevated the war's moral purpose. After the war, the Republican-controlled Congress pushed through other measures designed to bring blacks into a state of equality with whites. On December 6, 1865 the Thirteenth Amendment was ratified, abolishing slavery in the United States. On March 2, 1867 Congress passed the Reconstruction Act, which sought to end legal discrimination against blacks in Southern states by setting up five military districts in the South governed by officers who were appointed by newly elected President Ulysses S. Grant, a Republican. The act was passed in response to a proliferation of Black Codes enacted by Southern legislatures to limit the rights of blacks and keep them in a position of political and economic subservience. The Act was backed up a year later with the ratification of the Fourteenth Amendment that made blacks citizens of the United States and assured them of due process under its laws.

The South responded to these legal steps with terrorism. Groups of ex-Confederate soldiers, many of them former riders on antebellum slave patrols, banded together to form the Ku Klux Klan and Knights of the White Camelia. The Klan effectively intimidated Southern blacks and their white supporters through a program of marauding, mayhem, and murder that discouraged them from voting and prevented them from exercising the rights granted them under federal laws. A national administration presided over by Andrew Johnson, who sympathized with white Southern planters, looked the other way. By 1870, the year the Crafts returned to Georgia, the Republican Party behind the reforms had lost its sway over national politics, and racism in the South remained virulent. The majority of "free" blacks were denied educational and economic opportunity and were struggling under a system of sharecropping and peonage that differed circumstantially very little from slavery.

Georgia, through its Black Codes and Klan activity, led the South in defiance of federal efforts to give blacks equality. Though the Klan had been formally disbanded in 1869, its members continued their depredations against blacks. Harassment of black voters played a major role in weakening the Republican Party in the South.

In spite of the dangers facing them, William announced at the annual meeting of the Massachusetts Anti-Slavery Society in January 1870 that he and Ellen intended to return to Georgia, buy a plantation, and start an industrial school and cooperative farm. The Crafts left for Georgia in April, a few months after the Fifteenth Amendment had been ratified, and found there conditions for blacks little changed from when they had left over twenty years before. Most blacks were now working for their former owners for little or no pay, and there were no schools for rural black children.

After a reunion with William's sister Sarah in Macon, the Crafts went to Savannah, where they formed a business partnership with a black man who had leased a plantation called Hickory Hill across the state line in South Carolina. Ellen opened a school teaching children during the daytime, adults in the evening. William managed the plantation with the help of tenant farmers. They produced a substantial crop in the first year. In the autumn, after the crops had been harvested, the Klan visited them one night wearing their hooded robes ("ghosts of the Confederacy"), set fire to the school and barn, but spared their lives. The Crafts lost a quarter of the capital they had brought back with them from England.

They returned to Savannah and tried for a year to operate a hotel with their son Charles. When that failed, they leased a run down eighteen hundred acre plantation called Woodville nineteen miles south of Savannah. In sad disrepair after the plundering by Sherman's troops, the plantation had the advantage of being cheap. The Crafts leased it for three hundred dollars a year with an option to buy and set about rebuilding it. Four tenant families moved in, and Ellen opened another school. Classes were offered at night in the main house dining room. Seventeen people, adults, and children attended.

The Crafts were struggling financially. They had spent two thousand dollars the first year to get the plantation running, but took in only one hundred and fifteen dollars when they sold their crops. Their partner pulled out and demanded to be paid for his work. William went to the North to seek help from his friends in the anti-slavery movement. He stopped in Washington and met with President Grant seeking a position as minister to Liberia, but the post was not vacant. He then spent a year lecturing in New York and New England raising funds. When he returned to Georgia, he had enough money to buy Woodville.

The plantation had prospered under Ellen's management. She had purchased a team of oxen for plowing and had planted crops of rice, cotton, corn, and peas. She had set up a school in a large barn serving about a dozen children. She also taught at night and ran a Sabbath School. On Sundays, the barn was used as a church by itinerant preachers.

By 1874, three hundred acres were under cultivation, and a one and a half story schoolhouse had been built. Brougham, who had returned from England the studied at Howard University in Washington, took on the teaching responsibilities at the school. Thirty students attended, studying reading, writing, arithmetic, and geography. Ellen taught the black women, most of whom had been field workers as slaves, housekeeping skills such as sewing, cooking, and cleaning. Ellen also broke the cycle of corporal punishment the women had absorbed from their owners and were inflicting on their children. She taught the families to resolve conflicts without resort to violence. Ellen also served as a nurse and caregiver to residents of the plantation who needed help.

For his part, William had become active in Republican politics. He ran for the state senate in 1874, and in 1876 he represented his district in state and national Republican conventions. But due to the harassment of Republican voters, most of whom were black, Republican influence was on the wane in the South. William continued to travel to the North, lecturing about conditions in the South and raising money to support their enterprise.

Woodville, the only black plantation in Bryan County, was prospering. Seventy-five boys and girls attended Ellen's school. Sixteen families lived on the farm. Ellen had purchased more livestock, built another barn to house them, and offered tenant farmers favorable terms that drew them away from rival plantations. The success of Woodville created resentment from white planters. One of them sent a slanderous letter to a friend in Boston, Barthold Schlesinger, the German consul, who had it published in local newspapers. The letter accused the Crafts of spending the money they were raising in the North on themselves. Though William published a rebuttal calling the charges untruthful and sued Schlesinger for libel, the smear had its intended effect. William's supporters withdrew, and even Wendell Phillips testified for Schlesinger at the libel trial, which William lost. Ellen testified eloquently about the accomplishments of Woodville, but the panel of all white judges denied the Crafts' claim. The story was picked up by the *Savannah Morning News,* and soon even black people in Georgia were complaining about the Crafts.

The Crafts returned to Georgia after the libel trial to face the deteriorating conditions of Reconstruction. Blacks were losing the right to vote and hold office. Most were working as sharecroppers for their former owners. Some were caught up in the corrupt peonage system, under which blacks would be arrested on false charges, imprisoned and fined, then freed as indentured servants to the white man who had paid their fine, a roundabout way of returning them to slavery. A convict-lease system worked similarly, with proceeds from the lease going to the local sheriff who had arrested the black.

After their return to Woodville, the Crafts were forced by their shrunken finances to give up their school, but the plantation survived with the help of tenant families who remained loyal to them. Daughter Ellen was sent to school in Boston. Alfred was educated at a school somewhere near Savannah. William Jr. visited them from England for a short while but returned to England to live.

In 1890 the Crafts left Woodville to live in Charleston, South Carolina, with their daughter Ellen, who had married a physician and Republican activist, Dr. William Crum. Brougham and Alfred found jobs with the United States Postal Service. Ellen died in 1897 at the age of seventy-one and was buried at Woodville. William died three years later, aged seventy-six.

The Crafts never succumbed to the racism that formed the basis of life in the American South. They endured it, and in their own way, triumphed over it. But this racism continued to drive public policy and relations between blacks and whites in the American South for the next fifty years until the federal government once again intervened during the 1950s and 1960s. Racism's thinly veiled presence in our current political climate can be seen in the oft-repeated claims that Barack Obama, born in Hawaii of a black Kenyan father and a white woman from Kansas, is not a real American.

Thorstein Veblen (Courtesy of Carleton College Archives,
Thorstein Veblen Collection.)

Thorstein Veblen

Prologue

As the industrial revolution transformed American life during the second half of the nineteenth century, it brought with it new variations on old patterns of human social and economic relationships. Industrialization brought urbanization and with it new roles for men and women in the family and the workplace. Heavy concentrations of population, and wide disparities of wealth, and opportunities for consumption of goods and services, created new modes of social distinction and status within the new social and economic hierarchy. One of the most astute and penetrating observers of this emerging social order was a rustic Norwegian farmer's son from Minnesota named Thorstein Veblen.

Veblen saw in the new social arrangements the recurrence of archaic patterns of competition, rivalry, and dominance by predatory elites. He articulated his social theory in a series of articles and books written in a ponderous and often tortured style that baffled and annoyed all but the most determined readers, of whom there were few outside the realm of academia.

His vision of the unfolding industrial world order was bleak and found few adherents. The eccentricities of his personal life and his unconventional relations with women damaged his career and weakened his credibility. But his indictment of the rising trend of consumerism, his sardonic recognition of the spiritual emptiness at its core, called into question the myth of "progress" that underpins Americans' optimistic faith that tomorrow will be better than today. His skepticism about the direction American culture had taken under the impetus of industrialization marked him as an iconoclast and marginalized him as a social thinker. Nevertheless, his theory of "conspicuous consumption" as the driving force of America's social and economic life has become an accepted part of our native vernacular, as relevant now as when he coined the term more than a century ago.

Thorstein Veblen – An Adam Longing for Eden

Following its Civil War, American society experienced a prolonged and profound transformation under the forces of industrialization that the war itself accelerated. The development of steam and then internal combustion machines, the spread of railroads and telegraph wires, the rise of factories, and the movement of populations from dispersed rural areas to concentrated urban centers produced lasting changes in how people lived and worked and how they thought about the purpose of their lives. Machines replaced people as the main producers of goods and the generators of wealth. The handicraft era of sustenance farmers, skilled artisans, and small independent businessmen rapidly faded. The people who owned the machines—a small capitalist class—shaped society and determined its direction. The government was put in the service of the machine, enacting laws that facilitated the spread of industrialization and favoring its owners over the workers who served the machines. This process, which evolved during the period between the Civil War and the First World War, ushered in the modern world.

Railroads were the primary engine of industrialization. The effects of the railroad infrastructure laid down over eighty years beginning in the 1820s were felt across all segments of American society, altering its geography, its commerce, its politics, its social life. The spread of railroads changed the country physically and morally and led to the rise of the modern capitalist state.

The biggest changes wrought by the railroads were in finance and politics. The railroads needed money to lay track across a vast continent and build engines and cars to run on it. A symbiotic relationship developed between the railroad companies and the state and federal governments.

This relationship enriched the railroad entrepreneurs and the politicians who aided them at the expense of the public. Legislators gave both land and tax incentives to railroads to enable them to capitalize. The land was used as collateral for bond issues sold to investors in America and Europe, giving birth to the financial services industry on Wall Street. Politicians were rewarded for the giveaway with railroad stock and the opportunity to buy choice parcels of land along the routes. Thus began a cozy relationship between industry and government, which throughout the Gilded Age, under predominantly Republican administrations, passed laws—including protective tariffs—favorable to the capitalist class, while ignoring or suppressing the needs of the enormous working class on which the greatest burdens of industrialization fell.

The tendencies towards social injustice and economic inequality that were inherent in this alliance of the wealthy with the powerful erupted into public view during the Great Railroad Strike of 1877. The strike was a response by workers for the Pennsylvania Railroad to a showdown between John D. Rockefeller of Standard Oil, and Tom Scott, the president of the railroad, who cut wages and laid-off workers to compensate for his losses in a rate war started by Rockefeller.

Seventeen strikers were killed and over sixty wounded throughout the forty-five-day confrontation that ensued between striking workers and federal troops. Other worker uprisings soon followed: The Haymarket Square Riot in Chicago (1886), the Homestead Strike at Andrew Carnegie's Pennsylvania steel mill (1892), and the Pullman Strike (1894) that shut down rail traffic west of Detroit, Michigan. These protests indicated the depth and breadth of workers' dissatisfaction with the conditions of their labor and their lives. All told, there were more than 650 railroad strikes between 1877 and 1894.

At the other end of the economic spectrum were families like the Vanderbilts, who in 1883 invited more than 1,000 guests to their Fifth Avenue mansion for a masquerade ball that cost $250,000 ($6M in today's currency). The social purpose of the ball was to upstage the Astors, who ruled New York society and had snubbed them. Guests arrived dressed as French aristocrats in powdered wigs and danced quadrilles until dawn. But the ball had the unintended effect of creating a public backlash against the excessive display of wealth and frivolity in a city teeming with miserable immigrant laborers living in slums. New York's *The Sun* tutted, "Old sober-minded men ask themselves whether it is advisable to make such a display of wealth and luxurious living at a time when the working classes are in a state of serious fermentation all over the world."

——•——

Into these turbulent and transforming times a strange genius was born, whose commentaries on capitalism, its origins and consequences for society and the people who live in it, startled his contemporaries and continue to baffle the academic world. His name was Thorstein Veblen.

Veblen was born on June 30, 1857, four years before the outbreak of the Civil War. His parents, Thomas Veblen and Kari Thorsteinsdatter Bunde, were Norwegian immigrants who had married in Norway in 1847 and then emigrated to the United States after losing their land in Norway to swindlers.

Thorstein was the sixth of twelve children, three of whom died in childhood. His parents were hardy pioneers who had settled in a Norwegian community, acquired land, built a home, and developed a prosperous farm. They were insular and largely self-sufficient, growing their food, making their clothes. They were sober (no tobacco or alcohol), industrious (Thomas was a carpenter and cabinetmaker, Kari served the community as a midwife), not religious, interested in books, politics, and public affairs. They venerated learning and sent all their children to school, unusual for farmers.

Thorstein did not have a robust constitution or the "get ahead" ambition of his brothers. He was somewhat frail, prone to sickness, and avoided the heavy farm work whenever possible. He preferred to retreat to the attic of the house where he could read old almanacs and newspapers in solitude. He had a fondness for practical jokes and sly humor. Late in his life, a celebrated author and scholar, he encountered an unwelcome admirer who had trekked to his front door. He passed Veblen on his way out of the house, dressed, as always, in rumpled rustic clothes. The visitor asked if Veblen was inside. Veblen answered, "He was there when I left," and continued on his way past the baffled visitor. Thorstein's brothers thought him eccentric and "queer," but Kari considered him her favorite for those very qualities.

When Veblen was seventeen, his parents enrolled him in Carleton College and Preparatory School in Northfield, Minnesota, ten miles from their farm. Thomas bought a small parcel of land near the college and built a cottage on it where Thorstein and his siblings could live while getting their educations. Buckboards brought provisions regularly from the farm. Veblen completed an eight-year program in six years and delivered a graduation speech on John Stuart Mill that dumbfounded the faculty by its brilliance, making his parents proud.

While at Carleton, Veblen met Ellen Rolfe, who would become his first wife and trouble him throughout his academic career. Veblen proposed to Ellen when he was eighteen, she sixteen, but she turned him down. They were finally married in 1888 when Veblen was thirty-one, Ellen twenty-nine.

After graduating from Carleton, Veblen taught for a year at a Lutheran high school in Madison, Wisconsin. Ellen also became a teacher, but suffered a nervous breakdown and went to Colorado to recuperate. Veblen left Madison in 1881 to follow his brother Andrew to Johns Hopkins University in Maryland to study philosophy. A year later, dissatisfied with the program there, he transferred to Yale, where he studied philosophy under President Noah Porter and social theory under William Graham Sumner, an advocate of laissez-faire economics. Thomas paid the tuition, mortgaging the farm to borrow money. Veblen received his Ph.D. in Philosophy from Yale in 1884, and although he was awarded the Porter Prize for best essay of the year, he was unable to secure an academic appointment. Philosophy was a field imbued with theology, and Veblen's skeptical attitude made him suspect. Once, when asked what church he attended, Veblen replied mischievously, "Moravian," a sect known for its sympathy towards Native Americans, who were widely feared and distrusted. The truth was that Veblen did not attend church at all.

Veblen returned to the family farm, where he remained for three years, loafing and reading. In 1886, doctors investigating his low blood pressure and slow pulse discovered that he had a small heart. This organic weakness kept him on the edge of poor health for most of his life.

In 1888 Veblen proposed to Ellen again and over the objections of both their families—Thomas regarded them as "two sick people"—they were married. They moved into the summer home of Ellen's family in Stacyville, Iowa, and lived on the income from investments that Ellen had received from her wealthy father. This was an idyllic time for the couple, who kept livestock, tended a garden, and took picnics to boating outings on a nearby river. They loafed, read, and talked. Veblen was translating some old Norse sagas that were eventually published as *The Laxdaela Saga*. But later, it was revealed that their marriage was probably never consummated. After her death, an autopsy showed that Ellen's reproductive organs had never fully developed, making her physically incapable of sexual intercourse.

Veblen continued seeking academic posts, and when none were offered, he decided to study for a doctoral degree in economics, a field free of religious doctrine. He obtained a fellowship to enter the graduate program at Cornell and moved to Ithaca alone. Ellen remained at Stacyville, apparently at Veblen's request, creating the first of many separations that would mark their marriage. Ellen joined him for the second year of his fellowship. After receiving his degree, Veblen, accompanied by Ellen, moved to Chicago to assume a position at the newly established university endowed by John D. Rockefeller. Veblen's mentor from Cornell, J. Laurence Laughlin, had been appointed Chair of the Economics Department and brought Veblen with him to teach a graduate course on socialism. Laughlin also appointed Veblen editor of the influential *Journal of Political Economy*. Veblen's salary for the year was $520, Laughlin's $7,000.

Over the next several years, Veblen drifted away from Ellen, though they continued to live together. Friends remarked that they were fundamentally incompatible. Ellen was mystical, loquacious, and sociable; Veblen was coldly scientific, taciturn, a loner. Ellen had become a socialist after reading Edward Bellamy's *Looking Backward* and threw parties for her socialist friends that Veblen either skipped or observed in silence. He was not a socialist. Ellen was also a careless housekeeper, and her constant chatter made it difficult for Veblen to work. Eventually, he took a separate apartment that he used during the week as a study.

Veblen became enamored of a beautiful graduate student named Sarah Hardy, who was drawn to his erudition and iconoclasm. They took long walks around the campus, and she assisted Veblen with his writing. Unbeknownst to him, she was secretly engaged to Warren Gregory, a lawyer from California who came to Chicago in 1893 to take her to the Columbian Exposition.

Sarah's ambition, or rather her mother's ambition for her, was to become the president of Wellesley College. Although Sarah was unable to complete her degree work in Chicago because of illness, she did manage to obtain a teaching position at Wellesley. But after only a few weeks there, she suffered a nervous breakdown and had to be hospitalized. Veblen seemed drawn to neurasthenic women, of whom there were many during the Gilded Age. Veblen may have probed the sources of this malady in an essay he wrote titled "The Economic Theory of Women's Dress," which argued that women's fashions were designed primarily to display the purchasing power of their husbands.

Veblen corresponded with Sarah during her hospital stay and then as she recuperated at her father's home in Hawaii. In January 1896, she passed through Chicago on her way west and spent time with Veblen. His letters to her, consoling and encouraging, hint at deeper feelings he is reluctant to express. Perhaps to discourage Veblen, Sarah wrote him for advice on the proposal of marriage she had received from Warren Gregory. He advised her to marry only for love, as any other motivation would only bring her unhappiness. He then disclosed his feelings for her: "I love you beyond recall," he penned plaintively. Two months after receiving this letter, Sarah married Warren Gregory.

Veblen wrote to Ellen, who had separated from him and taken up residence in Idaho. He confessed his love for Sarah and said, "I am not your husband, in fact." He then asked her to initiate divorce proceedings in Idaho, presumably to avoid the possibility of scandal in Chicago that might harm both him and Sarah. Ellen wrote back her refusal to do this, copied the letter, and mailed the copy to Sarah Gregory.

In the summer of 1896, Veblen traveled alone to England to visit William Morris, a leader of the Arts and Crafts Movement. In the fall, he resumed his teaching duties in Chicago. Ellen had returned from Idaho to live with him. Their marriage continued in its unhappy pattern for eight years, a period during which Veblen produced some of his most significant writing—*The Theory of the Leisure Class* (1899), *The Theory of Business Enterprise* (1904), and the essays "The Instinct of Workmanship and the Irksomeness of Labor," "The Beginnings of Ownership," and "The Barbarian Status of Women."

Veblen had become friends with Professor Oscar Triggs and his wife Laura, who lived in the same apartment building as the Veblens. In the summer of 1904, Veblen traveled alone to Europe, where the Triggs were also traveling with their infant son. When he returned, Ellen struck. She reported to President William Rainey Harper gossip that Veblen had been seen traveling with Mrs. Triggs and that Mrs. Triggs had been seen at late hours of the night leaving the separate apartment that Veblen kept in Chicago. Harper summoned Veblen to his office and asked him to sign a statement that he would not have anything further to do with Mrs. Triggs. Veblen responded with the disclaimer that "he was not in the habit of promising not to do what he was not accustomed to doing" and instead submitted his resignation. Ellen moved to Oregon, where she had staked a timber claim on Mt. Hood.

Sometime during that year, Veblen met Ann Bradley Bevans, the woman who would eventually become his second wife. Ann was married to an architect, and they had two daughters, Becky and Ann, but her husband was philandering, and at the time Veblen met her, her marriage was unraveling. She was an independent and resourceful woman, a socialist like Ellen, and a suffragette. She separated from her husband and moved with her daughters into a shack left over from the Columbian Exposition near the Illinois Central Railroad tracks.

Veblen continued to ignore the social proprieties of the times. He and Ann, both married, both separated from their spouses but not divorced, spent the summer of 1905 together in Woodstock, New York, at her sister-in-law's home. The following summer, they vacationed together on Washington Island in Wisconsin. The openness of their relationship gave offense to some of Veblen's academic colleagues, but Veblen was indifferent to their opinions.

Veblen had applied for a position at Stanford, and in the spring of 1906, President David Starr Jordan offered him $3,000 to teach an undergraduate course on "The Economic Factors in Civilization." Veblen had become something of an intellectual celebrity due to the stir created by *The Theory of the Leisure Class* and, to a lesser degree, *The Theory of Business Enterprise*, so Jordan may have felt that Veblen was a good catch, despite the gossip in his wake.

Perhaps to satisfy the respectability requirements of Stanford, perhaps because he was unable to abandon her, Veblen went to Oregon and brought Ellen with him to Palo Alto at the start of the academic year. They rented a beautiful property called Cedro adjoining the campus. The house had been built for a relative of Leland Stanford. It stood on fourteen acres, encompassing a five-acre garden, a barn, and space for livestock. Veblen kept chickens, cows, and two horses, one of whom, named Beauty, he rode in the hills above Cedro.

Ellen soon discovered that Ann was writing regularly to Veblen. When she learned that Ann intended to divorce her husband and move to Berkeley to enroll in the University of California, she returned to Oregon. From there, she wrote to Sarah Gregory, now living in Berkeley, disclosing the sorry state of her marriage to Veblen. Veblen was socializing with the Gregorys, and with his colleague Wesley Mitchell, who taught at Berkeley.

After Ellen moved out of Cedro, three students moved in to help maintain the property, and Veblen built a cabin on a promontory overlooking the sea. He rode there often on Beauty, and the suspicion grew that he was rendezvousing with Ann. Veblen's friends warned Ann that her visible presence in Veblen's life was endangering his career. Meanwhile, Ellen had moved to Carmel-by-the Sea and had also bought property adjoining Cedro, where she built a cabin, which Veblen considered a watchtower. At the end of the 1908 academic year, Veblen gave up his lease on Cedro and told the students he was going away. But the likelihood is that he moved up to the promontory to be with Ann.

The following year Ellen began to make allegations of impropriety against Veblen to President Jordan. Veblen had informed her that he intended to seek a divorce on the grounds of desertion. She offered to resume living with him, an offer Veblen declined. Ann, now divorced, returned to Chicago, then took her daughters with her to live near Grangeville, Idaho, in a log cabin called "Nowhere."

Veblen had applied to Jordan for a leave of absence during the 1909-1910 academic year so that he could pursue studies in Scandinavia. Perhaps he wished to move beyond Ellen's reach. Jordan was initially disposed to grant the leave, but he changed his mind after Ellen's complaint. Ellen had provided Jordan with copies of her correspondence with Veblen and her letters to Sarah Hardy as proof of Veblen's transgressions against conventional morality. As Harper had before him, Jordan confronted Veblen with the allegations. Veblen denied nothing and tendered his resignation from Stanford. Ellen left Carmel to become a patient at a sanitarium.

In December 1909, Veblen left Palo Alto by train to join Ann in Idaho. He brought Beauty with him. It was snowing when he arrived. He rode Beauty from the train station in Grangeville to Nowhere through a sudden winter blizzard and arrived near death from double pneumonia.

Ann devoted herself to nursing Veblen back to health. She sent her daughters to live with relatives to give herself totally to the task. A doctor prescribed calomel, a supposed wonder drug that contained mercury and was used to treat a wide range of ailments, including pneumonia. Veblen somehow survived the mercury poisoning, but his teeth were permanently damaged, and his already frail constitution further weakened.

After Veblen recovered, he returned to Palo Alto and applied for a grant from the Carnegie Institution to research the evolution of racial characteristics. Although he received enthusiastic letters of support from colleagues and a letter of recommendation from President Jordan, he was not funded. Instead, Herbert Davenport, a former student from Chicago who was now the Chair of the Economics Department at the University of Missouri, obtained an appointment for Veblen in his department. Ann and her children came to Palo Alto and stayed in a cottage near Veblen, who left alone for Columbia, Missouri, at the end of the year. Veblen boarded with the Davenports and savored Mrs. Davenport's mince pies.

In the summer, Veblen joined Ann and her daughters at a cattle ranch near Ashland, Oregon. They lived in a tent and cooked on an open fire, like natives. Somehow, Veblen was able to write under these primitive circumstances. He made progress on *The Instinct of Workmanship and the State of the Industrial Arts*, which was published in 1914.

Over the next three years, the pattern of Veblen's and Ann's patchwork life together continued. He taught at Missouri during the academic year, and they spent summers together, usually in remote western locales where they could enjoy privacy and simplicity. One year they were in Taos, New Mexico, the next in Colorado. Ann studied stenography in Chicago, then went to New York looking for work. Not finding any, she took the girls with her to live in Lindsborg, Kansas, a four-hour train ride from Columbia. Ann may have met Veblen occasionally in Topeka on holidays and weekends. In January 1912, Ellen divorced Veblen in a California court, finally releasing him.

In the summer of 1914, Veblen telephoned Ann, who was in Chicago, staying at her parents' house with Becky and Ann. He proposed marriage to her, and when she accepted, her brother-in-law, a conservative professor of geography who despised Veblen, struck her on the side of the head with a rifle butt, knocking her to the floor. Ann never reported this assault, and she told Becky, who had witnessed it, not to speak of it to anyone. Veblen never knew.

Veblen and Ann were married on June 17, 1914, in Chicago. They went to Norway for their honeymoon. They were in Europe when World War I erupted and were fortunate to get return passage to America. Back in Columbia, they enjoyed a lively social life with Veblen's colleagues. Ann cooked their meals and typed Veblen's manuscripts. He was writing *Imperial Germany and the Industrial Revolution*, a book that foresaw the alliance between Germany and Japan that brought America into World

War II. They spent summers on Washington Island, where Veblen had bought a property and built two cabins, one for living, the other for writing.

In 1917 Ann became pregnant, a surprise to her since she had entered menopause, though only in her late thirties. During the seventh month of her pregnancy, she delivered a stillborn boy. Ann had once declared that she wanted to bear the child of a great man, and the loss of this baby seemed to unhinge her mind. She became depressed and was kept from suicide by Veblen's intervention. He came upon her pointing a pistol at her breast and stopped her with the question, "What would your children think?"

Veblen left Missouri in 1918 to take a position with the Food Administration in Washington. The appointment ended after a few months, at which point Veblen moved to New York to become one of the editors of *The Dial*, a progressive journal that included John Dewey and Lewis Mumford on its editorial board. The Veblens found an apartment on Riverside Drive in Manhattan.

At a Thanksgiving dinner that year, Ann had a breakdown. She left the apartment amid the festivities, did not return until late in the evening, then disappeared the next day again. She had become paranoid that Veblen's life was in danger, and she wanted to have a meeting with President Wilson. She refused medication, was admitted to Bellevue, then transferred to Mclean Hospital in Massachusetts for treatment. She was never discharged, and died there from a pulmonary abscess on October 7, 1920, with Veblen at her bedside. She was forty-three years old.

Veblen's career frustrations continued. In 1919 the editors of *The Dial* were summoned to testify before a committee of the New York state legislature that was investigating subversives. All of *The Dial's* staff, including Veblen, were subsequently discharged. He then became one of the founders of The New School for Social Research, along with John Dewey and Wesley Mitchell, among others. He lived in an apartment provided by the school and was looked after by two ladies, Alice Broughton and Mildred Bennett. He supported both his step-daughters while they attended the University of Chicago. By 1922, The New School was struggling to survive. Of the founders, only Veblen remained, his salary paid by donations. He continued to publish, *The Engineers and the Price System* in 1921, *The Laxdaela Saga,* in 1925. He heard from Ellen, who had become a Christian Theosophist and had joined a religious community in Central California. She warned him of dire events about to strike New York and invited him to join her. She died in 1926.

In 1926 Veblen returned to California with his step-daughter Becky, who had given up her ambition for a career in medical research to care for him, as she had promised her mother. Veblen's health was poor, his spirits low. They stayed briefly in San Diego near Veblen's brother Andrew, then moved back to Palo Alto. Veblen died there of heart failure on August 3, 1929, three months before the stock market crashed.

Such, in abbreviated form, is the story of Thorstein Veblen's sad and often painful personal life. His poor health, his ironic passivity in the face of treachery and injustice, his fatal proclivity for mentally unstable women, brought him great suffering. But what of his mind, with its formidable intelligence and deep knowledge of humanity? What did he see when, from his Olympian detachment, he looked at America during its period of industrial transformation?

———•••———

Veblen had arrived in Chicago to teach at the new university at the height of the Gilded Age. It was one year before the Columbian Exposition put on display the wonders of the latest technologies, and one year before the financial panic triggered by overextended railroads pushed the country into a depression that closed hundreds of banks and sent urban unemployment soaring to twenty-five percent in Pennsylvania, thirty-five percent in New York, and forty-three percent in Michigan. The cultural contrast between the agrarian Norwegian community in which he was raised, with its emphasis on artisanship, thrift, and group solidarity, and the polarized classes of the city, in which a small capitalist class wallowed in luxury while the underclass that labored long hours at machines struggled to survive, was pronounced and perhaps shocking to his sensibilities. His family background, combined with his wide-ranging scholarship and independent reading, gave him a unique perspective from which to view the new industrial society.

Veblen sought to understand and describe the economic relationships operating in the society around him. To do this, he examined these relationships from a historical perspective, bringing to bear on them the newly forming disciplines of psychology, anthropology, and the evolutionary science of Darwin. He saw man's economic behavior not as a reflection of abstract "laws" of supply and demand and social utility as explained by classical economists like Adam Smith, but rather as the result of a cumulative process of change whose roots lay deep in the prehistoric past. He believed that two persistent factors were shaping this behavior: man's instinctual make-up, his genetic inheritance, on the one hand, and the institutions—what Veblen called "habits of thought"—that arose as a result of his struggle for existence, became embedded in his culture, and were perpetuated as the community's received wisdom and rules of behavior. In the modern state, these "habits of thought" are formally codified in a constitution and the laws flowing from it, and they operate informally as customs, norms, and other widely accepted attitudes. This institutionalized thinking grows out of and shapes economic behavior in a constantly unfolding process. Habits of thought are altered, sometimes drastically, as technological innovations are added to the culture.

Veblen identified three primary instincts as the keys to man's survival and progress: "the instinct of workmanship," which made man productive and gave him pride in a job well done; "the parental bent," which fostered both nurturing within the family and concern for the welfare of others; and "idle curiosity," man's speculative, inquisitive tendency that produced scientific discovery and enabled technological progress.

Veblen believed that there was a period in human development in which man's instincts and his institutions were in equilibrium and reinforced one another in a harmonious way. He called this the period of "peaceable savagery." It was characterized by group struggle for subsistence through agriculture and herding, cooperation among members of the community, simple technology, poverty, and the absence of warfare. It was a matriarchal society in which cultural institutions supported the altruistic and productive instincts on which the survival of the group depended. The Pueblo Indian communities of the American southwest were one example of this stage of human development.

Man fell from this Edenic state when the community's advancing technology enabled production of a surplus of goods that were not shared equitably amongst all the members of the group. This stage of human development marked the transition to barbarism and brought with it the institution of private property, the concept of ownership, slavery, increasing inequality of wealth, and an emphasis on "status emulation and rivalry" as a sign of distinction between members of the group. Patriarchy replaced matriarchy during the barbarian period. Veblen believed that barbarism began when men seized women as "trophies of the chase," held them in subservience as private property, assigned to them the productive labor on which survival of the group depended, and appropriated the products of this labor to themselves. Thus arose the predatory institutions that contaminated man's altruistic tendencies and bent them to selfish ends. In his writings, Veblen tried to show that this contamination was evident in all areas of modern society's culture—commerce, education, religion, the arts, politics. Put in the simplest terms, Veblen was explaining how greed replaced altruism as the dominant "habit of thought" in human society.

In Veblen's scheme, barbarism was succeeded by civilization, which fell into two phases: the handicraft era, extending from the late feudal period to the eighteenth century, and the machine age, ushered in by the industrial revolution, whose social and economic consequences Veblen saw all around him as he left the agrarian world of his Norwegian community and entered the mainstream culture of America. In the machine age, the community's enormously productive technological resources were owned and controlled by a small capitalist class—"the vested interests"—while the vast majority of men and women—"the underlying population"—performed the productive work but shared only marginally in its output. Veblen's analysis of the sources of economic inequality may seem at first glance to echo the doctrines of Karl Marx. But while Veblen saw class distinctions between capital and labor, he could find no evidence of Marx's class struggle unfolding historically through a dialectical process that would culminate with the formation of a classless society. Instead, Veblen saw "status emulation" as the driving motivation towards "pecuniary distinction" among members of the group, with all classes on the social ladder participating to the extent they could afford. In other words, according to Veblen, "status emulation" had become institutionalized as the motive force governing economic behavior.

These foundational principles of Veblen's social theory were laid down in a series of essays that he wrote after his arrival in Chicago. The first was titled "The Economic Theory of Women's Dress" (1894). In it, Veblen sardonically and satirically analyzed how the function of women's clothing was purely ornamental, designed to give evidence of her incapacity for useful work, and her subservience to the male who outfitted her as proof of his ability to spend lavishly and wastefully. He followed this up in 1898 with "The Instinct of Workmanship and the Irksomeness of Labor," which explained how workmanship had been contaminated by the predatory state of mind; "The Beginnings of Ownership," which traced private property to the capture and enslavement of women; and "The Barbarian Status of Women," which argued that, socially, the wealthy pampered women of the Gilded Age were descended directly from the captives of barbarian men. Veblen then expanded on these ideas in the book that made him famous, *The Theory of the Leisure Class* (1899).

In *The Theory of the Leisure Class,* Veblen sought to explain how the "vested interests" gain and hold economic power, and how they display their power through elaborate social rituals of "conspicuous consumption," "conspicuous waste," and "conspicuous leisure." Veblen regarded conspicuous consumption and conspicuous waste as modern forms of economic rivalry more subtle than the barbarian's displays of "booty" and "trophies of the chase," but no different in spirit. Conspicuous waste is proof of one's membership in the leisure class, of one's exemption from useful work, of one's status as a predator rather than a producer. Veblen defined leisure as "the non-productive consumption of time. Time is consumed non-productively (1) from a sense of the unworthiness of productive work, and (2) as an evidence of pecuniary ability to afford a life of idleness."

Veblen linked the formation of the leisure class to the subjugation of women in the barbarian stage of evolution, as society transitioned from matriarchy to patriarchy. "In the sequence of cultural evolution, the emergence of a leisure class coincides with the beginning of ownership [the capture of women] . . . The early differentiation out of which the distinction between a leisure and a working class arises is a division between men's and women's work in the lower stages of barbarism. Likewise, the earliest form of ownership is an ownership of the women by the able-bodied men of the community."

Veblen enlarged on this idea and showed its continuing traces in the modern community.

> The ownership of women begins in the lower barbarian stages of culture, apparently with the seizure of female captives. The original reason for their seizure and appropriation seems to have been their usefulness as trophies. The practice of seizing women from the enemy as trophies gave rise to a form of ownership-marriage, resulting in a household with a male head. This was followed by an extension of slavery to other captives and inferiors, besides women, and by an extension of the ownership-marriage to other women than those seized from the enemy. The outcome of emulation under the circumstances of a predatory life, therefore, has been, on the one hand, a form of marriage resting on coercion, and on the other hand, the custom of ownership. The two institutions are not distinguishable in the initial phase of their development; both arise from the desire of the successful men to put their prowess in evidence by exhibiting some durable result of their exploits. Both also minister to that propensity for mastery, which pervades all predatory communities. From the ownership of women, the concept of ownership extends itself to include the products of their industry, and so, therefore, to the ownership of things as well as of persons.
>
> In this way, a consistent system of property in goods is gradually installed. And although in the latest stages of the development, the serviceability of goods for consumption has come to be the most

obtrusive element of their value, still, wealth has by no means yet lost its utility as honorific evidence of the owner's prepotence.

This passage shows many of the key features of Veblen's style and method: his simultaneous application of anthropology, psychology, and evolutionary theory to identify and explain the origins and unfolding of the institutions of ownership and marriage; his matter-of-fact tone in presenting an unflattering portrait of relations between men and women; the satiric intention behind the inflated language of the final sentence, which mocks both its subject ("the owner"), and the pompous language of the pedant found in academic writing. Veblen then brings his analysis down to the time of his contemporaries.

> As the latter-day outcome of this evolution of an archaic institu-
> tion, the wife, who was at the outset, the drudge and chattel of the
> man, both in fact and in theory—the producer of goods for him to
> consume—has become the ceremonial consumer of goods which
> he produces. But she still quite unmistakably remains his chattel in
> theory; for the habitual rendering of vicarious leisure and consump-
> tion is the abiding mark of the unfree servant.

Veblen asserts that the leisure class, by its position at the top of the economic scale, sets the standards of behavior to be emulated by the classes below it. All members of society subscribe to the principle of emu-lation and resort to conspicuous consumption and conspicuous waste as demonstrations of their "reputability" to the extent that their economic means permit.

> The leisure class stands at the head of the social structure in point of
> reputability; and its manner of life and its standards of worth, there-
> fore, affect the norm of respectability for the community. The obser-
> vance of these standards, in some degree of approximation, becomes
> incumbent upon all classes lower in the scale. In modern civilized
> communities the lines of demarcation between the social classes have

grown vague and transient, and wherever this happens, the norm of reputability imposed by the upper class extends its coercive influence with but slight hindrance down through the social structure to the lowest strata. The result is that the members of each stratum accept as their ideal of decency the scheme of life in vogue in the next higher stratum, and bend their energies to live up to that ideal. On pain of forfeiting their good name and their self-respect in case of failure, they must conform to the accepted code, at least in appearance.

The basis on which good repute in any highly organized industrial community ultimately rests is pecuniary strength; and the means of showing pecuniary strength and so of gaining or retaining a good name, are leisure and conspicuous consumption of goods. Accordingly, both of these methods are in vogue as far down the scale as it remains possible . . . No class of society, not even the most abjectly poor, foregoes all customary conspicuous consumption . . . Very much of squalor and discomfort will be endured before the last trinket, or the last pretence of pecuniary decency is put away.

Veblen summed up the significance of conspicuous consumption as the measure of social reputability in the following sardonic passage:

Throughout the entire evolution of conspicuous expenditure, whether of goods or of services or human life, runs the obvious implication that in order to effectually mend the consumer's good fame, it must be an expenditure of superfluities. In order to be reputable, it must be wasteful. No merit would accrue from the consumption of the bare necessities of life, except by comparison with the abjectly poor who fall short even of the subsistence minimum; and no standard of expenditure could result from such a comparison, except the most prosaic and unattractive level of decency.

Veblen clarified the meaning of waste, as he was using the term. "It is here called 'waste' because this expenditure does not serve human life or human well-being on the whole, not because it is waste or misdirection of effort or expenditure as viewed from the standpoint of the individual consumer who chooses it." This observation reveals Veblen's moral outlook on the values of a society that elevates conspicuous display over the satisfaction of basic human needs. Veblen saw conspicuous waste operating in all the areas of man's social life, not merely his economic decisions.

> The principle of conspicuous waste guides the formation of habits of thought as to what is honest and reputable in life and in commodities. In so doing, this principle will traverse other norms of conduct which do not primarily have to do with the code of pecuniary honour, but which have, directly or incidentally, an economic significance of some magnitude. So the canon of honorific waste may, immediately or remotely, influence the sense of duty, the sense of beauty, the sense of utility, the sense of devotional or ritualistic fitness, and the sense of scientific truth.

In short, across the entire spectrum of man's life, all of his attitudes, his "habits of thought," have become corrupted by the principle of conspicuous waste.

Veblen's most scathing commentary on the unproductive and predatory social role of the leisure class was directed at the men and women of the Gilded Age.

> Conspicuous consumption of valuable goods is a means of respectability to the gentleman of leisure . . . He consumes freely, and of the best, in food, drink, narcotics, shelter, services, ornaments, apparel, weapons and accouterments, amusements, amulets, and idols or divinities . . .
>
> It goes without saying that no apparel can be considered elegant, or even decent, if it shows the effect of manual labour on the part of the wearer, in the way of soil or wear. The pleasing effect of neat and spotless garments is chiefly, if not altogether, due their carrying the suggestion of leisure—exemption from personal contact with industrial processes of any kind. Much of the charm that invests the

patent-leather shoe, the stainless linen, the lustrous cylindrical hat, and the walking-stick, which so greatly enhance the native dignity of a gentleman, comes of their pointedly suggesting that the wearer cannot when so attired bear a hand in any employment that is directly and immediately of any human use . . .

The dress of women goes even farther than that of men in the way of demonstrating the wearer's abstinence from productive employment. It needs no argument to enforce the generalisation that the more elegant styles of feminine bonnets go even farther towards making work impossible than does the man's high hat. The woman's shoe adds the so-called French heel to the evidence of enforced leisure by its polish; because this high heel obviously makes any, even the simplest and most necessary manual work extremely difficult. The like is true even in a higher degree of the skirt and the rest of the drapery which characterises woman's dress.

The Theory of the Leisure Class was widely read in Veblen's time and made him something of a literary celebrity. William Dean Howells was one of his early champions, and Progressives relished his skewering of "the vested interests" and his implicit classification of them with the barbarians of an earlier era. However, most of his contemporaries in the field of Economics regarded this book as a piece of literary satire, not social science. They were not ready to accept his eclectic methods of historical analysis and his disregard for data and statistics. But behind the satire, Veblen was serious in intent, as was evidenced by his next book, *The Theory of Business Enterprise*, which explored the relationship between industry—the productive capacity of the community—and the businessmen who controlled the means of production either through ownership or management, and directed it towards their desire for profit rather than towards the general welfare.

As he had done in his discussion of the origins and function of the leisure class, Veblen projected forward into the contemporary scene archaic concepts of ownership and exploit to expose the underlying forces operating in the realm of commerce. Although Veblen was merely speculating on the sources of ownership and private property, his speculations led him to some provocative and original theories about the economic organization of modern society. One of his most powerful insights was the distinction between exploit and industry. This led him to differentiate between what he called industrial and pecuniary employments, that is, between those who make goods and those who make money.

> Leaving aside the archaic vocations of war, politics, fashion, and religion, the employments in which men are engaged may be distinguished as pecuniary or business employments on the one hand, and industrial or mechanical employments on the other hand. In earlier times, and indeed until an uncertain point in the nineteenth century, such a distinction between employments would not, to any great extent, have coincided with a difference between occupations. But gradually, as time has passed and production for a market has come to be the rule in industry, there has supervened a differentiation of occupations, or a division of labour, whereby one class of men has taken over the work of purchase and sale and of husbanding a store of accumulated values. Concomitantly, of course, the rest, who may for lack of means or of pecuniary aptitude, have been less well fitted for pecuniary pursuits, have been relieved of the cares of business and have with increasing specialization given their attention to the mechanical processes involved in this production for a market. In this way, the distinction between pecuniary and industrial activities or employments has come to coincide more and more nearly with a difference between occupations.

Veblen saw in the separation of economic functions the beginnings of the modern dilemma of alienation—alienation of the worker from the product of his labor, which now becomes a good in the hands of a businessman who sets a price on it and sells it for a profit, and alienation of the businessman from the worker and from his own sense of workmanship, since he values products not for their intrinsic social utility but for the price they can command in the marketplace.

The everyday life of those classes which are engaged in business differs materially . . . from the life of the classes engaged in industry proper. There is an appreciable and widening difference between the habits of life of the two classes; and this carries with it a widening difference in the discipline to which the two classes are subjected. It induces a difference in the habits of thought and the habitual grounds and methods of reasoning resorted to by each class. There results a difference in the point of view, in the facts dwelt upon, in the methods of argument, in the grounds of validity appealed to; and this difference gains in magnitude and consistency as the differentiation of occupations goes on. So that the two classes come to have an increasing difficulty understanding one another and appreciating one another's convictions, ideals, capacities, and shortcomings.

Veblen believed that the technological base of the community, its industrial capacity, was the product of group life throughout human history. It was the cumulative output of the instinct of workmanship and should be used to promote the general welfare. Its appropriation by a pecuniary class, the businessman, for his narrow self-interest, he viewed in the same light as the exploits of the barbarian who seizes captives and reserves to himself the products of their labor. In the modern arrangement of industrial life under capitalism, the instinct of workmanship—key to man's survival as a species—had been turned into the servant of the profit motive.

Veblen traced the origins of capitalism to the development of accountancy in the ancient civilizations of the Middle East. Accountancy is a system of valuing all things on the sole criterion of price. This system gives the businessman an incentive to manipulate markets to maximize, not productive output, but the financial return on investment. Tariffs instituted at the behest of businessmen who wish to avoid competition are a crude example of this price manipulation. Veblen regarded the substitution of profit considerations for productivity as a form of sabotage of the community's industrial capacity.

There are many measures of policy and management both in private business and in public administration which are unmistakably of the nature of sabotage and which are not only considered to be excusable but are deliberately sanctioned by statute and common law and by the public conscience . . . The common welfare in any community which is organized on the price system cannot be maintained without a salutary use of sabotage—that is to say, such habitual recourse to delay and obstruction of industry and such restriction of output as will maintain prices at a reasonably profitable level and so guard against business depression . . .

The mechanical industry of the new order is inordinately productive. So the rate and volume of output have to be regulated with a view to what the traffic will bear—that is to say, what will yield the largest net return in terms of price to the businessmen who manage the country's industrial system . . .

In any community that is organized on the price system, with investment and business enterprise, habitual unemployment of the available industrial plant and workmen, in whole or in part, appears to be the indispensable condition without which tolerable conditions of life cannot be maintained.

Veblen took the implications of the price system a further step when he pointed to it as a cause of warfare between nations, warfare supported by the institutions of patriotism and nationalism. World War I provoked this analysis.

Veblen considered war not an innate tendency of man, but the result of his predatory institutions. In *Imperial Germany and the Industrial Revolution* (1915), he argued that Germany, as a dynastic state with its strong Prussian tradition of imperialism, was more bellicose than the democratic nations, and would remain so unless her institutions were reformed. Germany had grafted onto a feudal social system the advanced technology first developed in Great Britain, and this technological leap had fortified her imperialistic tendencies by greatly expanding her capacity for warfare. He predicted, correctly, that unless Germany and Japan, another feudal dynastic state, were converted to democratic institutions, they would pose a continuing threat to world peace. But Veblen did not believe that democratic nations like the United States and Great Britain were without bellicose tendencies. Their foreign relations were conducted, more or less, with a philosophy of "live and let live." As with other social and economic policies followed by the state, the decision whether to go to war rested with the vested interests, whose principal motivation was protecting their property rights and preserving their position at the top of the social and economic scale. The institution of private property, its roots deep in the violent exploits of the early barbarians, is the seed from which warfare on a national scale grows, in Veblen's view.

The only way that Veblen saw to guarantee a lasting peace was to eliminate the institution of private property, a prospect for which he held out no hope. He mocked himself for even bringing up the possibility. "Taken at its face value, without unavoidable prejudice out of the past, this question of a substitute to replace the current exploitation of the industrial arts for private gain by capitalistic sabotage is not altogether above a suspicion of drollery." He had no alternative to propose in its place and had quickly become disillusioned with the outcome of the Bolshevik Revolution in Russia. He resigned himself to a fatalistic acceptance of the status quo, which included recurring outbreaks of economic depression and war.

Veblen found operating in the institution of war the same spirit of emulation and status rivalry that animates members of all the social classes in the community and motivates their behavior. At the state level, this spirit of emulation expresses itself as nationalism and patriotism—rivalry with the people of another nation, as in sport. So long as these institutions have currency with the general population, the vested interests will be able to mobilize the common man in support of war when they deem such a step necessary. Veblen expounded on the nature and function of patriotism in his typical mordant and sardonic style.

> The patriotic spirit is a spirit of emulation, evidently, at the same time that it is emulation shot through with a sense of solidarity. It belongs under the general caption of sportsmanship, rather than

workmanship. Now, any enterprise in sportsmanship is bent on an invidious success, which must involve as its major purpose the defeat and humiliation of some competitor, whatever else may be comprised in its aim. Its aim is a differential gain, as against a rival; and the emulative spirit that comes under the head of patriotism commonly, if not invariably, seeks this differential advantage by injury of the rival rather than by an increase of home-bred well-being . . . Patriotism is of a contentious complexion, and finds its full expression in no other than warlike enterprise; its highest and final appeal is for the death, damage, discomfort, and destruction of the party of the second part . . .

The patriotic spirit is at cross purposes with modern life, but in any test case, it is found that the claims of life yield before those of patriotism; and any voice that dissents from this order of things is as a voice crying in the wilderness.

The turn of events after World War I soured Veblen. The possibility of a lasting peace enforced through a confederation of democratic states faded with the collapse of Woodrow Wilson's plan, which Veblen supported, for a League of Nations. And under the administrations of Warren Harding and Calvin Coolidge, the business of America once again became business, with all that implied for chicanery and financial manipulation of the industrial plant. His vision of the future was, in his terms, pessimistic, as he could foresee only a continuation of those evolutionary social forces he had identified and described in his portrait of the modern industrial community. It would be more of the same: "The scale of things is to be larger, the pace swifter, and the volume and dispersion of [the] leisure class somewhat wider." Surely this sums up the state of affairs in twenty-first-century America. One wonders how Veblen might connect the proliferation of digital technology controlled by an elite engineering class with the growing inequalities of wealth and the shrinking of the middle class.

Veblen has been faulted for offering his readers a comprehensive explanation of the sources and causes of society's ills and inefficiencies without proposing a solution. The problem for Veblen was that, given his analytical framework, he saw no solution other than a revolutionary overturn of the vested interests, an event that he considered highly improbable given all the institutional forces at work. In 1921 he wrote a book called *The Engineers and the Price System* in which he suggested that the industrial capacity of America could be put to more efficient and equitable use if it were managed by the engineers and technicians—the men of workmanship—who were indispensable to its functioning, rather than by businessmen who wished only to exploit it for their profit. This takeover of the country's industrial apparatus would have to be accomplished by a general strike that would bring the entire economy to a standstill. But Veblen held no illusions that such a revolutionary spirit was at work in the community of engineers. Quite the contrary. In Veblen's view, they were as contaminated with the values of the leisure class as the vested interests that employed them.

> By settled habit the technicians, the engineers and industrial experts, are a harmless and docile sort, well-fed on the whole, and somewhat placidly content with the "full dinner pail" which the lieutenants of the Vested Interests habitually allow them. It is true, they constitute the indispensable General Staff of that industrial system which feeds the Vested Interests, but hitherto at least, they have nothing to say in the planning and direction of this industrial system, except as employees in the pay of the financiers.

Thus, "anything like a Soviet of Technicians is at the most a remote contingency in America."

Veblen spent the last five years of his life in rustic isolation, his health broken, his finances shaky, his reputation as a major social theorist waning, except among a small cadre of devoted followers. In 1925 he was offered the Presidency of The American Economic Association, but he turned it down, some said because he dreaded giving the acceptance speech. But when the Great Depression struck just three months after his death, reformers in the administration of Franklin Roosevelt looked to his writings for inspiration, if not for ideas, on how to correct the inequities in America's economic and social systems in order to protect "the underlying population" from the depredations of the "vested interests."

Today Veblen's dismissal of the contributions of the business class seems quaint; his neglect of the role of government in regulating the economy short-sighted. His legacy is his method of analysis, his insistence on the nexus of personal motives and historical forces. He pioneered a new way of looking at the social organism that continues to have relevance to today's social problems.

Veblen's importance to America's cultural history is as a visionary who understood in the most profound way possible his country's transition from an agrarian to an industrial way of life. His contribution was to identify and explain the web of interconnecting forces that were shaping the national character during this change. He antagonized conventional minds both by his lifestyle and his radical social theories. He questioned Americans' perception of themselves as unique and exceptional people by showing the derivation of their mode of life from ancient cultures and traditions. But he was too much of a non-conformist to be tolerated, let alone celebrated. Words that he wrote in the essay "The Intellectual Pre-Eminence of Jews in Modern Europe" may be taken as his self-portrait.

> For him, as for other men in the like case, the skepticism that goes to make him an effectual factor in the increase and diffusion of knowledge among men involves a loss of that peace of mind that is the birthright of the safe and sane quietist. He becomes a disturber of the intellectual peace, but only at the cost of becoming an intellectual wayfaring man, a wanderer in the intellectual no-man's land, seeking another place to rest, farther along the road, somewhere over the horizon. They are neither a complaisant nor a contented lot, these aliens of the uneasy feet, but that is, after all, not the point in question.

CHAPTER 7

Thomas Merton

Prologue

The life story of the Cistercian monk Thomas Merton is an existential journey undertaken by a man seeking a meaning for his life that the industrial civilization described by Thorstein Veblen could not provide. Merton sought meaning in a spiritual quest for union with God, and to find it, he gave away all his possessions, except for a few books, and recused himself from mainstream American society into the sanctuary of a Trappist monastery.

But Merton was a man of contradictory and passionate character, pulled between his longing for the solitary experience of God and his love for the world and its people. Orphaned as a teenager, Merton early in his life sought solace in the worldly pleasures of London and New York. Dissatisfied with his aimless way of living, shamed by indiscretions, and facing induction into the US Army during World War II, Merton entered the Gethsemani monastery in the backcountry of Kentucky, where he remained for the remainder of his life.

There, the tensions in his character persisted. He became a mild but insistent dissenter against the conventions of his order by demanding the complete solitude of a hermitage where he could pursue a mystical communion with God. But the outside world remained a constant magnet for his thoughts and energies, and he wrote voluminously on the major public issues of his time: the nuclear arms race, civil rights, and the Vietnam War. His application to these issues of Christian principles honed through the discipline of monastic life often challenged the official positions of the Catholic Church, leading to temporary censorship

Thomas Merton (Photo by Sybille Akers. Used with permission of the Thomas Merton Center at Bellarmine University.)

of his writing. However, his voice would not be silenced, and before his untimely accidental death, he gained international recognition for his humanitarian message and example.

Thomas Merton – The Restless Hermit

Thomas Merton was one of the most exceptional cultural and spiritual figures of twentieth-century America. A prolific and best-selling author who wrote poetry, fiction, memoir, and spiritual meditations, a gregarious socializer and bon vivant with a fondness for whiskey and jazz, a man with a strong awareness of social injustice and suffering who spoke out boldly about civil rights, disarmament, and war, Merton retreated from the secular world at the age of twenty-six to join one of the most severe and restrictive religious orders of the Catholic Church, the Cistercian Order of the Strict Observance, also known as the Trappists. His life without and within the monastery was a long struggle to reconcile contradictory tendencies in his character: an insistence on personal independence and the sovereignty of his own will, and a need to engage with the world, find acceptance from others, and earn their love and respect. He sought through his dedication to the religious life to resolve the dualities of his nature and reach the wholeness of his deep self but carried these warring impulses even into his life as a hermetic monk. His powerful story illuminates the existential dilemmas that challenge all of us now living in a world of technological forces that are radically transforming us physically and spiritually.

Merton was born on January 31, 1915, in Prades, France, a small village in the Eastern Pyrénées. His parents were artists and wanderers. His mother, Ruth Jenkins, was from Ohio, the daughter of Martha Baldwin and Samuel Jenkins, a successful businessman who owned a stationery-bookstore in Zanesville, Ohio, then became a salesman for New York publishing house Grosset & Dunlap. After schooling at a private academy in Massachusetts, Ruth went to Paris to study art under Percyval Tudor Hart, a Canadian artist and teacher. There in 1911, she met the painter Owen Merton, also studying under Hart. Owen was from New

Zealand, the son of Alfred Merton and Gertrude Grierson, a teacher. Owen's parents encouraged his artistic talents, and at the age of seventeen he left New Zealand to study art in London, then went to Paris to participate in the artistic ferment flourishing there. When he and Ruth met, they were both twenty-four years old, trying to launch careers as painters.

In 1914, as war threatened, Hart moved his studio to London. Ruth and Owen followed. On April 7, 1914, they were married in an Anglican ceremony. By the time Tom was born, they were living spartanly in Prades, from where Owen sent his paintings to London for gallery shows. After the outbreak of World War I, the Mertons in August 1916 moved to Douglaston, Long Island, to live with Ruth's parents and her brother Harold. Owen rented a house in Flushing from a tavern keeper, started a garden to grow his food, and earned money playing the piano in silent movie theaters. On November 2, 1918 Tom's brother John Paul was born, marking a turning point in Tom's early childhood development.

Ruth was a devoted if somewhat detached and clinical mother. She held high expectations for Tom, watched his behavior closely, and kept a journal of his growth and activities she called "Tom's Book." After the birth of John Paul, her attention to Tom slackened, though she homeschooled him. Then in September 1921, when Tom was six years old, Ruth was diagnosed with stomach cancer and hospitalized. She refused to let her children see her ill. She wrote Tom a letter telling him she was dying and would never see him again. On the day of her death, October 3, Tom was taken to the hospital but not allowed to be with her. This cruel abandonment set the stage for Tom's later difficulty believing that women could love him. Tom and John Paul were sent to live with their grandparents and uncle in Douglaston. Tom was enrolled in the Douglaston Elementary School, which he initially disliked. A year later Owen moved to Bermuda, seeking a better climate in which to live and work, and took Tom with him, leaving John Paul with the Jenkins family. Thus began a pattern of dislocation, separation from family, and loss that persisted throughout Tom's childhood.

In Bermuda, Owen fell in love with Evelyn Scott, a novelist married to the artist Cyril Kay Scott. With Cyril's tolerance, Owen and Evelyn conducted an open affair. Tom's life in Bermuda was unhappy. He disliked Evelyn intensely. He was placed in a school where he struggled until his father withdrew him. While Owen painted and carried on with Evelyn, Tom was left alone at the boarding house where they lived. Evelyn abused Tom emotionally, with cruel remarks about his deceased mother. After a year of this, Tom was sent back to Douglaston. Owen, Evelyn, and Cyril took their ménage à trois on an excursion to France and North Africa.

In the fall of 1924, Owen became ill and went to London for treatment. He broke off his relationship with Evelyn and returned to Douglaston in July to retrieve Tom. Owen then went again to France, taking Tom with him but leaving John Paul with Sam and Martha. Tom, who was setting down roots in Douglaston and forming friendships with boys his age, reluctantly went with his father.

Owen settled them in the medieval village St. Antonin-Noble-Val in the Midi-Pyrénées. He boarded Tom at the Lycée Ingres in Montauban, a place that Tom grew to hate for its prison-like atmosphere. But Tom overcame initial bullying from the French students with his pluckiness and brilliance in languages. Over the next two years, he begged his father unsuccessfully to remove him from the school. Owen bought land in St. Antonin and made plans to build a house on it. In the summer of 1926, Sam and Martha brought John Paul to France for a visit. They met Owen and Tom in Paris, then traveled to Switzerland. Sam embarrassed Owen with boorish displays of his wealth, throwing coins in the street to begging urchins.

In May 1928, following a successful show of his work in London, Owen withdrew Tom from Lycée Ingres and moved them to Ealing, a suburb of London, to live with Owen's aunt Maud and her husband, Benjamin Pearce. Tom, now age thirteen, was enrolled at Ripley Court, a school in Surrey run by Benjamin's sister. Sam Jenkins paid the tuition.

In July 1929, Owen returned to St. Antonin to sell his property and retrieve his paintings. On his way back to London he collapsed on the train and had to be hospitalized in Middlesex. Recovered, he took Tom with him on a vacation trip to Scotland, but collapsed again and went to London for treatment. After Tom returned to Ealing, the Pearces told him that his father was suffering from an inoperable malignant brain tumor that would end his life.

Tom matriculated to Oakham, a small public school located in a market town in the Midlands. Sam again covered the cost of tuition. Tom adapted well to the school. His wide interests and colorful background made him popular with the other students. He competed in rugby, track, and cricket, and endured the ritualistic bullying prevalent in the public schools of that day. He attended the twice-daily chapels and was exposed to Anglican class-consciousness. The headmaster, recognizing Tom's intellectual gifts, customized his curriculum, allowing him to study the modern languages in which he excelled in addition to the traditional Latin and Greek.

Sam, Martha, and John Paul visited Tom during the summer of 1930. Sam informed Tom that he was establishing an annuity for him and his brother that would give them financial independence through their school years. He chose Tom's godfather, Dr. Tom Bennett, to be his guardian until he reached the age of twenty-one. On January 18, 1931, thirteen days before Tom's sixteenth birthday, Owen Merton died, leaving Tom an orphan.

For the next several years, while he continued his studies, Merton lived under the supervision and guidance of his godfather Tom Bennett and Bennett's wife, Iris. The Bennetts were sophisticates who lived in an elegantly furnished London apartment and exercised highbrow tastes in literature, music, and the performing arts. They introduced Merton to the literature of D.H. Lawrence, James Joyce, and Ernest Hemingway. During visits to their flat, Merton amused himself at jazz clubs and wandered the streets of London, where he discovered the glaring inequality between slum life and his godparents' life of comfort and plenty. The contrast sparked in Tom a literary interest in communism. He read Marx and Engels.

Merton lived adventurously for an orphaned teenager. He made summer trips alone across the Atlantic Ocean to visit the Jenkins and John Paul. On one of the crossings, he pursued a romance with a woman twice his age who indulged him no further than instruction in bridge.

While in America, he went to the 1932 Chicago World's Fair and found work as a midway barker outside an erotic exhibition titled "The Streets of Paris." In New York, he spent time in the Greenwich Village studio of the painter Reginald Marsh, getting his first taste of bohemia. During the school year at Oakham, Merton made solitary vacation trips to Europe, walking through the Rhineland and the south of France. Twice he went to Rome. On the second trip, after his graduation from Oakham, he discovered the early Byzantine Christian churches and spent many hours exploring them. He also visited the Trappist monastery at Tre Fontane. On this trip, he had experienced the spiritual presence of his mother and father and had the urge to pray for them. He recorded his emotional confusion about this impulse in the journal he was keeping.

Merton continued to prosper at Oakham. In his final year, he was appointed house prefect and given spacious living quarters. He was also selected to be the editor of the school literary magazine. In December 1932, he went to Cambridge to take the scholarship examination for Clare College. He passed the exam, was given a scholarship, and in the fall of 1933 at age eighteen entered Cambridge.

At Cambridge, Merton lost his way. He fell in with a rowdy crowd, skipped lectures, spent too much time drinking in pubs, and ran up debts, alarming Tom Bennett. He brought women to his rooms at Clare College in violation of the rules and made one of them pregnant. Bennett summoned him to London for a reckoning. He worked out a financial settlement for the unwed mother and promised Merton not to inform the Jenkins about the scandal. He warned Merton that his behavior was jeopardizing his scholarship. At the end of the academic year, Merton once again traveled to New York to be with his family. Bennett wrote to him that his scholarship was unlikely to be renewed and advised him not to return to England. To apply for resident alien status in the United States, Merton had to go back to England to complete paperwork. This done, he sailed back to New York and in January 1935 enrolled as a sophomore at Columbia University.

Merton entered Columbia with the intent to prepare for a career as a journalist and decided to pursue a curriculum in the social sciences. He also plunged into the social and literary life of the university. He joined the Alpha Delta Phi fraternity and competed for the track and cross-country teams. He submitted articles and cartoons to the campus humor magazine, *Jester*, and more serious writing to the *Columbia Literary Review*, which was edited by Robert Giroux. Merton presented himself to the Columbia community as a worldly dandy. He wore three-piece suits and a felt hat and sported a watch chain on his vest. He circulated a rumor that he had left behind in England a pregnant girlfriend. He frequented bars and nightclubs, where he smoked and drank excessively. He was living with the Jenkins family in Douglaston and commuting into New York on the railroad. He fell in love with a girl from Long Island. His life continued along the same aimless, pleasure-seeking path that he had followed in England, and that had led nowhere.

The change began in his junior year. On his way to one of his social science classes, he mistakenly sat down in the classroom where Mark Van Doren, a brilliant and inspirational professor, taught a yearlong course on Shakespeare. In this class, Merton discovered the power of literature to make life comprehensible, to impart wisdom and understanding. He found in Van Doren a mentor who would ultimately nudge him through the door to religious life. And in the circle of students who gravitated to Van Doren, Merton made life-long friends who shared his sense of discomfort with the modern world. The most important of these friends were Robert Lax, Edward Rice, and Sy Freedgood. Merton remarked their significance in his best-selling autobiography, *The Seven Storey Mountain*: "Our friendship would work powerfully to rescue us from the confusion and the misery in which we had come to find ourselves, partly through our own fault, and partly through a complex set of circumstances which might be grouped under the heading of the 'modern world' and 'modern society.'"

Merton's feelings of displacement and alienation were aggravated in October 1936 by the death of his benevolent and supportive grandfather Sam Jenkins. After Sam's wife Martha died the following summer, Merton moved away from his family home in Douglaston to avoid the supervision of his uncle Harold and into a room on 114th Street near the university. His brother John Paul was then a junior at Cornell.

Literary influences were beginning to shape Merton's life and give it a more meaningful direction. Etienne Gilson's *The Spirit of Medieval Philosophy* introduced Merton to the Catholic concept of God. Bob Lax recommended that he read Aldous Huxley's *Ends and Means*. Merton wrote a review of it that was published in the *Columbia Literary Review*. The book awakened in Merton an awareness of the reality of a supernatural order that is accessible through prayer, detachment, and love. Huxley argued that humankind could not realize good ends as long as it uses evil means, such as war. He characterized man as captive to his animal nature and its material desires. He offered asceticism as a way for man to free his spirit to form a union with God. But Huxley distrusted Catholicism and preferred the Eastern approach to spirituality made through Buddhism.

Merton received his AB degree in January 1938, then enrolled in the graduate school of English. "This registration in the graduate school represented the first remote step of a retreat from the fight for money and fame, from the active and worldly life of conflict and competition," Merton wrote in *The Seven Storey Mountain*. He chose the Romantic poet William Blake as the subject of his Master's thesis, which he titled "Nature and Art in William Blake." Blake's radical spirituality, as expressed in his poetry and painting, had a profound effect on Merton. Blake exemplified in his life and his art the destiny of the outsider whose inner spiritual revolution brings him to a Reality beyond the grasp of the man who lives by reason alone. "As Blake worked himself into my system," Merton relates, "I became more and more conscious of the necessity of a vital faith, and the total unreality and insubstantiality of the dead, selfish rationalism which had been freezing my mind and will for the last seven years."

That summer, Merton met another spiritual guide, the Hindu monk Brahmachari, who pointed him in the direction of his ultimate vocation. Merton was introduced to Brahmachari at Grand Central Station in New York by Sy Freedgood. Brahmachari, sensing that Merton was groping his way towards a religious conviction, urged him to read St. Augustine's *Confessions* and *The Imitation of Christ* by the fourteenth-century monk Thomas à Kempis.

Merton spent the summer of 1938 researching his thesis on Blake. His reading ranged from the thirteenth-century Christian mystic Meister Eckhart to the Zen Buddhist D.T. Suzuki. Work on this thesis proved to be a turning point in Merton's spiritual development. "By the time I was ready to begin the actual writing of the thesis, that is around the beginning of September 1938, the groundwork of conversion was more or less complete . . . I began to desire to dedicate my life to God, to his service."

Merton took his first tentative steps into the embrace of the Catholic Church when in August he canceled a Sunday date with his girlfriend to attend a Mass at the Church of Corpus Christi a few blocks from Columbia. Merton was struck by the religious sincerity of the congregation and the sermon on Christ delivered by a young priest. Though he left the church in the middle of the service, fleeing out of a sense of his unworthiness to be there, he felt changed by the experience.

He was reading the poetry and life of the English Jesuit priest Gerard Manley Hopkins. One day in October, he put down his book, walked to Corpus Christi Church, and told the parish priest, Father Ford, that he wanted to become a Catholic. Father Ford arranged for him to receive instruction from Father Moore, the young priest who had delivered the sermon. On November 16 he was baptized a Catholic in a ceremony witnessed by Ed Rice, Bob Lax, and Sy Freedgood. He made his first confession, then took communion.

In *The Seven Storey Mountain*, Merton writes that he "makes a mess" of the first year after his baptism because he does not know how to live a Catholic life. He quickly fell back into his old dissolute routines. He faults his own character. "The one thing I needed most of all was a sense of the supernatural life, and systematic mortification of my passions and my crazy nature." He recognized that he had been converted in his intellect only, not his will.

In February 1939, Merton received his AM degree in English. He intended to continue his studies towards the Ph.D. and began work on a dissertation on Hopkins. He moved to Greenwich Village, where he wrote poetry and book reviews that were published in *The New York Times* and the *Herald Tribune*. He spent the summer in Olean, New

York, with Bob Lax and Ed Rice. All three were writing novels. Merton brought his novel, *The Labyrinth*, back with him back to New York and placed it with Naomi Burton, an agent at Curtis Brown, after it was repeatedly rejected.

World War II was approaching. It filled Merton with horror. He felt personally responsible for it. "When we went back to New York, in the middle of August, the world I had helped to make was finally preparing to break the shell and put forth its evil head and devour another generation of men."

As his classes at Columbia resumed, Merton went into crisis about his future. Following a night of heavy drinking, he announced to his friends that he believed he should enter a monastery and become a priest. He admitted his inability to live a religious life by himself. "I needed a Rule that was almost entirely aimed at detaching me from the world and uniting me with God, not a Rule made to fit me to fight for God in the world." He sought advice from Dan Walsh, a philosophy professor from whom he had taken a course on Thomas Aquinas. Walsh suggested he investigate the Cistercians, also known as the Trappists, one of the most severe and ascetic Catholic orders. Merton felt the Trappists would be too hard for him, especially given his somewhat fragile health. Walsh then arranged for Merton an introduction to Father Edmund at the Monastery of St. Francis of Assisi on 31st Street. Father Edmund encouraged Merton to apply for entrance into the novitiate in August 1940.

In the summer of 1940, Merton returned to Olean with Bob Lax. He was drawn to St. Bonaventure's, a Franciscan college, and moved into a dormitory there. As the date for his entry into the monastery approached, Merton grew fearful that his past life might disqualify him for the priesthood. He decided to go to New York and confess all to Father Edmund. After hearing Merton's confession, Father Edmund advised him to withdraw his application. Shattered, Merton sought solace in the confessional of a nearby Capuchin church. The priest there told Merton that he was unfit for any religious order and the priesthood.

Merton returned to Olean and applied for a teaching position at St. Bonaventure's. He had decided to become a writer and teacher and to pursue a life as a monk outside the monastery. He joined the secular Third Order of the Franciscans and wore a scapular under his clothes. He bought a breviary and received instruction in its use from the librarian at St. Bonaventure's, Father Irenaeus.

As the New Year began, two pressures pushing in radically different directions were bearing on Merton, one secular, one religious. In February, he applied to go on a retreat at Gethsemani, the Trappist monastery in Kentucky that Dan Walsh had recommended. His application was accepted, and in April he spent a week there working and praying with the monks. He rhapsodized over their devotion to God. "They were the least and the last of men. They had made themselves outcasts, seeking outside the walls of the world, Christ poor and rejected of men." He wanted to join their order but believed that their way of life was closed to him, and was too fearful of broaching the subject with the abbot. Before leaving Gethsemani, he went through the Stations of the Cross and at the last one prayed to God to become a Trappist. He returned to St. Bonaventure's, resumed his teaching duties, and began work on a new novel, *The Journal of My Escape from the Nazis*.

The other pressure came from the world. He received a notice from his draft board to appear for a physical exam. He applied for non-combatant status as a conscientious objector. At his physical exam, he was rejected for service on account of his missing teeth. Merton's position on the war followed orthodox Catholic doctrine, which sanctioned "just wars"—wars of defense.

During the spring term, Merton met Catherine de Hueck Doherty, a Russian immigrant who had come to St. Bonaventure's to speak about her work at Friendship House in Harlem, and to chide her fellow Catholics for averting their eyes from the suffering and injustice being inflicted on American negroes. Merton offered to volunteer at Friendship House over the summer. Moved by what he found there, he agreed to join Catherine in her work during a second visit she made to St. Bonaventure's in the fall. But while on a retreat at Friendship House over Thanksgiving, he changed his mind after a luncheon conversation with Mark Van Doren, who encouraged him not to give up his calling to the priesthood. When he got back to St. Bonaventure's, he spoke to Father Irenaeus about his desire to join the Trappists at Gethsemani and recounted his experience with Father Edmund. Father Irenaeus told Merton he saw nothing in his past that would prevent him from entering a religious order, but wondered if the Trappists were the right order for him. Merton then wrote again to Gethsemani but did not dare disclose that he was coming as a postulant who wished to enter the novitiate.

Merton received an invitation from the abbot to return. This was followed by another summons from his draft board to report for a second physical exam. When Japan bombed Pearl Harbor on December 7, Merton decided to leave St. Bonaventure's before the end of the term to avoid conscription. He wrote his draft board that he was about to enter a monastery. He gave away all his possessions except for a few clothes and books (Blake, Hopkins, his breviary, his Bible), sent his literary manuscripts to Mark Van Doren, and boarded a train for Louisville. "I belonged to God, not myself," he wrote in *The Seven Storey Mountain*. "And to belong to him is to be free of all the anxieties and worries and sorrows that belong to this earth, and the love of the things that are in it."

Merton had chosen for his retreat from the secular world one of the oldest and most rigorous orders of the Catholic Church, the Cistercians of the Strict Observance. The Cistercians were founded in 1098 in the village of Cîteaux (Latin name *Cistercium*) near Dijon, by a group of Benedictine monks who wished to follow the sixth-century Rule of St. Benedict. The Rule was built upon three vows—stability, fidelity to monastic life, and obedience. All three of these vows would test and at times, be challenged by Merton during his twenty-seven years as a monk. The Rule also required silence, though not in the form of a vow. Cistercian monks communicated through a special sign language, and spoke only when addressing a superior or in case of emergency. Cistercian life was structured around a routine of prayer, worship, meditation, singing, and manual labor in the fields to grow their food. It was a communal life in which the monks worshipped together, worked together, ate together, and slept together in large dormitories. Privacy and solitude were scarce.

The Trappists took their name from a reform movement that began in the seventeenth century out of a desire to return the order to the austere principles on which it had been originally founded. The reform movement was initiated by Armand Jean de Bouthillier de Rancé, the abbot of La Trappe Abbey in Normandy. The Trappist monastery in Kentucky was founded in 1847 by Father Paulinus, the prior of the Melleray monastery in France. Overcrowding at French monasteries and political upheavals in the country were spurring emigration of monks to North America. Father Paulinus purchased fourteen hundred acres from the Sisters of Loretto, who were operating an orphanage on a farm called Gethsemani, in a region of rolling hills and beautiful forests. In October 1848, a colony of forty-four monks led by Father Entropius set out to build a monastery on the farm. After an adventurous journey in the course of which they nearly lost all their possessions, they arrived at Gethsemani shortly before Christmas, almost to the day of Merton's arrival there. Writing a history of the Trappists in *The Waters of Siloe*, Merton gave his reasons why men become Trappists:

> The Trappists are the most austere order they could find, and Trappist life was that which least resembled the life men lead in the towns and cities of our world. And there is something in their hearts that tells them they cannot be happy in an atmosphere where people are looking for nothing but their own pleasure and advantage and comfort and success.

Merton arrived at Gethsemani in the dead of night after all the monks had gone to bed. The monk on duty at the gatehouse greeted him with the question, "Have you come to stay this time?" Merton spent several days in the guest house, where he caught cold by leaving the windows open to the freezing winter air, a gesture of mortification that was undercut when the master of novices came to interview him and remarked on the vanity of Merton's display. Merton began his interview with the master of novices by repeating the confession he had made to Father Edmund of the Franciscans. The master of novices arranged for Merton to meet with the abbot, Dom Frederic Dunne, and on December 13, he was accepted as a postulant to the choir.

After a two-month trial period as a postulant, Merton entered the novitiate as a choir monk and was issued the rough medieval wardrobe worn by the novices. Underwear consisted of a long denim shirt, long drawers, stockings tied to the drawers, and socks. Over this, in winter the monks wore a robe, a scapular, and a cowl, all made from heavy wool. The clothing chafed the skin and weighed twenty pounds. The summer wardrobe was lighter—flannel shirts, a robe of duck, scapular, and cowl made from cotton. On their feet the monks wore clumsily fitted work shoes similar to army boots.

Personal comfort was shunned by the Trappists, who believed the way to God involved a struggle between the senses and the will. The sensory experience was focused on detecting God in the world; gratuitous sensory pleasure was regarded as a distraction. The monks ate simple, tasteless food—bread, soup, vegetables—with plain wooden utensils. Eggs and meat were excluded from their diet except during sickness. The monks slept in small dormitory cells on straw mattresses spread on boards. They wore their habits, which often became tangled as they slept. The cells were separated by partitions with a curtain covering the entrance. Snoring monks often kept Merton awake. Furniture in the cell was limited to a crucifix, a holy water stoup, a few pegs. From one of the pegs hung "the discipline," a small cord whip used for self-flagellation on the back. Hygiene was spartan. The monks shaved once a week and had haircuts once a month. There were no bathtubs and only three showers for the entire population, which numbered over one hundred when Merton entered Gethsemani. The showers were locked and could be used only with permission.

Few personal indulgences were allowed. Novices were given twenty minutes each week to select a book from the library, subject to approval by the master of novices. Merton had a small box in the scriptorium where he stored his few books, poems he had written, and some letters. Monks were permitted to send and receive mail four times a year but were restricted to writing no more than half a page. The abbot screened all correspondence. Regulations controlled every aspect of the monk's life, even to the way he held his cup while drinking. Each day the monks participated in the Chapter of Faults, an assembly during which they confessed their lapses in carrying out the Rule and bore the accusations of other monks. Penance might include scourging with the whip.

In many ways, life at Gethsemani resembled the life of a prisoner in a penitentiary or a soldier in a fort. The difference was that monks were always free to leave, with or without the consent of the abbot. Merton needed this severe external structure to tame the impulses that had shamed him, and to free him to pursue his quest for the experience of his divine nature. What to others might seem as confinement, Merton saw as the ultimate security. "I was hidden in the secrecy of His protection," Merton wrote in *The Seven Storey Mountain*.

Merton plunged into the regimen at Gethsemani with his usual exuberance, and within a year began to show signs of weakening health, exacerbated by his poor diet and heavy workload. Health issues would plague him throughout his years at the monastery, periodically requiring trips to St. Joseph's Infirmary in Louisville for treatment. To lighten his workload, Dom Frederic assigned Merton to translate religious books and pamphlets from the French. Although translation hardly tapped Merton's deep talents as a writer, it opened the door for him to practice his craft and set the stage for what would be a prolific career as a writer in Gethsemani. Merton had brought his poems with him to the monastery and continued to write poetry until it was temporarily forbidden him.

In July 1942, Merton's brother John Paul visited him while on his way to England to fight in the war. John Paul had left Cornell for Canada, where he joined the Royal Canadian Air Force. During his brief stay at Gethsemani, John Paul became a Catholic, was baptized, and took communion with Tom in the chapel. Once in England, he met and married the Englishwoman Margaret Mary Evans. On April 16, 1943 he was killed when the bomber he was flying crashed in the North Sea while on a mission to Germany. The crew survived the crash and was rescued, but John Paul died at sea from his injuries and was buried there. Tom wrote the moving elegy "For My Brother: Reported Missing in Action, 1943," which begins with the lovely lines "Sweet brother, if I do not sleep/My eyes are flowers for your tomb."

At the end of the year, Bob Lax, born a Jew but now a converted Catholic, visited Merton at Gethsemani. When he left, he carried with him the poems Merton had been writing and showed them to Mark Van Doren, who passed them along to James Laughlin, the publisher of New Directions. Laughlin issued the poems in 1944 under the title *Thirty Poems*. This volume was Merton's first published book. A second collection, *A Man in a Divided Sea*, was published in 1946.

Merton was ambivalent about his dual role as writer and monk. He was concerned that his writing might undermine his religious life by calling attention to himself, feeding his vanity and ambition. The question he faced was whether he was writing for God or himself. Fortunately for both Merton and the monastery, his abbot Dom Frederic saw Merton's talent for writing as a gift from God that should be used in God's service. Initially, he ordered Merton to perform purely scholarly writing tasks. But later, he urged Merton to write in a personal way about his spiritual journey and his search for godliness. The first such work was *The Seven Storey Mountain*, which Naomi Burton submitted to Robert Giroux, then an editor at Harcourt Brace. The book became a bestseller, bringing fame to Merton and Gethsemani, as well as a steady royalty stream that helped lift the monastery out of debt. Merton came to accept that his vocation as a writer and his vocation as a monk were joined. "It seems to me that writing, far from being an obstacle to spiritual perfection, has become one of the conditions on which my perfection will depend," Merton wrote in *The Sign of Jonas*. "If I am to be a saint—and there is nothing else that I can think of desiring to be—it seems I must get there by writing books in a Trappist monastery." This remark illustrates how well placed was Merton's fear that his writing might inflame his ambition. All in all, Merton wrote and published more than seventy books about the spiritual life, some highly personal like his journals and meditations, others more scholarly, dealing with Church history and doctrine. As we shall see, writing connected Merton not only to God but also to the secular world he had abandoned.

Merton moved steadily through the stages of his formal commitment to the Cistercian Order. In 1944 at the Feast of St. Joseph, he made his simple vows of "temporary profession" after being approved by those monks already professed. At this time, Merton gave up all his worldly possessions and wrote a will leaving part of his estate to the mother of the child he had never seen. In March 1947 Merton made his solemn vows, signifying that he had been accepted by the community forever.

Ironically, as Merton passed this milestone, he was beginning to question whether the Trappists were the right order for him. The issue was the order's emphasis on activity over contemplation. Merton felt that the routines at Gethsemani left him no time or space for the solitude that he believed was essential in following a contemplative life. He believed that it was contemplation, achieved in silence and solitude, which brought men close to God. The busyness of life at Gethsemani was an obstacle to this contemplative state. When Dom Frederic died in 1948, leaving behind a monastery in debt and in need of upkeep, his successor Dom James Fox embarked on an ambitious program to make farming a source of profit for the monastery. Royalties from *The Seven Storey Mountain*, which had sold 300,000 copies in its first year, enabled Gethsemani to purchase mechanized farm equipment. Merton was disturbed by the noise and ceaseless activity and made no secret of his discomfort. "We seem to think that God will not be satisfied with a monastery that does not behave in every way like a munitions factory under wartime conditions of production." Merton longed for the solitude and silence that nourished the contemplative state. In his meditations, published as *Thoughts in Solitude* in 1958, Merton extols the virtues of the solitary life. "The solitary life, being silent, clears away the smokescreen of words that man has laid down between his mind and things . . . Silence teaches us to know reality by respecting it where words have defiled it . . . When we have really met and known the world in silence, words do not separate us from the world nor from other men, nor from God, nor from ourselves because we no longer trust entirely in language to contain reality."

For Merton, contemplation was not merely a private escape into the company of God. It was the foundation for meaningful action, for a moral, godly life. "Contemplation means rest, suspension of activity, withdrawal into the mysterious interior solitude," he writes in *The Seven Storey Mountain*. But this contemplative state is not an end in itself. The highest perfection is reached when the fruits of contemplation are communicated to others, bringing about change. The aim of contemplation is to become joined to Christ, then bring Christ out into the world, if not by word, then by example.

Around the time that Merton made his solemn vows, he explored the possibility of transferring to another order, the Carthusians, an ancient hermetic order that gives each monk his own private living space, where he can remain for most of the day. Transfers from the Trappists to other orders of the Roman Catholic Church required the permission of the abbot of the monastery, the abbot general of the order, and the abbot of the applied-to monastery. Dom James Fox was opposed to Merton's transfer on several grounds and would not give his permission. The loss of Merton from the Trappists would receive publicity because of Merton's fame and would also have financial consequences for Gethsemani. And Dom James also believed the transfer was not in Merton's interest. He was familiar with the story of Merton's turbulent childhood and young manhood and regarded Merton as vulnerable to impulses that were harmful to his spiritual development. For this reason, he was loath to allow Merton even to leave Gethsemani on monastery business. Merton's few trips outside the monastery had been limited to hospital visits in Louisville and his naturalization as a US citizen. But Dom James recognized Merton's need for more privacy and solitude, both for his writing and his spiritual practices, and over the coming years made a series of accommodations that gave Merton time and space to be alone while remaining a monk at Gethsemani.

This began in 1948 when he permitted Merton to move into the book vault. Over the next several years, other mitigations followed. Dom James appointed Merton forester, enabling Merton to spend hours alone in the woods, which he loved. In 1952 Dom James allowed Merton to use a toolshed in the woods as a private retreat during certain hours of the day. Merton reveled in the pleasure afforded by this solitude. "My chief joy is to escape to the attic of the garden house and the little broken window that looks out of the valley," he wrote in his journal. The more Merton tasted solitude, the more he sought it. Merton continued to press Dom James for permission to transfer, and wrote to a fellow monk in Europe about joining the Camaldolese, another order with a strong hermetic component. Dom James remained adamantly opposed, but in 1955 agreed to appoint Merton as fire warden, an assignment that would require him to live in the woods in a watchtower, essentially giving him his hermitage. Instead, Merton chose to become the master of novices, a position that had become vacant. This position was second in importance to the abbot, as it entailed the training and supervision of the novice monks, and so thrust Merton back into the heart of the Gethsemani community. Perhaps the prospect of complete solitude daunted Merton. At any rate, this conundrum over solitude, and its temporary resolution, exposed the duality in Merton's character that craved both independence and engagement with others.

During this period of tension with his order and his abbot, Merton had been progressing through the church hierarchy. In 1949 he was made a deacon, and on May 26, he was ordained a priest and became Father M. Louis Merton in a ceremony attended by his editor Robert Giroux, his publisher James Laughlin, and his close friends Bob Lax and Ed Rice. In 1951 he was appointed master of scholastics, responsible for training the professed monks. In that same year he became a naturalized US citizen.

Merton's deepening engagement with the community of Gethsemani as master of novices gratified the gregarious side of his nature and marked the beginning of an outward movement that, over time, spread far beyond the walls of the monastery. This impulse in Merton towards the larger human community countered his desire for solitude and brought Gethsemani more and more into the public eye, straining both Merton and his order. But throughout his period of outreach and activism, he continued to press for permission to live as a hermit. He was putting into practice his belief in contemplation as the source of moral order in the world.

Merton enjoyed his role as master of novices, and the novices quickly grew fond of him, giving him the nickname Uncle Louis. (Speech was necessary for instruction.) Many of the novitiates who studied under Merton were familiar with his books, and some had come to Gethsemani after reading *The Seven Storey Mountain*. Merton spoke in an informal, often humorous manner and spiced his lectures with references to the outside world. He led the novitiates on walks in the woods, where he taught them to identify plants and animals. On hot summer days, he allowed them to remove their robes and swim in the monastery's ponds, a luxury that Dom James quickly forbade. Merton was unpretentious and accessible, holding private conversations with each novice once a week.

This personal contact sparked an interest in psychology and psycho-analysis that deepened his understanding of the apparent contradictions in his nature and the causes of social disease and disorder. John Endes, one of the monks who had entered the monastery in 1950, was a doctor who had been put in charge of the infirmary. He was concerned about the number of monks who suffered from nervous and digestive com-plaints—ailments that also plagued Merton. In a rare exception to his re-strictions on travel, Merton was permitted by Dom James to accompany Endes to Collegeville, Minnesota, to attend a two-week workshop on psychiatry featuring the psychoanalyst Gregory Zilboorg. Merton's plan to go into psychoanalysis was aborted after Zilboorg humiliated Merton in front of Dom James with the remark, "You want a hermitage in Times Square with a large sign over it saying, HERMIT." This dagger went to the heart of Merton's psychic dilemma but was cruelly thrust. Instead, Merton began meeting with the psychologist James Wygal in Louisville. Their sessions were more conversation than analysis. They listened to jazz records together and occasionally dropped into Louisville's jazz clubs. On one of his visits to Louisville, Merton experienced an epiphany standing on a street corner. Looking about him at the people coming and going, "I was suddenly overwhelmed with the realization that I loved all those people, that they were mine and I theirs, that we could not be alien to one another even though we were total strangers. It was like awakening from a dream of separateness . . ." Watching the people coming and going, Merton felt a powerful communion with them. They were all human beings like himself, blessed by God, if not aware of it. This experience fed his desire to project his spirituality beyond the confines of Gethsemani, to awaken the man in the street.

Through his reading and correspondence with writers and activists, Merton sought to widen his world. He was reading extensively in the secular literature of America, England, and Europe, as well as South American poetry. He was especially interested in understanding the culture of America's rival in the Cold War and immersed himself in Russian literature, music, and politics. He asked his agent Naomi Burton to send him a copy of Boris Pasternak's novel *Dr. Zhivago*, and after reading it, initiated a correspondence with the author. In October 1958 the Nobel Committee announced that Pasternak had won its literature award, but Pasternak was forced by his government to decline the honor and was expelled from the Union of Soviet Writers. Merton wrote articles about Pasternak, calling him a Christian anarchist who showed traces of Gandhi and the Russian mystics in his writing. Before his death in 1960, Pasternak wrote Merton to thank him for his support.

Merton was also corresponding with the Polish writer Czeslaw Milosz and the Zen Buddhist D. T. Suzuki. Milosz praised Merton for being a contemplative who had entered the world of action to address "the terrible questions." He urged Merton to read Albert Camus and Simone Weil. Merton's correspondence with Suzuki reflected his deepening interest in the religious traditions of the East that would culminate in his extended 1968 trip to Asia. In 1964 Merton received permission to travel to New York City to meet with Suzuki. Merton was interested in all religious traditions; he also studied Islam and the Sufi mystics. In a time of terrifying tension between East and West, Merton was seeking the core spiritual values that unite all of humanity.

In published articles and books, Merton began to speak out against war and argue for disarmament. He wrote a prose poem about the nuclear holocaust in Japan called *Original Child Bomb* that caused misunderstanding and controversy in both his order and the secular world. In *New Seeds of Contemplation* (1962), Merton addressed the psychological causes of war and prayed for peace.

> At the root of all war is fear: not so much the fear men have for one another as the fear they have of *everything*. We fail to recognize the evil in ourselves, project it onto others, then seek to destroy it by violence.
>
> The whole world is in moral confusion . . . Thus we never see the one truth that would help us begin to solve our ethical and political problems: that we are *all* more or less wrong . . .
>
> When I pray for peace, I pray God to pacify not only the Russians and the Chinese but above all my own nation and myself . . .

The passage is built on Merton's conviction that each individual contributes to the condition of war by his failure to confront his moral lapses, his propensity for violence. Merton's stand on disarmament and his advocacy of non-violence were at odds with orthodox Catholic doctrine, which sanctioned "just wars" (wars of defense) and by implication the right of nations to arm themselves for "nuclear deterrence." In an article published in May 1962 in *Jubilee,* Merton argued that the widespread destruction of civilian life caused by nuclear warfare made it unavoidably offensive and, therefore, unjustifiable. He cited a statement by a Catholic official close to the Vatican that all modern warfare is inherently unjust because of its widespread disaster and destruction. In 1963 Pope John XXIII's encyclical *Pacem in Terris* vindicated Merton's positions on war and nuclear weapons. But Merton's superiors in the Trappists forbade him to publish any writings on war on the grounds that it was inappropriate for a monk to do so because it "falsifies the message of monasticism." A book that Merton had written for publication for Macmillan titled *Peace in the Post-Christian Era* was blocked by the abbot general. To circumvent this censorship, Merton resorted to mimeographing his essays and letters on war and non-violence and circulating them through his networks. He had established friendships with several leaders of the anti-war movement, including Jim Forest from *The Catholic Worker*, W. H. Ferry from The Center for Democratic Institutions, and Daniel Berrigan, among others.

Merton's prominent role as a voice for peace and racial harmony was recognized publicly in 1963. He received the Pax Medal for his writings on war and nuclear arms. The University of Kentucky bestowed on him an honorary doctor of letters. In November, the Merton Collection opened at the Bellarmine College Library. Robert Kennedy was arranging for Merton to deliver a series of lectures at The White House, but the assassination of his brother John aborted them. Merton was uncomfortable with these accolades, fearful that he was becoming a cult figure and prey to vanity.

Throughout this period, Merton continued to press for changes in his living circumstances at Gethsemani. Despite his engagement with major world issues, he continued to chafe at the restrictions imposed by his order and to long for solitude. In May 1959 he wrote to several bishops inquiring if there might be hermitages in remote parts of their dioceses. He learned of possible openings in the British West Indies, Nevada, Cuernavaca, and Nicaragua. But his transfers continued to be opposed by Dom James and Rome.

To mitigate his refusals, Dom James permitted Merton to spend time in a plain cement block building located on a hill called Mount Olivet some distance from the monastery. The building had been constructed as a retreat center in conjunction with nearby Bellarmine College. It contained two rooms and a fireplace. Merton was allowed to spend a few hours each day at Mount Olivet, but could not sleep there. Gradually Merton's allotted time at Mount Olivet was expanded until in 1965 he was permitted to live there full time as a hermit. Merton named the hermitage St. Mary of Carmel after the patroness of his solitary vocation.

The stresses that Merton was under as monk, as master of novices, as writer and activist, were wearing down his health. He was suffering from bursitis and colitis and endured chronic back pain from a displaced disk injured during his days playing rugby in England. The skin on his hands became inflamed with a rash, and when it was discovered that he was allergic to sunlight, he had to wear thermal gloves when he went outside. His doctor told him that Gethsemani was ruining his health and suggested he leave.

In September 1963, Merton was hospitalized at St. Joseph's Infirmary in Louisville for treatment of a fused cervical disk. While he was there, four black children were killed by a bomb blast in Birmingham, Alabama. Censored by his order from speaking out publicly on war, Merton turned his attention to racism and the civil rights movement.

Merton saw in racism another sign of man's separation from God. Writing in *Conjectures of a Guilty Bystander* (1966) about his epiphany on the streets of Louisville, Merton said, "We [monks] are in the same world as everybody else, the world of the bomb, the world of race, the world of technology, the world of mass media, big business, revolution, and all the rest. We take a different attitude to all these things, for we belong to God. Yet so does everybody else belong to God . . . And if only everybody could realize this . . . If only we could see each other that way all the time, there would be no more war, no more hatred, no more cruelty, no more greed . . ." Merton approved of the non-violent protest being organized by Martin Luther King, Jr., but feared that the angrier, more confrontational stance of the Black Muslim movement would only exacerbate white hatred and resistance to reform.

At the end of 1964, Merton was allowed to spend his first complete day in his hermitage, and in September 1965 he gave up his duties as novice master and moved permanently to Mount Olivet, becoming Gethsemani's first hermit. After his retirement as abbot, Dom James also took up life as a hermit on the grounds of Gethsemani. Conditions in the small cottage, which initially lacked both plumbing and electricity, were even more spartan than in the abbey, but Merton relished his privacy and solitude. He wrote in his journal:

> I can imagine no other joy on earth than to have such a place to
> be at peace in. To live in silence, to think and write, to listen to the
> wind and to all the voices of the wood, to struggle with a new an-
> guish, which is nevertheless, blessed and secure, to live in the shadow
> of a big cedar cross, to prepare for my death and my exodus to the
> heavenly country, to love my brothers and all people, to pray for the
> whole world and offer peace and good sense among men. So it is my
> place in the scheme of things and that is sufficient.

Merton had promised Dom James that his routine in the hermit-age would closely follow that of the monks in the abbey, and he kept a diary of his daily activities that he shared with the abbot. Merton rose at 2:15 A.M.; prayed and meditated until 5:00 A.M.; took breakfast; read and studied until 7:30 A.M.; said the rosary; performed manual work and chores from 8:00 A.M. until 9:30, then went to the monastery for Mass and more liturgical offices, followed by dinner (noon meal) in the Infir-mary refectory. He returned to the hermitage for a "siesta" or light read-ing, then Vespers followed by meditation. At 2:15 P.M., he wrote for two hours and might take a walk; Vigils at 4:15; supper at 5:00, followed by Compline. At 6:00 P.M., he read in the New Testament, then meditated again. He retired for the night at 7:00 P.M.. Such was the life of a hermit at Gethsemani.

Merton continued to be plagued by poor health—skin problems, colds, flu, an injury to his eye from a tree branch. He developed dysentery from drinking polluted water from a spring behind the hermitage. His old neck injury pained him. These afflictions caused Merton to give up difficult physical labor. Instead, he wrote more. Between 1965 and 1967, Merton published six full-length books, in addition to his extensive correspondence and journal writing. He delighted in the solitude of his hermitage and the woods surrounding it. Always up well before dawn, he experienced the breaking of the day as a religious event—God bring-ing the world into being again, frogs croaking "OM," "the querulous, noisy, raw waking of the crows." He thrilled when one night lightning struck the hermitage, and wrote to Bob Lax, "I plan first to be struck by lightning from going to walk in thunderstorms," a remark that proved eerily prophetic.

In March 1966, while recovering from an operation to repair the fused disk in his neck at St. Joseph's Infirmary, Merton began a relation-ship with a young student nurse attending him that nearly caused him to break his vows and leave Gethsemani. Margie Smith was twenty-five years old, half Merton's age. She had read Merton's books and conversed with him about them and the new liturgy in the Catholic Church. In a lighter vein, they also discussed *Mad* magazine. Before leaving the hospital, Merton asked Margie for her address and told her he desired her friendship. He left a letter for her when he was discharged.

Margie wrote to him at Gethsemani, setting their relationship in motion. On his next visit to Louisville for a check-up, Merton met her away from the hospital. He was writing about her obsessively in his journal. They both recognized the perils of their attraction but continued to meet. On Derby Day, May 17, Margie came to Gethsemani along with other friends of Merton. They accompanied James Laughlin to the Louisville airport, and Laughlin saw that they were in love. He thought Merton was at grave psychological risk.

At another meeting in Louisville, Margie and Merton considered the implications of living together. For Merton, married to the Catholic Church, the move would amount to a divorce and a repudiation of his solemn vows. They continued to rendezvous. James Wygal told Merton he was risking disaster. In his journal, Merton wrote that he was contemplating marriage to Margie. He was drinking heavily in the hermitage.

Another monk reported Merton's liaison to Dom James, who then ordered Merton to end the relationship. He suggested that Merton should leave the hermitage and move back into the monastery. He saw Merton weakened by loneliness, and his fears about Merton's instability and impulsivity were being confirmed.

Merton continued to see Margie on trips to Louisville, in defiance of his abbot. His difficulty in ending the relationship caused Dom James to recommend that he return to the monastery and assume the duties of master of scripture. To avoid the loss of his solitude, Merton promised Dom James not to leave the hermitage without permission. In August, he wrote a letter to Margie telling her that he must remain a monk. Margie returned to her home in Cincinnati. Merton saw her twice more in October while at the hospital in Louisville, and in the summer of 1968 before he left on his trip to Asia, he telephoned her one final time. Merton, the monk, had suppressed the insurgency from Tom Merton, man of the world.

In the last two years of his life, Merton was freed up to pursue his deepest interests without restriction from his abbot or his order. The liberation occurred in stages and culminated in his extended trip to Asia in the fall of 1968 that ended with his accidental death.

Although Dom James continued to restrict Merton's travel during his final year as abbot, Merton's life within the grounds of Gethsemani became increasingly independent and comfortable. In the summer of 1967, the abbot general ended all censorship of Merton's books, freeing him to give full expression to his views on the Vietnam War, whose continuing escalation appalled him. His bursitis had become so painful that he had to use a tape recorder for the composition of his essays, and he underwent another operation to relieve it. In July he received permission from Dom James to say Mass at the hermitage, and he had a special altar built for that purpose. Later the hermitage was enlarged by the addition of a chapel and a bathroom. Merton was also preparing all his meals at the hermitage and thus lived almost entirely independent of the community.

The hermitage did not lack for comforts. Merton had a refrigerator and stocked his pantry with wine and beer. He had a phonograph that enabled him to listen to jazz and classical music. He frequently entertained visitors there: Sy Freedgood, Naomi Burton, Daniel Berrigan, Joan Baez, his fellow Kentuckian Wendell Berry, the poet Denise Levertov, and the photographer Ralph Eugene Meatyard. Occasionally, Merton would go into Louisville to hear live music in clubs. He was corresponding with Coretta King to arrange a retreat for her husband, a plan that came to an end when Martin Luther King, Jr. was killed in Memphis, Tennessee, on April 4, 1968. Two months later, Robert Kennedy was assassinated in Los Angeles, putting the nation through yet another trauma.

In January 1968, Merton learned from his friend Dom Jean Leclerq of a monastic ecumenical conference to take place in Bangkok in December, and in March he received an invitation from Leclerq to attend and give a talk. The new abbot at Gethsemani, Dom Flavian Burns, approved of Merton's participation and ended the travel restrictions that had kept him on a short leash. In May, Merton traveled to California to lead a conference for Trappistine nuns at Our Lady of the Redwoods in Humboldt County. He spent two weeks there, and on his way back to Gethsemani visited the Benedictine abbey Christ in the Desert in New Mexico.

Merton left Gethsemani again on September 10 to start his Asian trip. First, he went to Anchorage, Alaska, and Santa Barbara, California, where the Center for Democratic Institutions is headquartered, to give talks. He then explored the California Central Coast for possible hermitage sites but concluded that the region was too heavily developed. He departed for Asia on October 15 from San Francisco, where he had stayed with the poet and bookseller Lawrence Ferlinghetti.

Merton's mission to Asia was motivated by his belief that the West needed an infusion of spiritual energy and inspiration from the East. He had become concerned that the West, with its deepening reliance on technology and its relentless pursuit of material progress, had become spiritually barren, that lacking a religious dimension western man's life had become meaningless. He wrote in his Asian journal that it fell to the monk to revive the spiritual impulse in western man. "It is the peculiar office of the monk in the modern world to keep alive the contemplative experience and to keep the way open for modern technological man to recover the integrity of his inner depths."

Merton was especially interested in the power of Zen Buddhism to bring men into contact with Reality. He had read and corresponded with the Zen Buddhist D.T. Suzuki, and conveyed his belief in common ground between Buddhism and Christianity in his essay "A Christian Looks at Zen." Merton admired Zen for its disregard of doctrine, for its insistence on pure experience. Zen asks the question, "Who is this 'I' that exists and lives? . . . The Zen experience is a direct grasp of the *unity* of the visible and invisible . . . Zen, then, aims at a kind of certainty: but it is not the logical certainty of philosophical proof . . . It is rather the certainty that goes with an authentic metaphysical intuition . . . The purpose of all Buddhism is to refine the consciousness until this kind of insight is attained." The nonsensical koans that form the basis of much instruction in Zen are deliberately absurd, designed to destroy our linguistic preconceptions and rational explanations. They aim to puzzle and bewilder the logical mind, to move past it to "enlightenment." Enlightenment is the empty mind that, like a mirror, reflects on reality from pure consciousness.

Merton launched himself on a whirlwind tour of Asia that took him to major cities in Thailand, India, Singapore, and Ceylon. He met with important religious figures, including the Dalai Lama, Chogyam Trungpa Rimpoche, and Chatral Rimpoche, a Buddhist hermit who confessed to Merton that after thirty years of meditation he had never once achieved the state of "perfect emptiness" that he sought. Merton's most profound experience occurred in Ceylon (Sri Lanka), at Polonnaruwa, the site of gigantic statues of the Buddha. Of this visit, he wrote in his Asian journal, "Looking at these figures I was suddenly, almost forcibly, jerked clean out of the habitual, half-tied vision of things, and an inner clearness, clarity as if exploding from the rocks themselves, became evident and obvious . . . The rock, all matter, all life, is charged with dharmakaya [Reality] . . . Everything is emptiness, and everything is compassion . . . I know and have seen what I was obscurely looking for."

Merton arrived in Bangkok on December 6 and went to the Red Cross Center south of the city where the conference—Aide à l'Implementation Monastique—was being held. He was assigned a room on the ground floor of a two-story, four-bedroom cottage, sharing it with three other monks. On December 8, he delivered his talk, "Marxism and Monastic Perspectives." Hearkening back to his brief boyhood flirtation with communism, Merton declared that only in monastic life was the communist ideal "from each according to his ability, to each according to his need" realized. The talk was not well received. He was tired after his talk, having spent a sleepless night kept awake by yowling cats. He went back to his cottage to shower and nap. At about three P.M. a monk in an upstairs bedroom heard a noise and a cry from below. He went down to investigate but received no response when he knocked. An hour later he returned to retrieve from Merton the key to the cottage and discovered Merton lying on the wet stone floor in his underwear with a large floor fan lying on his chest. Burn marks ran down his side. Merton had been dead for over an hour, electrocuted by a short in the room fan as he tried to turn it on in his wet bare feet. His body was flown back to Kentucky in a US Air Force bomber and identified by John Endes. Merton was buried in the cemetery at Gethsemani.

In the story of Thomas Merton we come upon the problem of alienation in the modern technological society, and one man's response to it. Merton was an archetypal outsider, a man without family, without a country, without belief in the meaningfulness of the social and political imperatives of his time. He faced the dilemma described by various twentieth-century social philosophers such as the French existentialists, the Marxist Herbert Marcuse, the political theorist Hannah Arendt. The dilemma was the diminishment of man by his technological inventions. Arendt, in *The Human Condition*, traced this loss to the invention of the telescope, through which man discovered that the Earth was not the center of the universe, that the Sun did not orbit around it as his senses had told him for centuries. From this discovery, man fell into a state of doubt in which he could trust only what he had made himself and so separated himself from the natural world and God's manifestation there.

Marcuse, a thinker who influenced Merton, saw modern man as a prisoner of his social institutions who had lost the capability of distinguishing between society's need and his own, thus becoming "one-dimensional man." Men sought to fulfill themselves by meeting the needs that society imposed on them through various forms of propaganda, including advertising and "news," to the neglect of their own personal, interior needs as unique human beings. The mass of men live with no consciousness of their servitude to the social machine. Of this mass man, Marcuse wrote contemptuously, echoing Veblen, "The social controls exact the overwhelming need for the production and consumption of waste; the need for stupefying work where it is no longer a real necessity; the need for modes of relaxation which soothe and prolong this stupefaction . . ."

Merton sought in the Catholic Church the security and stability and permanence that had eluded him in his secular life. The monastery at Gethsemani gave him the family he had always lacked, and the opportunity to seek a meaningful interior life in contemplative union with God. His was a character marked by profound tension between the need for perfect solitude and the need for communion with others. He resolved this contradiction by becoming a hermit who shared with the world the discoveries of his interior journey through his writing.

Sergeant Brummett Echohawk (Photo courtesy of Mark Ellenbarger.)

CHAPTER 8

Brummett Echohawk

Prologue

If Thomas Merton saw in World War II a crystallization of the horrors of twentieth-century modernity, the Pawnee Indian Brummett Echohawk saw in it opportunity—the opportunity to validate the depth to which Native Americans were truly *American*: patriots, not a people set apart. Echohawk was proud of his heritage as a member of the Pawnee tribe, and especially of his family ancestry with its strong warrior tradition, but he saw his lineage as merely one thread in the larger fabric of American life and history. The war enabled him to put the warrior tradition of his Indian nation in the service of a larger national cause and to demonstrate that Indians could not only serve their country, but they could also set the standard for bravery and skill as fighters.

Echohawk not only fought with distinction; he used his war experience to make himself into an artist. After his honorable discharge from the Army, he used his art to fuse Native American culture with mainstream American culture through his paintings, cartoons, and narratives. Though many Americans might see their indigenous people as a race apart, Echohawk insisted that they be seen and accepted as having an equal claim to American patrimony as do people whose origins are in Europe, Africa, or Asia. Both through his life example and his art, he countered white stereotypes of Indians as incapable of achieving parity with their countrymen.

Brummett Echohawk – Plains Warrior

Brummett Echohawk is the name of a full-blood Pawnee Indian who fought in World War II with the famed US Army 45th Infantry Division, known as the Thunderbirds for its high percentage of Native American soldiers. The name Echohawk carries a long tradition of military service in Brummett's family. Brummett has explained its origin. "My grandfather won the name in the field of battle . . . 'The hawk does not sing' . . . Because he was a man who did not sing of his praises like the hawk did not sing, but the people echoed everything he did, so thus Echo-Hawk, a warrior whose deeds are echoed."

The name points not only to a tradition in Brummett's family but also to a proud tradition among the Pawnees of fierce and fearless warriors who have served their country. In 1866 Congress had authorized the recruitment of Indians to serve as scouts in the US Army. Native Americans had played a role in American military affairs since the days of the French and Indian War. Belligerent parties sought their assistance for their knowledge of the land and other tribes and their warrior skills—stealth, tracking, bravery. Indians also fought in the American Revolution and the Civil War. During these conflicts, the Indians had no real loyalty to their "allies." They chose sides according to their tribal interests, hoping to partner with the most acceptable victor. Sometimes an alliance with whites gave them an advantage in their conflicts with tribal enemies.

After the Civil War, the federal government viewed Army service by Indians as a path to assimilation, a way to merge Native American culture with mainstream culture. Pawnee warriors also saw advantages in the service—pay, respect from whites, and an opportunity to continue their plains traditions in combat. The scout program was the beginning of Native American military allegiance to the United States. The first member of Brummett Echohawk's family to serve was his grandfather *Te-ah-ke-kah-wah Who-re-ke-coo* (He Makes His Enemies Ashamed). In 1876 Howard Echohawk became a scout for the US Army unit sent against the alliance of Lakota Sioux, Northern Cheyenne, and Arapaho that had defeated the US 7th Cavalry Regiment at Little Big Horn and killed its commanding officer, Lt. Colonel George Armstrong Custer.

———•———

Brummett Echohawk's father, Elmer Price Echohawk, was born May 18, 1892. He attended the Pawnee Agency Boarding School, then transferred to the United States Indian School at Carlisle, Pennsylvania, where he roomed with famed Indian athlete Jim Thorpe. In September 1910, the year he left Carlisle, Elmer married Alice Jake, an orphan whom he had met at the school. They moved into a four-room house on a farm four miles from Pawnee, Oklahoma, a town incorporated in 1894. Together they had four children. Brummett was born on March 3, 1922, named for his grandmother's brother Bromet Taylor. When Brummett was two years old, his grandfather Howard died.

At age five, Brummett attended the Pawnee Agency Boarding School. The school used a militaristic approach towards the goal of transforming Native Americans into Americans. The students wore heavy, uncomfortable woolen uniforms poorly suited for the heat of the plains, and followed a strict daily regimen. Though often homesick, Brummett adapted well during his four years at the school and began to exhibit his talent for drawing there.

On January 1, 1929, Alice Echohawk died from pneumonia. Elmer also became ill and unable to care for his children. Brummett and his brothers went to live with their uncle George Echohawk, his wife Lucille, and their four children in a two-story house outside Pawnee. Brummett grew up hunting, fishing, horseback riding, and swimming in the Arkansas River with his cousins.

In the early 1930s, George moved his family to Albuquerque, New Mexico, where Brummett attended high school while his older brothers studied at the University of New Mexico. George returned to Oklahoma towards the end of the 1930s. Brummett moved back in with his father, who had survived a serious illness, continued high school, and was named the captain of the football team. In April 1939, before graduating from high school, he joined the National Guard.

While Brummett was attending school in Albuquerque and Pawnee, far away in Europe, events were unfolding that would have a profound effect on his life. In Germany, Adolph Hitler rose to power on an appeal to German nationalism and denunciations of the onerous burdens placed on Germany by the Treaty of Versailles. He led the Nazi Party to electoral victory, was appointed chancellor in 1933, and in the following year, became dictator of the Third Reich. In 1936 Italy invaded Ethiopia, Franco started a civil war in Spain, and Japan went to war with China. Hitler and Mussolini formed the Rome-Berlin Axis and set the stage for World War II. In March 1938 Germany annexed Austria; two months later she seized the Sudetenland in western Czechoslovakia, then invaded Prague and conquered all of Czechoslovakia, breaking promises Hitler had made to England's Prime Minister Neville Chamberlain. In August 1939 Hitler signed a non-aggression pact with Stalin; Germany and Russia then agreed to divide Poland. The following month Britain and France declared war on Germany. By June 1940, Germany had overrun Denmark, Norway, Belgium, and Holland. She had captured Paris and established the collaborative Vichy government in France. England stood alone against Germany, which began an air assault and prepared for an amphibious invasion. On May 11, 1940, Winston Churchill became Prime Minister.

Across the pond, President Roosevelt realized that America would be drawn into the war but faced strong isolationist sentiment from Congress and an American public reluctant to become involved in another bloody European conflict. He authorized material aid for England and took steps to rebuild America's army, which in 1939 was poorly equipped and had only 500,000 men in uniform. In September 1940, Congress passed a conscription act calling for the induction of an additional 800,000 men. That same month, Roosevelt signed papers placing the 45th Infantry Division—the National Guard unit that Brummett Echohawk had joined—on active duty. Ten days later, Japan joined the Axis by signing the Tripartite Pact with Germany and Italy, pledging unity should America enter the war.

The 45th Infantry Division had the largest number of Native Americans soldiers in the US Army. One-third of its members came from tribes in Oklahoma, New Mexico, Colorado, and Arizona. Ironically, the origins of the National Guard were the state and local militias formed to protect western settlers from hostile Indian tribes in areas beyond the reach of the US Army. The 45th grew out of a territorial militia formed in New Mexico during the Mexican-American War.

In World War I, the Oklahoma National Guard was composed of two regimental units, the 179th and 180th Infantry. They saw action in France as part of the 40th Division in 1917. Although Brummett Echohawk's father Elmer Price Echohawk had enlisted in the Army during World War I, the war ended before he was sent overseas. After the war, the 179th and 180th Regiments became part of the 45th Infantry Division, which was established in Oklahoma City in 1925. The division included two other regiments, the 157th and 158th. Each regiment numbered approximately three thousand men. Brummett was assigned to the 2nd Squad, 2nd Platoon, B Company, 1st Battalion, 179th Regiment. His platoon sergeant was Phillip Gover, a Pawnee Indian whom Brummett knew. Most members of B Company were also Pawnee.

The insignia of the 45th had been a swastika—a mystical symbol common in many Indian tribes. In April 1939, around the time that Brummett enlisted, the swastika was replaced by the image of the Thunderbird, regarded by Native Americans as a magical bird that brings rain, thunder, and lightning.

In September 1940, the Thunderbirds began their training as an integrated unit of the US Army at Fort Sill, Oklahoma, under the command of Major General William S. Key. When the division was fully equipped and organized, it moved in February 1941 to Camp Barkeley near Abilene, Texas, for more advanced field training. Brummett was promoted from Private First Class to Corporal after being made an instructor in judo and bayonet training. (He weighed 126 pounds.) In the late summer, he participated in the Louisiana Maneuvers, two months of war-games involving 470,000 troops. During the maneuvers, Echohawk's regiment distinguished itself when it fought off an entire "enemy" division for three days, an achievement that foreshadowed its heroics in Anzio. The 45th was singled out for special commendation by the General Staff, recognition that would lead to the division playing a prominent role in the invasion of Italy.

During the exercises, Corporal Echohawk came close to shooting then Lieutenant Colonel Dwight D. Eisenhower. Brummett had been assigned to guard a payroll shipment and was given orders to shoot anyone who came within the secure perimeter area where footlockers full of money were stored. During the night, Eisenhower inadvertently entered the area, then fled when he saw Brummett's rifle aimed at him. The two men later met by chance in an elevator in Washington, D.C., and joked about the incident.

On December 7, 1941, Japan launched a surprise attack against the US Navy's Pacific fleet at Pearl Harbor, Hawaii, and the United States entered the war. In January 1942 German U-boats began to attack American ships in the Atlantic off Cape Cod. America was at war in two major theaters requiring enormous manpower and productive capacity to sustain.

Following America's entry into the war, the 45th Infantry Division underwent a rigorous training program to prepare it for the most dangerous form of combat, amphibious landings. Brummett was shuffled among various camps around the United States, chosen to simulate the different conditions of terrain and weather that the 45th would encounter on the field of battle. Eisenhower had assigned the 45th to join General George Patton's 7th United States Army in North Africa, the staging ground for the Allies invasion of Italy. During these preparations, Brummett's father Elmer Price Echohawk died, and Brummett was given a five-day furlough to attend his father's funeral in Oklahoma.

On May 25, 1943, the Thunderbirds moved to Camp Patrick Henry near Norfolk, Virginia. From there they were loaded onto ships at Hampton Roads. On June 4, they sailed for North Africa with a convoy of twenty-five ships protected by destroyers. Brummett Echohawk and the other men of the 1st Battalion, 179th Regiment, were on board the flagship *USS Leonard Wood*.

On June 22, the convoy arrived at Mers El Kibir, a harbor seven miles from Oran, Algeria, and dropped anchor. The Allies were preparing to launch Operation Husky, the largest amphibious operation in US military history. Under the command of General Eisenhower, it involved nine Allied divisions—115,000 British troops, 66,000 American soldiers, 3,200 ships, and 4,000 aircraft. Its objective was Sicily, the first stage of an invasion of Italy designed to draw German forces away from both the eastern front and northern Europe, where plans for Operation Overlord, the invasion of Normandy, were underway. Sicily was defended by 50,000 German troops and 315,000 Italian soldiers. During the month-long battle Hitler sent an additional 40,000 German troops to Sicily.

On July 5, the Thunderbirds sailed from Mers El Kabir. Once at sea, the secret orders were opened, and the men learned that their destination was the southwestern coast of Sicily. Maps were distributed, and the troops were given information about the terrain and the enemy defenses. As they plowed towards the landing area, they were joined by ships carrying the 1st Infantry Division from Algiers and the 3rd Infantry Division from Bizerte. General Montgomery's 8th Army was headed for the southeast coast, its objective to capture Syracuse.

Minutes before midnight on July 9, the invasion armada dropped anchor in the Gulf of Gela off the coast of Sicily on a moonless night. Brummett and the rest of the troops watched from the decks of their ships as the aerial and naval bombardment of the beachhead lit up the darkness. Landing craft were lowered into the water, and at 0345 on July 10 the first assault wave went ashore. Echohawk's unit was one of the first to reach land. Their objective was to sweep south and capture the town of Scoglitti, from where they could protect the right flank of the 3rd Battalion, whose objective was the town of Vittoria, near the Comiso airfield. The airfield was the prize. Capturing it would weaken the German Luftwaffe and give Allied planes a foothold on the island. Brummett, now Sergeant Echohawk, later sketched on paper he had found in a captured building the appearance of the men in his battalion as they came ashore carrying fifty pounds of equipment.

Inventory of a Thunderbird warrior's armament as he waded through the surf to the beach:

> M1 Rifle mounted with bayonet
> 24 blocks of TNT tied to chest
> 25 feet of explosive primer cord
> Web cartridge belt holding 80 rounds
> Two bandoleers each holding 48 rounds
> Two hand grenades, one in each trouser pocket
> Steel helmet covered in mosquito net
> Gas mask
> Wire cutters
> Entrenching shovel
> Life preserver
> Two canteens
> First aid packet
> Combat pack holding personal items

This equipment was attached to a woolen uniform worn with canvas leggings above GI shoes with leather soles and rubber heels.

On the first day of the invasion, Echohawk's battalion, encountering only mild resistance, took Scoglitti and captured twenty-five enemy soldiers. The 3rd Battalion seized Vittoria, the town closest to the Comiso airfield. Brummett later wrote these words about his first day of combat: "Even though I was very scared, which made me human, I lived up to those words; men of men, a warrior whose deeds are echoed."

On the morning of July 11, Brummett's regiment began its attack on the Comiso airfield, which was strongly defended by German troops. Colonel Robert Hutchins, Commanding Officer of the 179th, moved Echohawk's battalion northeast from Scoglitti to the regiment's left flank while the 2nd and 3rd Battalions advanced on the airport in two columns, backed up by a battalion of the 157th. After a brief but fierce fight, the 179th captured the airport at 1610. Echohawk killed his first enemy soldier during the battle for Comiso.

The Thunderbirds moved north towards the city of Palermo on Sicily's northwest coast, behind the retreating Germans. Italian troops had offered little resistance, and by July 12 were no longer a serious combat threat, although they did continue sniping attacks on US forces. The Germans, heavily outnumbered by the combined Allied armies, and lacking support from their Axis partner, had little choice but to fight delaying actions as they withdrew towards Messina at the northern tip of the island, just across from the toe of Italy. After they captured the key town of Nicosia, General Patton relieved the Thunderbirds with the 3rd US Infantry Division. He assured the men he was not dissatisfied with their performance. "I hope you know how good you are," he said, "for everyone else does. You are magnificent." The 45th moved away from the combat arena to a bivouac area five miles to the west of Cefalu on the Tyrrhenian Sea for three weeks of rest after twenty-two days of continuous combat. The Thunderbirds had lost 275 men killed, 573 wounded, and 141 missing in action. They had taken 11,266 prisoners and killed or wounded uncounted hundreds of enemy soldiers.

A key element of the 45th's success was its use of night patrols to locate enemy positions, assess their strength, and bring back intelligence to the command post staff for use in planning. Brummett Echohawk and other Native Americans in Company B were often assigned to these patrols. It was dangerous work requiring stealth and daring, qualities that Indians took pride in possessing. Brummett, eager to prove himself a Pawnee warrior worthy of the name Echohawk, undertook both official and unofficial night patrols, often with results that provided comic relief from the grim horror of war.

Echohawk's "ad hoc" patrols avoided the enemy by following game trails visible only by the light of the night sky. On one outing, his men reached the north coast of Sicily in advance of other Thunderbird units. They found a hand-car powered by two bicycles at a rail yard. Echohawk left part of his patrol at the yard and headed for the nearest town on the hand-car with several other Indian soldiers. The town was occupied by a large force of German and Italian soldiers. Echohawk boldly led his men into the town, where a German officer spotted the Thunderbird insignia on their uniforms as he drove by. Before the vehicle could turn around, Echohawk and his men slipped into a movie theater that was showing the World War I film *Sergeant York*, starring Gary Cooper speaking dubbed Italian. Echohawk told the attendant that the Americans had captured the town, then the patrollers sat down to watch the movie. After a while, they ventured out and made their way to the empty town square, where they lowered the Nazi flag and replaced it with a wine bottle carrying the note, "This town captured by Pawnee Indians." They were fired upon as they pedaled back to the rest of their platoon but escaped unharmed. They had penetrated sixteen miles behind enemy lines and brought back a good story to their company commander.

On another occasion, Echohawk led a patrol in the vicinity of San Mauro Castelverde to locate German panzer positions. The patrol entered the town under darkness and hid in a church close to German headquarters. After gathering intelligence about the German presence in the town, they walked into a house occupied by German soldiers sleeping after a meal of bread and wine. The Indians appropriated the leftovers and deposited a live grenade as a calling card in the pack of one of the dozing German soldiers.

At their bivouac on the beach at Bagheria, near Cefalu, the Thunderbirds rested, relaxed, ate cooked food instead of K-rations, and bathed in the sea. They were entertained by Bob Hope, Francis Langford, and Jack Pepper. Before they received their new orders, General Patton addressed them, delivering more praise mixed with a warning. "Your division is one of the best if not the best division in the history of American arms. I love every bone in your heads, but be ever alert. Do not go to sleep at the switch, or someone's liable to slip up behind you and hit you on the head with a sock full of shit, and that's a hell of an embarrassing way to die."

On August 17, Messina, the last German stronghold, fell. Sixty-thousand German troops and 62,000 Italian soldiers fled across the Strait of Messina to the Italian mainland to join the defense being built against the expected Allied invasion. The campaign for Sicily was over. The Thunderbirds were detached from Patton's 7th Army and assigned to the

5th Army under Lt. General Mark W. Clark to participate in Operation Avalanche, the invasion of Italy.

————•————

At the beginning of September 1943, the Allies launched Operation Avalanche. The strategic purpose of this invasion had been determined at a meeting of Churchill and Roosevelt held on August 9 in Quebec. The aim of the invasion was to distract Germany by an assault on its southern flank that would relieve pressure on the Russian front and dilute German defenses against the planned invasion of Normandy.

On September 3, Italy surrendered unconditionally to the Allies, and Hitler was forced to pour more of his divisions onto the Italian peninsula to stem the Allies' advance. Ultimately the Allied invasion would achieve its objectives of liberating Italy and thinning Germany's defenses, but only at a terrible cost in casualties. Skillfully placed German entrenchments in Italy's mountainous terrain that favored defense, exceptionally severe weather, and tactical mistakes by Allied commanders in the field took a heavy toll on British and American soldiers.

On September 9, the armada carrying General Clark's 5th Army arrived at the Gulf of Salerno. In the early morning hours, the US 36th Infantry Division went ashore at Paestum and was met by withering fire from artillery, mortars, and machine guns while parachute flares lit up the beach. The Germans had known the Allies were coming. As dawn broke, the Luftwaffe strafed the troops on the beach and the landing barges.

The next day, around noon, Echohawk's regiment, which had been waiting in reserve at sea, came ashore with orders to capture a strategic bridge on the Sele River, then advance north to Eboli, about seventeen miles inland. Facing them were two German panzer divisions.

As Brummett Echohawk's 1st Battalion advanced towards Eboli, they were surrounded by German tanks from the 16th Panzer Division. Here Brummett suffered his first injury of the war and experienced the trauma of seeing friends and comrades-in-arms brutally slain in battle. The men of Company B and Company C became caught in the Persano Trap. The concussion from an exploding shell ruptured Brummett's eardrums. As Company B fixed bayonets and ran forward in an attempt to take the town of Persano, they passed the remains of Company C, which had been surprised by nine German tanks carrying one hundred German soldiers. The men of Company C, including Indian friends of Echo-hawk, had been destroyed by German fire while they rested on the road with their packs off. Echohawk marched past their burned and mangled bodies on his way to Persano.

Later during the three-day battle that raged for possession of Persano, Echohawk's squad was assigned to hold a position on a trail near the Sele River. Eight German MIV tanks approached, heading for the beach. Echohawk and three other soldiers lay in a dry ravine below them. Echo-hawk stood up and shot the commander of the lead tank as he stood in the turret. Using only rifle fire and anti-tank grenades that Echohawk had recovered from dead American soldiers, the squad stopped the advance of the tanks. For his actions in this engagement, the commander of Company B, Colonel Glen Lyon, recommended that Brummett Echohawk be awarded the Congressional Medal of Honor.

Based on such episodes in Italy, Echohawk built a reputation among his officers and fellow enlisted men for being a soldier who disregarded danger and risks in battle, who walked where others feared to tread. After the war, Echohawk traced his bravery to a meeting he and other Pawnees had held with a tribal elder before they left Oklahoma. The elder told them that only one of them would die in the war. During the landing at Salerno, a Pawnee Indian was killed. Brummett believed he had passed the test of death. The elder's prediction was based on an old Pawnee legend designed to instill courage in its warriors. The legend held that in any battle involving Pawnees, only one man would die.

Before the struggle for the Salerno beach was over, the Germans launched a counter-attack employing two hundred tanks accompanied by infantry. Heavy naval bombardment and unyielding defense from the Thunderbirds repelled them. The Germans, as they had done in Sicily, withdrew to regroup at another line of defense. The Allied advance inched up the leg of Italy, encountering stiff German resistance at every stage.

After a month of continuous fighting, the Thunderbirds approached the town of Faicchio, located in the heights above the Volturno River. During the fierce three-day battle that ensued, Echohawk suffered another concussion injury that further damaged his hearing and caused other internal injuries. Echohawk's squad was leading Company B through dense woods spaced by vineyards. They came under machine gun and mortar fire. As Echohawk was crossing a vineyard, his bayonet caught in a strand of wire supporting the vines and pulled him up short. A mortar shell landed in front of him, embedded in the mud and exploded, knocking him backward. Believing he had been hit and not wanting to draw fire to his rescuers, he ran for cover behind a low wall. He lay in the mud with his ears ringing and his stomach churning. The medic who examined him found no visible wounds, so Echohawk rejoined his men in their attack on Faicchio. Had his bayonet not snagged the wire, Echohawk would probably have been killed by a direct hit from the mortar shell.

Concussions from exploding shells are violent events that frequently occur on the battlefield, causing unseen injuries that can have serious consequences. Following his second concussion hit, Echohawk began draining fluids and lost most of his hearing. His safety was in jeopardy because he could not detect incoming artillery or small arms fire. He compensated by watching his comrades' reactions and copying them.

The battle for Faicchio turned the town into a no man's land, with Germans on the north and Allies on the south. On October 18, the 159th Regiment relieved the 179th on the front lines, and three days later the entire division was replaced by the 34th Infantry Division and given nine days rest. The Thunderbirds had been in continuous combat for forty-three days. During that period, Echohawk's regiment had absorbed double the casualties of the Sicilian campaign: 133 killed, 619 wounded, and 157 missing in action. The weather and terrain had also thinned their ranks. The constant exposure had caused a high number of malaria and physical exhaustion cases. Evacuated sick totaled 978 officers and enlisted men. Battle-tested veterans were replaced by inexperienced soldiers fresh from basic training. Additionally, their commanding officer Colonel Robert Hutchins was forced by illness to relinquish his command to Colonel Malcolm R. Kammerer. During its month-long slog up the Italian peninsula, the Thunderbirds had advanced two hundred miles and had liberated 274 towns and villages.

Early in November, the 45th was on the move again, joining the rest of the US 5th Army's advance towards the Germans' Winter Line, a string of heavily fortified positions stretching through the mountains above the Garigliano River and the town of Venafro. Field Marshal Albert Kesselring, the commander of Germany's forces in southern Italy, had withdrawn his troops behind this line to stop the advance of the Allies. Here, in terrain so steep that the troops had to be resupplied with rations and ammunition brought in by pack mules, Echohawk suffered injuries that removed him from action for the remainder of Operation Avalanche.

A German shell exploded in the tree under which he was standing, knocking him unconscious and sending shrapnel into the other members of his squad. When he awoke, he was coughing blood and discovered that his platoon had retreated, leaving him for dead. Bleeding from his wounds, Echohawk made his way down the mountain after coming across a medic who injected him with morphine. He reached a battlefield aid station, where he passed out again. He woke up in a field hospital removed from the combat area and was then transferred to an evacuation hospital where doctors removed the shrapnel from his flesh and bandaged his wounds. He bunked next to two wounded German soldiers, who observed as one morning an officer entered the hospital tent and awarded Echohawk a Purple Heart Medal. He was then transferred to a hospital in Naples, and from there to the 33rd General Hospital near Bizerte, Tunisia.

The Allied 5th Army stalled at the Winter Line. On November 15th, General Clark, with the concurrence of General Sir Harold Alexander, Eisenhower's deputy commander in the Mediterranean theater, stopped the offensive to rest his men. Early in January 1944 the division was pulled out of Venafro and sent to Naples to join preparations for Operation Shingle, the Allied invasion at Anzio whose objective was the capture of Rome. The stalemate at the Winter Line continued until May.

———•◆•———

Early in January, while the Thunderbirds were resting from one hundred and ten days in combat, and being entertained by Joe E. Brown and Humphrey Bogart at an open-air theater in Faicchio, Brummett Echohawk, still recovering from his wounds at the hospital near Bizerte, was trying to get back into action. Learning of a training program for fighter pilots, Brummett applied. But though his application was supported by three letters of recommendation from officers in his regiment, he was turned down. Hearing stories of his depleted unit in the hills of Venafro, he decided to rejoin his comrades. When the hospital staff refused to discharge him because his wounds had not entirely healed, he went AWOL, sneaking out of the hospital at night and hitching a ride from an Arab who took him to the coast. He hid at the edge of the Bizerte airfield until he saw a transport plane ready for takeoff. He stowed aboard the plane, and when it landed, he found himself back in Sicily. After hiding behind some barrels on the airstrip, he stowed away on another flight that deposited him in Naples, where MPs were waiting for him. Disbelieving Echohawk's explanation of his intentions, the MPs called him a deserter and began to rough him up. He fought back using his judo skills and escaped into the streets. He encountered Bill Mauldin, the cartoonist of the 45th Infantry Division, who agreed to hide him in his apartment. There, Brummett showed his battlefield sketches to Mauldin, who bestowed his approval.

Having learned that the Thunderbirds were about to ship out for another amphibious assault, Echohawk made his way to the Naples harbor. There he was arrested again and thrown into a stockade after brawling with the MPs, who had infuriated him by slandering Indians. Fortunately, an officer from the 45th happened by, recognized Echowhawk, secured his release, and arranged for him to be transported back to his regiment, which was preparing to sail for Anzio.

The invasion at Anzio was designed to make an end-run around the German forces protecting Rome with its defenses along the Winter Line. The Allies were employing a two-pronged assault, one by land, the other by sea, in an attempt to split the enemy's forces. But the commander of the assault on Anzio, Major General John Lucas, had serious misgivings about the likelihood of success. He worried that he did not have enough troop strength to push the enemy back.

The invasion of Anzio took place in waves spread over a week because the Allies did not have enough ships to move the entire VI Corps from Naples to Anzio, a distance of one hundred miles, all at once. The first wave, carrying the 3rd US Infantry Division and the 1st British Division, arrived at Anzio on January 24th and landed without resistance. They moved three miles inland, then stopped their advance. Lucas's caution got the better of him. Unsure of the enemy's strength, wanting to have the entire VI Corps at his disposal, Lucas failed to advance his troops towards the strategic towns that opened the route to Rome. Instead, he secured the beachhead and waited. News of his hesitation infuriated Churchill, who was overseeing Operation Shingle from his bunker in London.

Echohawk's regiment, the 179th, boarded ships on January 23rd and arrived at Anzio in the early morning hours of the 25th. The 157th Regiment arrived on the 29th, followed by the 180th on the 30th. In the week that intervened between the arrival of the first and last units of VI Corps, Field Marshal Kesselring had brought in 71,500 German troops and two panzer units to form an impregnable ring around Anzio. Operation Shingle had caused Hitler to divert eight divisions to Italy. But the Allied forces were pinned down on the beach, their backs to the sea.

Echohawk's regiment came ashore in the early hours of the 25th and assembled near the town of Nettuno, south of Anzio. They were ordered to relieve the 504th Parachute Infantry Regiment at a defensive position south of the Mussolini Canal near Campo Morto, the "Field of Death." Activity there was limited to patrols. On February 1st, they joined the rest of the Thunderbirds in the center of the beachhead. Conditions on the beachhead were uncomfortable and dangerous. The terrain was flat and swampy, with little vegetation or land features to provide cover. The men dug foxholes, but the high water table flooded them. Blankets and a simple tent were their only protection against the freezing temperatures. Rain fell steadily. By day, the Germans shelled them from the higher ground above the Padiglione Woods. At night, they absorbed bombardment from the Luftwaffe. Men who sought to escape the misery of their foxholes were killed by enemy fire. The Germans, seeing the vulnerability of the VI Corps, were preparing a counter-attack to drive the Allies into the sea. They massed their forces behind Carroceto and Aprilia, a town referred to as "The Factory" because of its bleak Fascist architecture.

The Germans and the Allies had been contesting the towns of Carroceto and Aprilia, which guarded the road to Rome. British forces had captured Aprilia, but on February 8th, the Germans forced the Brits to withdraw and retook it. At a meeting on February 10th between Lucas, Major General William Eagles, Commander of the Thunderbirds, and Major General W. Penney, the British commander, it was agreed to send Echohawk's 1st Battalion in relief of the British 1st Division, with orders to attack Carroceto and Aprilia. They would be assisted by two companies of the 191st Tank Battalion. Lucas and Eagles were sending a battalion to do the work of a division, an almost suicidal assignment.

The attack began at dawn on February 11, preceded by Allied aerial bombardment. The Germans had intercepted a radio message and knew they were coming. Tanks waited for them behind Carroceto. Colonel Wayne Johnson led the 1st Battalion's assault at 0630, without the support of the American tank battalion, which had been delayed. Companies A and B were driven back from Aprilia by German tanks and infantry, after reaching some buildings at the edge of town. The battalion had suffered heavy losses and was reduced to fewer than two hundred men. Four Indians remained, among them Brummett Echohawk.

At 0353, on February 12, the 1st Battalion attacked again. Echohawk led a bayonet charge ahead of thirteen men across an open seventy-five yard plain. Wounded in the right hand and left leg from shrapnel, he was taken to an evacuation hospital on the beach. He returned to his company after the attempt to take Aprilia from the Germans had been abandoned. For his actions in the battle for Aprilia Echohawk was later awarded the Bronze Star.

On February 16, German forces mounted a massive offensive designed to push the Allies off the beach. Their path lay through the defensive position held by Echohawk's regiment. During the intensive artillery barrage that preceded the German advance, Echohawk was knocked unconscious by a concussion blast. The wounds he had received at Faicchio opened and began to bleed again. He was evacuated to the 17th General Hospital near Naples.

There he met the movie star Madeleine Carrol, who was volunteering for the Red Cross. After he showed her his battlefield sketches, she obtained drawing paper for him. Her interest brought Brummett's war artworks to the attention of the American press, which published them accompanied by an article written by New York Senator James Mead. Mead praised Echohawk for depicting "soldiers as they really are, seen by a man who sketched them as he fought with them . . . They aren't pretty pictures," Mead wrote, "but they portray the fighting GI as he wants to be portrayed."

In March 1944, the 17th General Hospital was bombed during an air raid. Many of the wounded soldiers being treated there were killed, but Echohawk survived by donning his steel helmet and taking cover under his bed. He was furloughed home to Pawnee. After his wounds had healed, he was assigned to an Army Ordnance Depot in Detroit, Michigan. At the end of the war, the Army discharged him honorably on August 15, 1945, at Camp Chaffee, Arkansas.

The stalemate at Anzio continued until May 1944 when Allied forces broke through the defensive ring protecting Carroceto and Aprilia and opened the road to Rome. On June 4, the first patrol entered the city, and Thunderbird units arrived in the afternoon. Two days later Operation Overlord was launched, and the Allies landed in Normandy. The 45th Infantry Division was detached from the VI Corps on June 16. It was transferred back to the Salerno beaches where it underwent training for a landing in Southern France. The men of the 45th landed on the Riviera coast between St. Tropez and Cannes as part of the US 7th Army under Lieutenant General Alexander Patch. The 45th pursued the retreating German army through France and into Germany. It reached Dachau on April 29, 1945 where it discovered railroad cars stuffed with thousands of rotting corpses. Horrified GI's summarily executed the German soldiers guarding the camp in what became known as the Dachau Massacre.

———•———

At the outbreak of World War II, the Indian population of the United States was approximately 350,000 spread over two hundred tribes speaking over fifty-five languages. Most Indians lived in reservations west of the Mississippi River. Twenty-five thousand Indians served in the military: 21,767 in the Army, 1,910 in the navy, 874 in the Marines, 121 in the Coast Guard. Additionally, several hundred Indian women served as nurses in the Women's Army Corps and the Navy's WAVES. A total of five hundred Indians were killed in the war, and another seven hundred were wounded. The 45th Infantry Division had the largest number of Indians of any military unit. It produced eight Congressional Medal of Honor winners, two of whom were Indians.

One important effect of World War II on Native American culture was to bring Indians into the mainstream of American life. The war took Indians from their reservations either to serve in the military or to work in the industries that supported and supplied the war effort. As a result, Indians received pay equivalent to whites, acquired literacy and job skills not available to them on their reservations, and became familiar with the customs and habits of city dwellers. The greatest dissolution of cultural differences between Indians and whites occurred in the infantry, where men facing the prospect of imminent death bonded in their common humanity and their dependence on each other for survival.

But many Native Americans struggled to reconcile their tribal heritage with the mainstream white culture that surrounded them. The majority of Indian veterans and war workers returned to their reservations after the war ended. Some quickly became dissatisfied with reservation life and went to the cities in search of employment, only to return if they could not find it. The unemployment rate for urban-dwelling Indians was fifteen percent, three times the rate for whites. The challenge facing Native American men after the war was how to sustain their tribal identity while functioning autonomously in the wider American culture. This was the challenge that Brummett Echohawk took up after the United States Army discharged him honorably from his service as a soldier.

While serving in the Italian campaign, Echohawk had consciously and deliberately used the war to affirm his identity as a Pawnee Indian. He fought with an awareness of the meaning of his name and strove to honor it. On the battlefield, he engaged in ritual practices of the plains warrior, such as scalping and counting coup on the enemy, as his ancestors had done in their battles. He courted the image of the Indian as a fearless fighter, always ready for battle, always ready to accept the most dangerous assignments. In his civilian life, Echohawk would continue to fuse his Pawnee heritage with his vision of himself as an American.

Following his discharge from the US Army, Echohawk embarked on a career as an artist that encompassed the visual arts, writing, acting, and public speaking. The central theme of his life's work was his pride in his Pawnee heritage and his belief that this heritage formed a vital part of the story of America. He became both a voice and an exemplar of his tribe, and an educator of non-Indian Americans.

His career as a visual artist had begun on the battlefields of Sicily and Italy. His realistic depictions of soldiers and battle scenes, though suppressed by the Army, impressed his comrades who recognized their truthfulness and encouraged Brummett to pursue his talent. While in Detroit, he began his formal training as an artist at the Detroit School of Arts and Crafts. Although, as an Indian, he was unable to benefit from the GI Bill (Indian lands could not be used as collateral for loans because they were held in trust by the federal government), he obtained a scholarship to study art at Dartmouth College through a Native American program. He left there after a short stay and enrolled at the Art Institute of Chicago, where he studied from the fall of 1945 to the summer of 1948. His first commercial sales were cartoons bought by Planters Peanuts for $1,000. He found employment as a staff artist for Chicago newspapers—the *Sun-Times*, the *Daily Times*, and the *Herald American*. He also worked as an announcer for WBKB in Chicago, opening another channel through which to communicate with the broad American public.

He then moved briefly to New York, where he worked in television, painted, and did commercial art. In 1950, while taking a sketching class at the Philbrook Art Center in Tulsa, he met Mary Frances McInnes. They married in 1952 and settled in Tulsa. Brummett supported them by working as an artist for a Tulsa oil company.

Over the next forty years, his career widened and deepened. He worked in a variety of genres, some commercial, some fine art. He drew cartoons and illustrations for magazines and books, painted extensively researched historical subjects in oil, exhibited, lectured, and gave workshops for other artists.

In 1954 he created a comic strip called "Lil' Chief" that was published in the local newspaper *Tulsa World*. The strip presented amusing scenes of Indians in the Old West, as witnessed through the innocent eyes of an Indian child. In one, Indian warriors are shown performing a ritual dance on the plains during a bright sunny day. The Lil' Chief wears a baffled expression as he notices that the medicine man casts no shadow. Brummett turned down a lucrative offer to syndicate the strip because the syndicators insisted on stereotypical caricatures of Indians that reflected whites' distorted and condescending views of Native Americans.

One of Brummett's major projects was to create a series of life paintings of the battle for Little Big Horn. Unable to obtain funding for the project, he instead did a series of charcoal paintings of an aged Sioux chief, Iron Hail, who, as a boy had witnessed the battle. He also did a painting of the fallen Custer titled "Hunter's Moon." Using ink wash, Brummett rendered another important event in Indian history with "Trail of Tears," the forced migration of thousands of Cherokees from their traditional lands in Georgia and South Carolina to a barren reservation in Indian Territory west of the Mississippi.

Brummett's reputation as an artist grew through exhibitions of his work in the Midwest and far west. His critics viewed him as an Indian artist who eschewed the mystical symbols and imagery found in most traditional Indian painting in favor of a realistic depiction of Indians and their culture executed in a classical fine art style. He showed his work at museums in Oklahoma, Missouri, Texas, and San Francisco. He also accepted commissioned work that reflected his strong sense of patriotism for the United States. Thomas Hart Benton, an artist he greatly admired, hired him to work on the mural Benton would paint for the Truman Memorial Library in Independence, Missouri. Echohawk clashed with Benton for creating in the mural a white man's version of Indians. One of Echohawk's paintings was hung in the US Department of State. Another, his portrait of Oklahoma Senator James Jones, was placed in the House of Representatives, where Jones had served as Chairman of the Budget Committee.

Echohawk drew on his military experience for his art. He was commissioned by the US Navy to create a mural of the battle for Anzio in which he had fought. The mural consists of a montage of scenes that culminate with the arrival of American forces in Rome. The mural was placed in the wardroom of the *USS Anzio*, a guided-missile cruiser that was commissioned in 1992. He painted portraits of Jack C. Montgomery and Ernest Childers, Congressional Medal of Honor winners from the 45th Infantry Division, that now hang in the division's museum in Oklahoma City. A painting that Brummett did of his fellow Sergeant from Company B, Phillip Gover, also hangs in the museum. Gover is shown in Indian regalia, naked from the waist up except for a medal and a bear claw necklace, the stump of the left arm amputated in Italy visible in the head-on view.

Brummett Echohawk also expressed himself as a writer and actor. He attended an English program at the University of Chicago while studying at the Art Institute. He later enrolled in a creative writing program at the University of Tulsa. His writing followed the pattern of his art. He wrote humorous stories, historical accounts, essays explaining his art, and an article satirizing the portrayal of Indians in Hollywood films, among many others. In one of his stories, "Con Man with Feathers," published in *Oklahoma Today*, a Pawnee Indian turns the tables on white hecklers in a bar by out-drinking them, then relieving them of their money with fake but convincing medicine man shows.

Having worked as an announcer for television stations in Chicago and New York, Brummett was comfortable performing in public. He acted in plays at Tulsa's Little Theater. His most significant role was as Sitting Bull in a production of Arthur Kopit's *Indians*. The play was also performed in Virginia, England, and Germany. The German performance attracted wide attention after details of his war record became known, and a German soldier Brummett had wounded in the ear, then sketched, came forward with his story. He also performed in the TV miniseries "Oklahoma Passage" produced by the Oklahoma Educational Television Authority. The show told the story of a fictional Cherokee family through six generations, from relocation in the 1830s to a modern space flight. Though Brummett was never called to Hollywood to work as an actor, he did serve as a consultant to MGM after he had helped form the American Indian Talent Guild of Tulsa and Hollywood, which pressed for more accurate depictions of Native Americans.

In his personal life after the war, Brummett suffered both hardship and loss. In 1984 his wife Mary was diagnosed with cancer. She died on January 8, 1986. Brummett then faced legal action over large medical bills he could not afford to pay. The hospital finally accepted a large painting in partial settlement of the debt. Brummett also struggled with Post Traumatic Stress Disorder. He experienced recurrent memories of horrifying combat situations that left him depressed, anxious, and angry. Fortunately, through his art, he was able to maintain healthy contact with reality and with other human beings. He died on February 13, 2006, three weeks short of his eighty-fourth birthday. He was buried in the Highland Cemetery at the edge of Pawnee, Oklahoma. He is still remembered by those who knew him as a unique and remarkable man who believed deeply in the value of his Pawnee heritage and its importance to American history. His own life was a testament to that belief. In the talk he gave to the Westerners of Chicago, Echohawk summed up "The Pawnee Story":

> It is a story of a once-great tribe that numbered close to 10,000 in the early 1800s and in 1900 numbered at 650. It is a story of an Indian tribe that chose not to fight "civilization" but to fight for it. It is a story of people who love their country.

Judy Baca (Photo courtesy of Judy Baca.)

CHAPTER 9

Judith Baca

Prologue

Judy Baca is a Chicana muralist who uses public art as an instrument of social change and historical correction. Her murals pay tribute to activists and workers, commemorate important events in American history, and remind us of the persistence of racial discrimination and social injustice that keep America's promise unfulfilled. Baca's background as the child of struggling Mexican immigrants, and her acknowledged status as a lesbian, have stirred her empathy for men and women living outside the mainstream of American society and fueled her artistry. Her talents as a visual artist and her skills as a community organizer have given her a prominent position in Los Angeles' cultural community and gained her international recognition. In her role as an educator, she is transmitting to a new generation of artists the power to awaken the conscience of society and to celebrate the achievements of America's diverse ethnic groups through public imagery.

Her work throughout a forty-year career has placed her in a long tradition of feminist commentators and reformers who have reminded us of our stated democratic ideals and of our failures to live up to them. The tradition has roots in early colonists such as Anne Hutchinson and Abigail Adams, who questioned the legitimacy of male dominance of public affairs, and was carried forward by numerous women who sought to reform deficiencies in the application of the country's founding principles. Harriet Tubman, a liberated slave, established the Underground Railroad that transported runaways through the South; Elizabeth Cady Stanton, Susan B. Anthony, and Alice Paul led the suffragette movement that culminated in the Nineteenth Amendment giving women the right to vote; Mary Harris Jones (Mother Jones) fought against unfair labor practices, became a socialist, and helped found The Industrial Workers of the World. Others, like Margaret Sanger, insisted on a woman's right to control the reproductive functions of her own body through birth control, a right that the US Supreme Court affirmed in its *Roe vs. Wade* decision.

Throughout American history, women have been at the forefront of efforts to extend the promise of individual rights to everyone, regardless of their sex, color, ethnic origin, or political persuasion. During the 1960s, when Baca's social consciousness was formed, these feminist streams gathered force in the women's liberation movement, announced by Betty Friedan with her book *The Feminine Mystique*, and fused with other movements demanding justice and equality—the civil rights movement, the anti-war movement—in a decade of upheaval, trauma, and rapid change. Baca's murals were inspired by these movements and gave expression to them and their origins. Her work continues today.

Judith Baca – Chicana Muralist

Along the concrete retaining wall of a flood control channel in Los Angeles' San Fernando Valley known as the Tujunga Wash stretches the world's longest mural, 2,754 feet of vivid and compelling imagery. *The Great Wall of Los Angeles* is the brainchild of Chicana artist Judy Baca, who oversaw its creation during five summers of painting between 1976 and 1984. The mural was painted by over four hundred youths whom Baca had recruited from the city's juvenile justice system and the barrios of East Los Angeles. It depicts the history of California, from pre-historic times down to the end of the 1950s, as experienced by the state's indigenous and ethnic populations—Indians, Mexicans, Blacks, Chinese, Jews—who settled the land and slowly built a civilization with their labor and their dreams. The mural is a work in progress. Another half-mile of imagery awaits completion of funding and design to bring the story of California to the end of the twentieth century.

Baca became a muralist by chance. While teaching art at an ethnically diverse Catholic high school in Mission Hills, California, Baca decided to encourage cooperation among her frequently feuding students by having them collaborate on the design and painting of a mural. Fired from her job in 1970 for participating in the Chicano Moratorium's protests against the Vietnam War, she was hired by the City of Los Angeles to teach art to seniors and elementary school children at parks in East Los Angeles, home to the city's large Mexican population. During downtime between her classes, she hung around the parks and became familiar with the youth gangs who laid turf claims to different parks and protected them from "trespassing" by rival gangs. She also took notice of their fondness for decorating their bodies with tattoos and painting graffiti on the walls of park buildings. She decided to bring members of rival gangs together to produce a mural. The result was *Mi Abuelita*, an archetypal portrait of Baca's grandmother painted on the bandshell at Hollenbeck Park. Sy Greben, the General Manager of the City Parks and Recreation Department, saw the mural being painted. Impressed by her ability to turn warring gang members into collaborative artists, he relieved her from her teaching responsibilities and hired her to direct the Eastside Mural Program. And so Judy Baca's career as a muralist began.

Baca was at home in the culture of the barrio because she had grown up in it. She was born on September 20, 1946, in Huntington Park, a mixed ethnic community in South Central Los Angeles. Shortly after her birth, her family moved to Watts, another mixed black and brown community. Her mother, Ortensia Baca, was unwedded, and her father, Valentino Marcel, was a serviceman in the US Navy stationed in Los Angeles. He left for the east coast after his discharge, and as a result, Judy grew up without ever meeting him.

She was raised in a family of women—Ortensia, Aunts Rita and Delia, who was retarded, and her grandmother Francisca, the *abuelita* of the mural, who was known in the neighborhood as a healer because of her use of herbal medicines. Francisca and her husband Teodoro had emigrated from Mexico to the United States during the early 1920s, following the revolution. Teodoro Baca was a small businessman who had been dispossessed of all his property except for a small cache of cash that Francisca had hidden in a water pitcher. Using this money, they migrated to La Junta, Colorado, a small farming community sixty miles from Denver where Mexicans had come to labor in the fields and on the railroad. The Mexicans lived in segregated housing, and their children attended segregated schools where they were scrubbed with kerosene "because all Mexicans had lice." Ortensia was born there in 1923. After her father died, Ortensia, eighteen years old, seeking a warmer climate and a less oppressive social environment, led the family on a move to California.

The Bacas arrived in Los Angeles just as World War II was about to lift the city and the country out of the Great Depression. The Mexican community in Los Angeles, already at the bottom of the socio-economic ladder, had suffered further slippage during the Depression. In 1936, seventy-seven percent of Mexican men in Los Angeles were working as unskilled or semi-skilled laborers. As unemployment grew, and the available labor pool swelled, Mexicans were the first to be laid off and the last to be hired. Many of them had only seasonal work in canneries and had to live on their meager earnings through the winter months. Women working in the garment industries were exploited by employers who demanded salary kickbacks, refused to pay the minimum wage, and deliberately used high turnover rates to keep their employees unsettled. With revenues from taxes falling, the city cut back on social services desperately needed by many Mexicans. Immigration policies tightened, quotas were lowered, and hundreds of thousands of Mexicans were forcibly repatriated. Many Mexicans who had reached the middle class voluntarily returned to Mexico. The social clubs and "mutualistas" that provided an important support network for Mexicans disappeared, further weakening the community.

In 1940, there were over one hundred thousand Mexicans living in Los Angeles, which had a total population of 1,500,000. The median income for a Mexican family was five hundred to seven hundred dollars below the federal standard for a decent living. This in a city they had founded and settled one hundred and sixty years before. It was into this environment that the Baca family arrived sometime during 1941.

The war years brought greater employment opportunities for Mexicans, but usually in the least desirable jobs doing difficult or dangerous work. In the Zoot Suit riots of 1943, young white servicemen attacked Mexican teenagers known as "pachucos" for the extravagant and foppish clothing they wore. The military police quickly suppressed the riots with no deaths on either side, but they brought into the open the racism that for decades had kept Mexicans in segregated neighborhoods and schools and made them objects of contempt in the Anglo-dominated society. This oppressive atmosphere isolated Mexicans in their barrios and intensified their need to hold onto their cultural traditions, religion, and language.

Ortensia found work at the Goodyear Tire Factory in Compton, not far from Watts. After Judy was born, she was raised by her aunts and grandmother. At home, with her mother and grandmother, Judy witnessed things being made by hand. The women designed and sewed all the family's clothes, and Francisca crocheted three-dimensional doilies into the shapes of flowers that she would place on tables around their home. Ortensia also amused Judy by drawing little portraits of her. The family was devoutly Catholic, and spoke only Spanish in the home, isolating Judy from the Anglo-European culture around them.

When Judy was six, her mother married an Italian named Clarence Ferrari, who worked as an upholsterer at the Lockheed Aircraft plant in the San Fernando Valley. The family moved to Pacoima, a mixed brown and black neighborhood near the plant. Francisca and Judy's aunts remained in Watts. Judy entered a public elementary school where she was not allowed to speak Spanish. Since Judy knew very little English and had difficulty keeping up with class lessons, her teacher allowed her to paint, an activity for which she showed aptitude and quickly came to love. She took art classes in junior high school and at Bishop Alemany, a private Catholic high school. There she amused her classmates by drawing caricatures of the nuns on blackboards and creating portraits of her friends on the covers of their notebooks.

Judy matriculated to California State University, Northridge, becoming the first member of her family to attend college. She studied art history, but when she was nineteen, she married, dropped out of college, and took a job at the Lockheed plant where her step-father worked. She was hired as an illustrator drawing machine parts. There she met an artist named Tomas, an older man who introduced her to watercolor painting. Judy resumed her studies at CSUN, received her degree in 1969, and took a job teaching art at Bishop Alemany, where she produced her first mural working with disaffected youth.

When Sy Greben appointed her Director of the Eastside Mural Program in the early 1970s, Baca began to develop the skills in community organizing and fundraising that would subsequently enable her to conceive and carry out the monumental Great Wall project. The City Parks and Recreation Department was paying her salary, but providing no funds to support mural projects. Baca held community meetings attended by gang members, their families, and small business owners at which she pitched her projects and sought donations. Initially, the community was resistant because people felt the gangs were fouling the barrios with their graffiti and giving Mexicans a bad reputation by their lawlessness. Baca was able to overcome this resistance by getting people to understand that the mural projects were channeling gang energies into constructive behavior and transforming the gang members in the process. Later, when Baca was writing a brief history of the Eastside Mural Program, she articulated the healing power of mural painting:

> Similar to the neighborhood I grew up in (Pacoima), [East Los
> Angeles] had cultural markers—graffiti—with roll calls written on
> the walls that told you who lived there, what the neighborhood was
> called, and who was from there. But this stylized iconography often
> triggered destructive conflict, part of the contesting of public space
> by rival gang members. I began working with gang members from
> different neighborhoods to establish networks between them to pro-
> mote peaceful solutions to such conflicts. Redirecting gang members'
> inclinations toward public expression via my own artistic training as
> a painter, we began painting murals as a way to create constructive
> cultural markers.

The success of the Eastside Mural Program led Baca, now divorced and living in the bohemian beach community of Venice, to propose to the Los Angeles City Council a Citywide Mural Program to be supported by Model Cities funding. At this point in her career, Baca began for the first time investigating the work of other muralists in Mexico and South America who were using public wall painting as a means of raising social consciousness and historical awareness among "la raza"—the people.

During fifty years from the early 1920s to the early 1970s, three great Mexican muralists—José Clemente Orozco, Diego Rivera, and David Alfaro Siqueiros—painted monumental murals on public buildings across Mexico that expressed the events and ideals of the Mexican Revolution. Though the themes, styles, and content of the murals varied according to the aesthetic sensibilities and interests of each of the artists, they had in common their recognition of the indigenous cultural identity of the Mexican people, their antipathy to colonial subjugation and rule, their criticism of foreign imperial intrusions on Mexico's sovereignty, and their affirmation of the dignity and value of the native cultural heritage of the Mexican people.

All three of "Los Tres Grandes," as they came to be known, were members of the Communist Party at one time, and all three studied art at the Academy of San Carlos in Mexico City under the painter Gerardo Murillo, also known as Dr. Atl, who can be considered the father of the Mexican mural movement. Atl began painting murals on the walls of public buildings in 1910, but his paintings were decorative, not political. His method, working with a collection of other artists, created a model followed by other muralists, especially Siqueiros. Atl's radical political positions influenced the artists who studied under him. He believed that art should reflect the social realities of the time and not serve simply as a vehicle for individual imaginative expression.

Siqueiros was the most politically radical of the three great Mexican muralists. Whereas Orozco saw human history as a stage on which clashed conflicting human tendencies of reform and reaction in a never-ending cycle, and Rivera looked to Mexico's pre-Columbian past for an idyllic and nostalgic representation of Mexico's true identity, Siqueiros in his murals expressed a vision of a socialist utopia brought about by revolutionary struggle that actualizes the potential for a just society through the equitable use of the full productive capacity of the industrial machine. During his life, Siqueiros fought in the Mexican Revolution and the Spanish Civil War. He was also jailed on two occasions in Mexico for his political activity.

Siqueiros spent three years in Europe between 1919 and 1921, where he absorbed several influences that shaped his approach to mural painting. In Paris, he met the painter Fernand Léger whose aesthetic of the machine appealed to him. In Italy he studied the frescos of the Italian Renaissance and the baroque architecture of Italian churches. He returned to Mexico in 1922 and painted his first mural in the stairwell of the Colegio Chico at San Ildefonso College in Mexico City, a work that was never completed, but that indicated Siqueiros' interest in combining mural painting with architecture.

Siqueiros was imprisoned for political activity in 1930. Upon his release, he came to Los Angeles to teach fresco painting at the Chouinard Art School. He experimented with new methods and materials, using a spray gun instead of brushes and industrial paints. He also formed a team of painters from his art class that he named "Block of Mural Painters," anticipating Baca's collaborative methodology by forty years. In 1932 he was commissioned to paint a mural at the Plaza Art Center on Olvera Street in the old Los Angeles pueblo. He called the mural *American Tropical* and did not attempt to soften its anti-capitalist message. Tropical America meant:

> Our land, our America, of undernourished natives, of enslaved Indians and Negroes, that nevertheless inhabit the most fertile land in which the richest and most ferocious people on earth lie. And as a symbol of the United States' imperialism, the principal capitalist oppressor, I used an Indian crucified on a double cross, on top of which stood the Yankee eagle of American finance.

The mural was whitewashed by the patron who commissioned it, but in 2012 it was fully restored through a ten million dollar project funded by the City of Los Angeles and the Getty Conservation Institute. In 1999 Judy Baca led a student mural project titled *Los Angeles Tropical* that was placed at the entrance to *American Tropical* as an homage to Siqueiros. Baca acknowledged her artistic debt to Siqueiros when she cited a statement he issued in 1922 as inspiring her work and the work of other muralists in Los Angeles: "We repudiate so-called easel art and all such art which springs from ultra-intellectual circles, for it is essentially aristocratic. We hail the monumental expression of art because such art is public property." This populist manifesto can be seen as the credo for Baca's career as a muralist.

After a false start, Baca succeeded in persuading the Los Angeles City Council to fund the Citywide Mural Program. An appropriation of $150,000 allowed Baca to purchase scaffolding, trucks, and supplies, and to pay stipends to her small staff of youths who had worked with her on previous murals. During the first year, forty murals were produced in ethnic communities across the city.

In developing the content for the murals, Baca followed the same procedures she had used in the Eastside Mural Program. She held community meetings to flush out concerns and issues that would shape the murals' design. "The content of the murals became stronger and stronger," Baca recalled in a 1986 interview. "There were pieces on immigration, there were pieces on drug abuse, there were pieces on police brutality, there were pieces on nature, and there were pieces on history." As the content of the murals became controversial with some of the more conservative constituents of the districts in which they were appearing, censorship was applied by local officials who threatened to withhold funding. Baca's supporters flooded the mayor's office with letters protesting the censorship pressure.

Rather than battle the city over the content of the murals, Baca turned to "Friends of the Citywide Mural Program," a group that included Zubin Mehta, Music Director of the Los Angeles Philharmonic, as well as several attorneys. The group helped her form a non-profit corporation called the Social and Public Art Resource Center. SPARC was established in 1974 "as an arts organization that could carry out mural programs in such a way as to animate public discourse and free expression of the diverse communities of the city without direct official intervention." SPARC was housed in Venice in an art deco building that had formerly served as a city jail. It shared space with the Citywide Mural Program. SPARC's first project was *The Great Wall of Los Angeles*.

The genesis of *The Great Wall* occurred when the US Army Corps of Engineers asked Baca to paint a mural in the Tujunga Wash at the border of Valley College in a neighborhood known as Valley Glen. The mural was to be part of a beautification project that would include a mini-park and a bicycle path. Baca went to see the wall. "I envisioned a long narrative of another history of California, one which included ethnic peoples. Women and minorities who were so invisible in conventional textbook accounts . . . I designed this project as an artist concerned not only with the physical aesthetic considerations of space, but the social, environmental, and cultural issues affecting the site as well." In 1975, Baca traveled to Mexico with her partner and SPARC co-founder Christina Schlesinger (a third co-founder was filmmaker Donna Deitch) and spent several months there studying murals as she prepared to execute the first segment of *The Great Wall*.

To create the mural, Baca assembled teams of workers, designers, and informants. The workers were young "Mural Makers," youths whom Baca recruited from the juvenile justice system and from low-income families in the barrios to prepare the wall and paint it under the supervision of artists who had designed the images. The content of the images was arrived at through collaboration with local historians, ethnologists, scholars, and members of the community. Funding for the project came from government agencies, including the juvenile justice system, the Summer Youth Employment Program, the US Army Corps of Engineers, and the Los Angeles County Flood Control District, as well as corporations, foundations, and individual donors. Additional support in the form of supplies and services came from small businesses and community organizations. Baca compared the scale of the project to the production of a Hollywood movie, or a military maneuver. She was functioning both as an artist/producer and social worker as she stitched together many disparate components of the Los Angeles community to create unique images of the city's origins.

The first segment of the wall was completed during nine weeks of painting in the summer of 1976 by a team of eighty youths, ten artists, and five historians. Along one thousand feet of the wall, it depicted the history of California from the time when saber-toothed tigers and mammoths roamed the grassy plains of the Los Angeles basin to the year 1910, by which time the foundations of the modern city had been laid down. One of the most important sections of this segment of the mural shows the founding of the pueblo of Los Angeles in 1781. Baca departed from the romantic myth of Los Angeles' settlement by the Spanish by revealing that of the twenty-two members of the first expedition, only one was Spanish. The remainder were Black, Mulatto, Mestizo, or Indian. They were farmers and artisans who had been recruited by the Spanish authorities in Mexico with the promise of land titles if they remained in Alta California, as it was then known, for at least ten years. These simple people were the city's first settlers.

Ten different artists had designed one hundred foot sections of the first segment. For the second stage of the project, Baca assumed more artistic control to ensure greater aesthetic integrity and smoother transitions between sections. This change in approach came about partly as a result of a trip that Baca made to Mexico in 1977 to study mural painting at the studio of David Siqueiros. Baca stresses the significance of this experience. "I learned about Siqueiros' concept of the musical ratio—of the harmonious musical ratio of composition—and his division of space, which is on a ratio of three to five . . . Well, that musical time is a way of creating a rhythm within the piece . . . Suddenly there's this like visual kind of connection between the forms, and it fits, clicks like pieces of a puzzle, right into place."

The second segment treated World War I, with emphasis on women's role in the war, the birth of the motion picture industry, and an homage to Thomas Edison, who was born in Zacatecas, Mexico and adopted by American parents.

The mural proceeds through the first five decades of twentieth-century California painted during the summers of 1980, 1981, and 1983. But her major concerns continued to be social injustice, racism, and the struggles of the poor. The wall reminds us of the essential role "minorities" have played in the development of California, and their frequent mistreatment. The scale of the project and its increasingly powerful imagery brought Baca to national attention. A four-page photographic spread in the December 1980 issue of *Life* described the mural as "one of the most extraordinary urban art projects in the U.S." and included a photograph of Baca painting the wall.

Work on *The Great Wall* continues today. In 2000 and 2001, SPARC received support from the Ford Foundation and the Rockefeller Foundation to continue work on the mural. In 2013 the National Endowment for the Arts granted SPARC $90,000 towards the costs of designing images for the remaining decades of the twentieth century. In 2004 SPARC produced a virtual 3-D model of *The Great Wall* in collaboration with UCLA's Digital Mural Lab, which Baca had established to extend the reach of mural production through the use of digital technology. The 3-D model is displayed on a 160 degree Imax screen at the Visualization Portal on the campus of UCLA, where Baca now serves as Vice-Chair of the César Chávez Department of Chicana/o Studies.

In 2001, SPARC initiated a restoration project to clean, repair, and repaint *The Great Wall*. Because the Tujunga Wash channels the primary water flow through the San Fernando Valley to the Pacific Ocean, the mural is vulnerable to erosion and other water damage during the Los Angeles' rainy season. A thirty-member restoration team that included a muralist, interns from universities around the country, local volunteers, and past participants of *The Great Wall* production performed restoration work during the summer. The restoration project was completed in 2011.

To encourage widespread suggestions for the content of the remaining segments of the mural, SPARC has created a page on its website through which artists may submit design proposals. One such proposal depicts an Aztec warrior dressed in indigenous costume and carrying a leaf blower on his back, a poignant comment on the ubiquitous Mexican gardeners making their living tending the manicured lawns of Los Angeles' suburbia.

One other important dimension of *The Great Wall* project is its role as a community healer. Many of the youths working on the wall needed social services to enable them to function as "Mural Makers." So Baca put in place counseling services, and shelters for battered kids and runaways. Baca sees this as an extension of the intercultural mission of The Great Wall. "What I've had to do is focus increasingly on the support services that will accomplish the goals of the interrelationship between the different cultures, which is the focus of *The Great Wall*," Baca says. "*The Great Wall* really then is just the tip of the iceberg. It's just really one part; the image is one part of the whole concept."

As the first stage of *The Great Wall* neared completion, a sixteen-year-old mural worker said to Baca, "We should take what we learned working with different nationalities here in Los Angeles to the world." So in 1987, SPARC began work on *The World Wall: A Vision of the Future Without Fear*, a portable installation of murals from countries around the world promoting the idea of peace. Baca was also motivated by her reading of Jonathan Schell's cautionary tale about nuclear warfare, *The Fate of the Earth*, published in 1982. Baca thought, "It was not imagining destruction that was so hard to us but rather imagining peace . . . If we cannot imagine peace as an active concept, how can we ever hope for it to happen?" Baca used workshops and brainstorming sessions she had developed during the production of *The Great Wall* to arrive at the concept of a portable mural composed of seven panels, ten feet by thirty feet each, that could be assembled into a one hundred foot diameter circle. The mural would be installed at locations around the world and viewed by audiences standing at its center or outside it.

The first four panels were created by Baca and several assistants. "Triumph of the Hearts" depicts the faces of four weeping figures holding candles while a fifth figure, wearing a small backpack and carrying a candle, strides purposefully away from them towards a distant horizon. Above him, a cloud of smoke carrying the wailing faces of the dead rises from the earth. Baca's caption reads, "The beginning of any movement of society towards peace: the individual taking action."

The central panel, titled "Balance," uses symbolism to express Native American and Eastern concepts of man living in a harmonious relationship with the world and showing respect for all life forms. "Triumph of the Hands" shows workers discovering the potential to use their hands in the production of goods that serve human needs and breaking their enslavement to the machine. In "Non-Violent Resistance," Baca's most powerful image, men and women lock arms and form a circle around a desolate wasteland littered with industrial debris and instruments of war. Baca is representing "the notion of using nonviolent means to create a societal transformation, to parallel the systems of the mainstream and create a psychic and political structure of transformation. The individual joins with others and forms a community of consciousness."

The World Wall had its premiere in June 1990 in Joensuu, Finland. A team of Finnish artists added the panel "Dialogue of Alternatives" that uses easily recognized symbols to convey a message of hope and transformation. The installation then traveled to Moscow, where it was exhibited for one week in Gorky Park. The Russian artist Alexi Begov contributed a panel he called "The End of the Twentieth Century." The piece is done in dark, brooding tones and features block-shaped figures reminiscent of Picasso's work in paintings such as *Seated Woman*. A crucified figure sets the tone of despair. At the base of the cross, a small child gazes fearfully towards the sky, crossing herself. Three adult figures, one of them blind, also gaze upwards, anticipating . . . what?

In 1998 "Compromise-Inheritance," an Israeli- Palestinian panel, was produced by three artists working with Baca at the Visual and Public Art Institute in Monterey, California, where she was teaching. Using bright colors and child-like figure drawings, the panel conveys the innocence of children, implying their need to grow up in an environment free from ancient animosities that breed terror and fear. A year later, in Mexico, two women artists created an eighth panel, "Tlazoltcotl: Creative Force of the Un-Woven." Using bold colors and drawing on imagery from Mexico's indigenous roots, the panel vividly expresses "the promise of a future reborn," suggesting that peace can be recovered when we establish contact with our common origins as human beings.

The World Wall, like its predecessor *The Great Wall*, remains a work in progress. Currently, a team of Canadian artists is working on a panel entitled "The Inuit Send the World a Canary," a mural that addresses the threat of global warming and the industrial desecration of irreplaceable natural resources. A major focus of the murals is the fight for Teztan Biny, a wilderness area that is the traditional home of the Tsilhqot'in people and is now the target of an industrial development proposal to excavate a huge open-pit copper-gold mine. The project would destroy a place recognized by anthropologists as a "cultural keystone." The struggle reached the Canadian Supreme Court, which recognized the Tsilhqot'in's aboriginal title and rights to the region.

The Great Wall spawned other mural projects in Los Angeles. In 1988 Mayor Tom Bradley asked Baca to develop a successor to the Citywide Mural Program. Titled "Great Walls Unlimited: Neighborhood Pride Program," it produced one hundred and five murals in almost every ethnic community of Los Angeles before being terminated in 2002 due to budget cuts. The creation of these murals followed the same pattern of community engagement and enlistment of youth apprentices that had characterized Baca's other collaborative mural projects. The program, added to Baca's previous work and the work of other muralists, made Los Angeles a national model for muralism and inspired other cities to launch mural programs.

Although Baca considers herself primarily an artist, her methods and message as a muralist suggest other vocations as well. She is a community organizer, a social worker, an activist, an entrepreneur, and an educator. Her murals educate the people who view them and teach skills and self-esteem to the young people who work on them. Baca's career as a muralist began in a high school classroom where she taught art. So it is not surprising that as her career as a muralist matured, and her reputation grew, she was recruited by academia. In 1994 she became a founding faculty member of California State University, Monterey Bay, in charge of its Visual and Public Art Institute. In a remarkable echo of the conversion of the old Venice jail into the headquarters for SPARC, the new university campus was a former military fort.

Baca's appointment came at a time of Chicano activism and protest at one of California's elite institutions, the University of California, Los Angeles. Since 1969, the time of the Chicano Moratorium, activists had been calling for a Chicano studies program at the university that would recognize the historical and cultural contributions Mexicans have made to American life. The proposal was resisted by the university administration and by some faculty members who wanted to preserve the traditional curriculum. The issue intensified in 1989 when a UCLA student film showed a Mexican woman having sexual intercourse with a donkey. Students demanded a core curriculum in Chicano studies taught by tenured professors. Administration inaction on these demands led to a mass rally on May 11, 1993, at which ninety-eight students were arrested and strip-searched. The administration's overreaction provoked a hunger strike by Chicano students, who set up a tent city on one of the campus's main plazas. The fasting students held out for a month. As a medical crisis loomed, the university's chancellor, Charles Young, agreed to the creation of the César Chávez Center for Interdisciplinary Instruction in Chicano and Chicana Studies, and to seven full-time core appointments to be made over the next three years. One of these appointments was offered to Judy Baca.

With this appointment, Baca brought mural making into the digital age. In 1996 she established the UCLA SPARC Digital/Mural Lab, located at SPARC's facility in Venice. Baca saw the lab as a place where formally enrolled UCLA students could experience the melding of community issues and art that is the hallmark of her work. By siting the lab at SPARC, Baca was immersing her students within an organization that was carrying out real-world mural projects in response to pressing social issues. She was removing the wall between academia and the raw world outside it.

The lab provides students with state-of-the-art digital technology with which to produce large-scale public murals. Using this technology, students combine a variety of hand-generated and digitally-derived images with traditional painting techniques to produce high-quality murals that are placed as permanent artworks in a wide array of communities and locations. The lab also functions as a production resource supporting mural projects initiated by communities around the world that wish to use art to reduce conflicts and racial or religious divisions. UCLA students have the opportunity to work as interns on these projects. Baca believes that mural making is a unique and powerful teaching tool. "You can teach anybody any content through the imaging process," she observes. "And it's learned in a way, by the transformation of its scale, that it can never be learned any other way. So it doesn't matter whether you're learning about the history of the Chumash Indians, or whether you're learning about a particular set of sociological events, literally any subject matter can be submitted to this process."

Since its founding, the Digital Mural Lab has produced several notable murals installed at locations in California, the United States, and Central America. The content of these murals continues to recognize the history and achievements of minority groups in America, especially Hispanics and Blacks, and to express their struggles for equality and social justice.

The first project of the lab involved a collaboration with the Cornerstone Theater Company, which was producing a play titled *The Birthday of the Century* to be performed outdoors at the California Plaza in downtown Los Angeles. The task for Baca's students was to create eight murals that would serve as backdrops on the set. Two of the murals, called The Birth Portal and The Death Portal, signified the lifespan of the century. The other six murals, "Witnesses to LA History," were portraits of individuals representing the city's cultural diversity: an Asian couple, a Gabrielino Indian woman, a teenage "cholo," an African-American slave woman who was freed in 1854 and became a community worker, a Pilipino farmworker, and an archetypal blue-collar worker surrounded by the industrial city he had built.

A second "Witness to LA History" project was initiated in 1997 when the Los Angeles Public Housing Authority asked SPARC to produce a permanent public art installation at the Estrada Courts, one of East Los Angeles' oldest housing projects and the site of numerous Chicano murals painted during the 1970s. The execution of this commission reveals Baca's working method with her students, who created art out of archival research and dialogue with community members that elicited family histories and photographs to illustrate them. The students and their collaborators installed six 8`x9` murals in the Estrada Courts Community Center.

In 1998, while a resident at Harvard University, Baca and her graduate students undertook what is undoubtedly her most personal mural project, *Memoria De Nuestra Tierra*. The mural shows the route her grandparents took from their home in Chihuahua through the portal of El Paso to La Junta, Colorado, set against the beautiful mesa landscape in which they settled. To develop the content for the mural, Baca followed her usual research procedure: locating old photographs, studying the history of the region, interviewing residents and scholars. Using computer technology, Baca blended photographic images and documents into the mural. The landscape was hand-painted at a small scale, then scanned into the computer at high resolution. The composite image was printed at the monumental scale of 10`x50` on digital aluminum tile and installed in the central terminal of the Denver International Airport. An accompanying text explains in detail the stories behind the images in the mural. The stories include a history of the Mexican Revolution and the ensuing migration of Mexicans to the United States, and the Ludlow Massacre of 1914, in which John D. Rockefeller's Colorado Fuel and Iron Corporation hired private detectives to fire on striking miners and then obtained the support of Colorado's National Guard to destroy the strike. Images of Rodolfo Gonzalez and César Chávez superimposed on buttes in the landscape remind viewers of the Crusade for Justice that began a national conversation about Chicano civil rights. Baca describes this stunning mural as:

> An excavation of the Chicano/ Chicanas complexity as indigenous
> people, and of their multiple identities as mixed Spaniards, Africans,
> and Asians living among newly immigrated Irish, Greek, and Italian

people. This is an excavation and a remembering of their histories. By revealing what is hidden, through pictorial iconography in the land, this mural is a kind of Mayan map not really intended to guide your path, but instead to tell you about the road.

Other significant mural projects carried out through the Digital Mural Lab include the Durango Digital Mural, produced in collaboration with Navajo, Latino, Ute, and Anglo high school students; an interactive mural commemorating the fiftieth anniversary of the Montgomery bus boycott that was exhibited in New York, Philadelphia, the District of Columbia, and Baltimore; a densely complex mural honoring the legacy of Chicano labor leader Miguel Contreras that was installed in the cafeteria of the Miguel Contreras Learning Complex, a high school in downtown Los Angeles.

Murals, as public art exhibited in unsecured exterior locations are vulnerable to degradation and damage from weather, aging, and vandalism by taggers. Murals painted on the walls enclosing freeways face the added risk of being painted over by Caltrans, the state's highway maintenance department, to cover graffiti and tags. As the mural movement in Los Angeles spread, SPARC became the focal point for requests from muralists and others in the community to maintain and protect the city's mural legacy. In 2008 SPARC established a Mural Rescue Program to address this need. However, as SPARC does not have funds in its operating budget to cover the costs of restoration projects, a fundraising effort must be undertaken for each mural in need of restoration work. To date, the Mural Rescue Program has accomplished the restoration of eight murals in Los Angeles and one in Guadalupe, Mexico.

Judy Baca remains active today as a muralist, educator, and lecturer. SPARC is currently engaged in a major fundraising campaign to continue the restoration of *The Great Wall*, to extend its narrative through the last four decades of the twentieth century, and to make the site a park that can serve as an international educational and cultural destination.

Baca sees herself as a healer and traces this calling to the example of her grandmother Francisca, who dispersed herbal medicines to the neighbors in her community. "I think all this work I have been doing is about healing," Baca says. "And it's about developing some kind of loving approach to the world, in which I can use my skills—I'm not a dancer or a singer, I make images—to heal a social environment and a physical environment."

CHAPTER 10

Warren Brush and Cynthia-Harvan Brush

Prologue

As we have seen from the preceding life stories, dissent from mainstream society and its prevailing attitudes can take many forms, in response to varying external pressures and personal circumstances. Not all dissent is overt and expressed through resistance to an existing condition or insistence on reform. Sometimes dissent from established norms is merely implied in the lifestyle choices that people make and the values by which they live. Such is the case with Warren Brush and his wife Cynthia, who have responded to the direction of modern life—built as it is around an escalating spiral of consumerism fed by technological progress and competition—by creating an alternate model of human community designed to be in synchronization and compatibility with natural systems and rhythms. Their gesture, in many ways, echoes the journey of Roger Williams and illustrates the persistence of the independent spirit in our ongoing American narrative.

They are reforming at the most fundamental level of human survival, agriculture, operating small, self-sufficient farms that are thoughtfully and deliberately integrated with the conditions and features of their local ecosystems. They are practicing permaculture, a method of designing human systems that accord with ecological principles and natural laws, and that therefore do not pose a threat to the health of the planet Earth, as do many of the current practices of agribusiness. Although their strategies for cultivating the land hearken back to practices followed by pre-industrial

Warren Brush and Cynthia Harvan-Brush (Photo courtesy of
Warren Brush.)

indigenous peoples, they are in the advance guard of efforts to slow and reverse human contributions to climate change that now threatens to disrupt civilization. Their alternative paradigm of human settlement is sustainable, efficient (i.e., waste-free), and healthy, and does not rely on the combustion of carbon releasing fossil fuels for energy.

Warren and Cynthia came to permaculture on a path that took them through various stages of healing: healing of their spirits through disciplined effort and tutelage; healing of others, especially children, through immersion in the natural world; healing of the land through caring stewardship. Along the way, they accumulated knowledge and experience that combined respect for indigenous attitudes towards the natural world with the best practices of modern environmental and agricultural science, creating a fusion of the old and the new. They then established two working farms in the mountains of Ventura County, California, as demonstrations of how humans can create sustainable methods of food production that operate in tandem with the ecosystems of which they are a part. The principles on which these farms operate have broad implications for humanity's response to climate change.

Warren Brush and Cynthia Harvan-Brush – Revolution from the Ground Up

The great issue of our time is the health of the planet Earth, our home, which has become diseased from our relentless and ever-increasing industrial activity. Since the period of the industrial revolution began, approximately two hundred and fifty years ago, humankind has been spewing into the atmosphere billions of metric tons of "greenhouse" gases formed primarily by our burning of fossil fuels to produce the energy that powers our way of life. These gases—carbon dioxide (CO_2), methane (CH_4), and nitrous oxide (N_2O)—remain in the earth's atmosphere for decades, trapping energy from the sun that would otherwise be released back through the atmosphere into space. As these gases have accumulated, the trapped energy has warmed the planet to temperatures outside the range of natural variability. During the middle of the twentieth century, this warming began to noticeably affect the earth's climate patterns, altering them in disturbing ways.

The changes in the climate have created undesirable impacts on natural systems and the human systems that depend on them. Rising temperatures are causing extreme heat events and melting polar ice sheets and glaciers, raising the seas to levels that jeopardize the coasts of continents. Rainfall patterns have been altered, creating droughts in some regions, flooding in others. Ecosystems and the organisms they support have been affected, changing the conditions for plant life, causing animals to migrate out of their traditional territories, and disrupting agriculture. The surplus of carbon in the atmosphere has been partially absorbed into the oceans, leading to acidification that threatens marine life and its habitat, especially coral reefs.

What human beings have been doing for the past two hundred and fifty years of economic and technological development has altered and thrown out of equilibrium the natural carbon cycle that has supported life on earth for eons—hundreds of millions of years. We have been tampering with the flow of cosmic energy that emanates from the sun and is continuously recycled through our air, land, and water, diverting it into human uses that are stressing natural systems that were functioning long before *homo sapiens* walked the earth.

We face a crisis in our relationship with the natural world, of which we are an inseparable part. How we respond to this crisis <u>now</u> will determine the future not only of our species but also of the manifold other species that share life on planet Earth with us. Can we become good stewards of our home, or will we continue to foul it in our endless pursuit of "progress?"

———•———

There have been many responses to the environmental crisis at both the macro and micro levels. These include studies by international groups of scientists that have led to national policies and regulations, advocacy by environmental groups such as The Nature Conservancy, and local efforts to encourage recycling of renewable energy sources by consumers.

But the most interesting response to the environmental crisis at the micro-level is the permaculture movement that formally began in 1978 in Australia with the work of Bill Mollison and David Holmgren, which drew from the natural farming philosophy of Masanobu Fukuoka. The movement has spread to Great Britain and the US through the activities of the Permaculture Institute. The word "permaculture" is a shortening of "permanent agriculture." It refers to a system of growing food that relies entirely on natural processes that are self-sustaining and in harmony with the wider ecosystem of which they are a part. The term has come to be extended to social culture as well through a vision of human society in which all people share equitably in the goods and services that society produces, at levels that are sustainable for all of us. In a permaculture world, wide disparities of wealth and poverty would cease to exist. But permaculture is an ethical system, not a political one, and does not advocate communism.

In its agriculture practices, permaculture integrates multiple-crop farming with sustainable natural ecosystem processes. It is an alternative to the unsustainable single-crop agriculture that is now being used to feed the world, but whose methods are contributing to global warming and leaving millions of people undernourished or in a state of starvation. Presently, agriculture in the US emits about ten percent of our greenhouse gases from livestock manure, chemical soil fertilizers, and single-crop rice production. Its methods also degrade the soil and remove vegetation that absorbs CO_2 from the atmosphere.

Permaculture, though local, small scale, and site-specific, is a response to our environmental crisis with far-reaching implications, for it embodies a new kind of relationship between human culture and nature that has applications across all sectors of our economic and social life. Western civilization, especially since the onset of the industrial revolution, has opened an ever-widening breach between man's world, artificially shaped by technology and urbanism, and the natural world, where everything has a necessary place that functions in the creation of equilibrium. Permaculture seeks to restore man to nature at the most basic level: food production.

———•◦•———

Fifty miles inland from the bustling seacoast city of Ventura, California, hidden from view in spacious Burges Canyon, and bordering the Los Padres National Forest, lies a demonstration of a future for agriculture and for human community, Quail Springs, a working permaculture farm which was co-founded by Warren Brush and Cynthia Harvan-Brush along with several of their friends and supporters. The farm is situated in the Upper Cuyama Valley (elevation 3,400 feet), a semi-arid high desert environment that receives on average less than eight inches of annual rainfall. The climate is Mediterranean: hot dry summers with temperatures above one hundred degrees, followed by cold, wet winters with below-freezing temperatures. This environment naturally supports a Piñon-Juniper woodland plant community dominated by sagebrush on level ground and chaparral on the hillsides. The setting makes Quail Springs an experimental site for drylands farming using permaculture methods that are adapted to the existing topography, climate, and soil conditions.

The farm is home to about fourteen permanent residents, ranging from children to elders, with many of them being men and women in their twenties and thirties who live in yurts and natural cob buildings (made from wood, straw, clay, and sand) scattered along the northern edge of the canyon. Here they receive maximum sunlight, the main source of energy for the farm's operations. Of Quail Springs' four hundred and fifty acres, only three are in cultivation for crops. The rest are left in their natural state but are used as forage for the farm's small goat herd, which provides the residents with milk, yogurt, soft and hard cheeses, and occasionally meat. The farm raises chickens and ducks for eggs and meat and breeds rabbits as a source of food and pelts. A food forest yields cucumbers, squash, melons, tomatoes, artichokes, lettuce, and kale planted in late spring, and root crops, including carrots, beets, and parsnips planted in late August. Potatoes, a ninety-day crop, are planted in March. Fruit trees yield apricots, pears, peaches, apples, figs, mulberries, and plums. Berries have started, but await more growth of the shading overstory.

The overstory and shrub layer also promote nitrogen fixation. Only natural fertilizers derived from compost are used to enrich the planting beds. The farm produces enough food to sustain, on average, twenty-two people eating three meals per day—residents, visitors, and participants in various educational programs that Quail Springs offers to the public.

Water, the lifeblood of all the farm's operations, comes from a perennial spring on the eastern border of the property. It now provides a flow of fifty gallons per minute, up from a mere trickle when the farm was acquired from its previous owner, a cattle rancher. The farm harvests only five gallons per minute, storing it in five large tanks. It allows the remaining forty-five gallons to water the land from the stream that meanders through the property, revivifying both the farm and the surrounding ecosystem.

The farm operates on the key permaculture principle of sustainability and regeneration of resources. As a village farm, it grows only enough food to support its immediate community. This need determines the number of animals it keeps as well as the number of annual crops it grows. Quail Springs is an interdependent human settlement that sustains itself by working with its surrounding community to provide those things they do not grow or forage, like pellet feed for the poultry, natural gas for stove cooking, and petroleum for the residents' motor vehicles. Solar panels use the sun's energy to provide electricity, natural materials are used to build shelter, and water is taken from the natural spring. Heating of the shelters during winter is fueled by firewood taken from the abundant woodland on the property, or from cultivated poplar trees whose bark has first been chewed off by the goats.

Quail Springs is a unique microcosm on Earth that both supports its occupants and educates the world around it on the principles and methods of creating sustainable human settlements in harmony with nature and interdependent with the people in the region where they live.

The Cuyama Valley has held human settlement since prehistoric times. The archaeological record shows that bands of Chumash Indians lived in the valley as early as 10,000 B.C., yet the people themselves claim to have lived there for over 30,000 years. ("Cuyama" is the Chumash word for "clam," a reference to fossilized clam shells found in the rock strata of the valley.) A Chumash village named Kuyam was located a few miles north of Quail Springs. The Chumash, who still live in the region and have for thousands of years, once lived as a stone-age people who survived by hunting and gathering. Because the valley's Mediterranean climate assured them of a year-round food and water supply, they were able to establish permanent villages. They built domed huts framed with willow poles and thatched with tule, made tools, utensils, and weapons from wood, stone, and bone, and clothing from plant fiber and animal skins. They hunted deer, bear, and rabbits, fished in the Cuyama River, which then flowed to the Pacific Ocean, and gathered over one hundred and fifty plants for food and medicine. Although the Chumash did not practice agriculture or keep domesticated animals other than dogs, they employed a variety of horticultural techniques, including pruning, sowing, weeding, burning, thinning, and selective harvesting that maintained them in harmonious balance with their ecosystem. These indigenous land management practices have been revived in the philosophy and applications being carried out at Quail Springs by its current residents.

With the arrival of the Spanish in the late seventeen hundreds, the sustainable land-use practices followed by the Chumash for thousands of years began to change. The Spanish built missions and forts and instituted agriculture and ranching to support the growing population of settlers. The Mexicans continued these occupations after their independence from Spain, as did the Americans who came to the valley after the Mexican-American War. A succession of alternating droughts and floods during the 1860s and 1870s devastated the cattle industry. Thousands of starving cattle were slaughtered, drastically reducing the herds. But homesteaders continued to arrive into the 1930s, working their small farms.

The valley also supported extraction industries. Phosphates used in fertilizer, gravel, sand, sandstone, and claystone were mined from the surrounding mountains. In 1950 the Richfield Oil Company developed a field that yielded 200,000,000 gallons of oil, the largest strike in the state. The company built the town of New Cuyama to house its workers.

These industrial activities, factored by increasingly large-scale agriculture, have markedly depleted the valley's groundwater reserves. A recently published study by the US Geological Survey of water usage in the valley from 1949 to 2010 found that the water table had dropped from its historical average of one hundred feet to well over four hundred feet and, in some cases, six hundred feet deep. The study said that the ongoing extraction rate is "unsustainable" because current mono-crop farming operations devoted to growing organic carrots and grain are draining the valley's groundwater reserves twice as fast as they can be replenished. The study warned that current practices, if continued, might bring farming in the valley to an end.

The Quail Springs property had been used during the twentieth century for agriculture and grazing. Overgrazing of cattle had denuded the landscape, allowing the natural water flow from the springs to exit the ecosystem, diminishing its ability to support both the livestock and the natural food chain of plants and animals. Unsustainable agricultural practices were moving the land towards desertification. In 2004 Warren Brush and his wife Cyndi, with support of the community that surrounded their first organizational endeavor, Wilderness Youth Project, using funds provided by a Santa Barbara family foundation, formed a non-profit corporation called True Nature Society and purchased the 450-acre Black's Ranch. They intended to develop a place for children and families to deepen their connection with nature and to learn about land stewardship. Over the years, the work with youth evolved Quail Springs into a place that demonstrates the feasibility of carrying out sustainable dryland farming on a high desert landscape and also provides a base for education programs designed to teach the principles and techniques of ethical land use to the broader community.

The path that brought Warren Brush and Cynthia Harvan to Quail Springs followed a circuitous route and leaps of faith guided by a deep intention to heal. Warren was born in Pasadena, California, in 1965 into what he describes as an upper-middle-class household. A sister, Kimberly, was born in 1961. His father, Bill, was a practicing psychologist. His mother, Donna, dealt antiques and was a professional puppeteer. They lived on the edge of a wood that Warren liked to explore as a boy. As an early sign of his independence and love of nature, Warren built himself a cabin in the woods. His parents encouraged his aptitude for the natural world, innovative thinking, and his free spirit.

Warren had an adventurous grandfather named Eugene who, at one point in his life, roamed the seas in a fishing boat, a man Warren calls "an edge dweller." When his family beckoned him to return to society to be with them, he took an office job at a trucking company that always left his heart yearning for the open road and the expanse of the seas. As he neared retirement, Eugene and his wife were long planning to go on a world tour. He died from a heart attack the very day after he retired and never took the trip for which he longed. Warren was fourteen when his grandfather died. The lesson he took from his grandfather's story was not to defer your heart's desire.

When Warren was fifteen, his parents lost all their economic wealth in a real estate investment that turned sour. After that debacle, his father could only find work as a janitor for the church where he worshipped, and could no longer support Warren. In that fortuitous crossroads of his parents' lives, they were led into a path of the heart. They spent most of the rest of their lives as puppeteers playing to thousands of children every year. Because of these family circumstances, Warren's life path took a new direction. He excitedly left the family nest and moved to Santa Barbara, managed to skirt the age regulations for renting an apartment, and found a job working at a Domino's Pizza. When he was eighteen, Warren was made the manager of a Domino's Pizza, and then at nineteen was offered his franchise site in nearby Goleta. He found a financial partner who took a forty-nine percent interest in the franchise and ran it successfully for over a year. He was on the rise in the growing company, and he was offered another franchise nearby in a small beach town a few miles south of Santa Barbara, which he ended up not accepting.

Despite his business success, Warren was not content. At this juncture, he read three books that affected him powerfully. One was Somerset Maugham's *The Razor's Edge*, whose main character becomes disaffected with western civilization. Another was Richard Bach's *Illusions*, which many readers of Warren's then age find spiritually uplifting in its message of compassion for the world. The third was Rainer Maria Rilke's *Letters to a Young Poet*. "Go into yourself," Rilke advises his correspondent. "Look inward."

One day while making a pizza, what was to be his last one with the company, Warren began to sob uncontrollably. He secluded himself in a closet and wept, out of sight of the astonished looks of his employees. When he emerged from the closet, he called his financial partner and told her he was selling out his interest in the business. Then he called People's Express, a discount airline with a long lead-time for reservations. He requested a canceled seat on a plane going anywhere. He was offered Brussels. He spent the next four months wandering Europe, reading, writing in his journal, musing on the meaning of his life. When he returned to Santa Barbara he enrolled in the local community college as a pre-med student. He also married and had a daughter named Anastasia. The couple separated amicably after two and a half years, sharing custody of their child.

While Warren attended university, he worked at the Hinchee Foundation, a non-profit corporation providing care for developmentally disabled adults. There, he and Cynthia Harvan met. Cyndi was born in Fresno in 1969 and grew up in a large family, where the sharing of music and good food was instilled through the many gatherings at her grandparents' house in the country. Her father, Mike, is a self-taught oil painter, chef (he learned from his father who was also a chef at their family-owned restaurant), tile worker, and gifted piano player. Her mother, Sandra, was a stay-at-home mom who ensured the family was always tended to, well-fed, and nurtured. She currently still spends many of her days now tending to the family's grandchildren. Cyndi has three siblings, a sister Tamara and brothers Mark and Brian. Her maternal grandfather, Douglas Bell, also lived with their family for fourteen years before he passed. When Cyndi was sixteen Mike and his wife Sandy moved the family to Santa Barbara to be near the ocean. Cyndi attended Santa Barbara City College after graduating from high school and studied dance. Her work at the Hinchee Foundation opened her heart in other ways.

Her patients became some of her most dear and profound teachers, who, by simply living their authentic lives, inspired an incredible passion for life in all of its forms.

A year after meeting and courting, Warren and Cyndi moved to Sausalito, California, where they lived on a sailboat anchored in the bay and supported themselves by running a home for three autistic children.

While Warren and Cyndi were living in Sausalito, they encountered a teacher who would further help to inspire and deepen their life-long learning journey and relationship with the natural world, through the art of tracking, the language of the birds, origin skills, and wilderness survival.

In 1994 Cyndi and Warren returned to Santa Barbara. Warren took a position at Transition House, a shelter for homeless families. Having experienced the healing powers of nature through immersion in wilderness training, Warren and Cyndi began to take the homeless children on adventure trips into nature on weekends. The children were mentored in nature awareness skills and other indigenous skills, such as how to make fires by friction, build shelters, forage for wild foods, and track animals. After working at Transition House for several years, Warren had another epiphany moment that came through the guidance of his friend Carl while they were kayaking together in the ocean. As Warren explained how transformative and empowering these wilderness experiences were for the homeless children, Carl urged him to "let go of the lamp post" and pursue his passion in wilderness education. Warren decided to resign his position at Transition House immediately. Cyndi supported him wholeheartedly, and when Warren told the Executive Director of Transition House what he intended to do, she suggested that he remain at Transition House for ninety days while he and Cyndi established their new venture. A volunteer at the shelter, learning of Warren and Cyndi's plans, introduced them to his parents, who owned land and a business in the Cuyama Valley and ran a small family foundation in Santa Barbara.

The philanthropists gave Warren and Cyndi free office space and their utilities for two years, and a check for $25,000 to enable them to launch Wilderness Youth Project, a non-profit organization dedicated to teaching young children survival skills and ethical land stewardship values through educational wilderness experiences. They also offered them the use of their 160-acre property in the Cuyama Valley for creating a basecamp. Their land adjoined Black's Ranch, and Warren and Cyndi often took the campers across the ranch to Quail Springs in search of animal tracks.

Warren and Cyndi, through their many and diverse life experiences, discovered a profound sense of the significance of patterns in human lives and nature and the possibility of recognizing and interpreting them through a combination of intuition and knowledge. Patterns exist that link the modern scientific world, with its rational approach to reality, to indigenous wisdom transmitted in dreams, visions, and stories. Warren writes: "All over the world, an ancient way of being has combined its elemental forces with the truths gained in the modern age to spark the fires of a new and imperative revolution. It is a subtle revolution of *knowing the story of where all that sustains us comes from, and of honoring those things deeply.*" This knowing brought them to recognize permaculture, which is based on the concept of making human systems consistent with the patterns of nature, and whose ethics and principles fit perfectly with their ongoing work. Through family connections—more patterns—Warren was led to study permaculture under its founder, Bill Mollison.

Mollison grew up in Tasmania, living in a small village whose residents followed a self-sufficient, subsistence lifestyle. While teaching at the University of Tasmania in 1974, he developed with David Holmgren the framework for a sustainable agricultural system based on a multi-crop of perennial trees, shrubs, herbs, fungi, and root systems—the antithesis of the prevalent mono-crop system being employed in large-scale commercial agriculture. Holmgren and Mollison described their method as permaculture, defined as: "The conscious design and maintenance of agriculturally productive ecosystems which have the diversity, stability, and resilience of natural ecosystems. It is the harmonious integration of landscape and people providing their food, energy, shelter, and other material and non-material needs in a sustainable way." (Quail Springs can thus be seen as an operational definition of permaculture.) The concept of permaculture has evolved to describe any human system that includes strategies for land access, business structure, and regional self-financing.

Not a cookie-cutter program, permaculture is a design method whose core principles of holistic integration of system elements for maximum yield and minimum waste are derived from other disciplines such as ecology, energy conservation, landscape design, and environmental science. These principles are underscored with permaculture's three-fold ethic of "earth care, people care, and fair share."

Mollison believes that sustainable human systems are possible only if designed to be in harmony with broader natural ecosystems, and he sees conventional agriculture as based on the false assumption of human superiority to nature, a paradigm he insists must be abandoned if human society is to survive. "Without permanent agriculture, there is no possibility of a stable social order," he wrote. "Conventional farming does not recognize and pay its true costs. The land is mined of its fertility to produce annual grain and vegetable crops; non-renewable resources [fossil fuels] are used to support yields; the land is eroded through over-stocking of animals and extensive plowing; land and water are polluted with chemicals."

The implications of permaculture move society and its members away from the chimera of endless growth based on consumerism and waste in the direction of a spiritual relationship to nature that is aligned with ancient indigenous practices but makes use of the knowledge gained through modern environmental science. "All we need to live a good life lies about us," Mollison reminds us. "Sun, wind, people, buildings, stones, sea, birds, and plants surround us. Cooperation with all these things brings harmony, opposition to them brings disaster and chaos."

Mollison and Holmgren developed a Permaculture Design Course that lays out all the elements that must be considered to create a sustainable, holistic human settlement system, regardless of its location. During the 1980s, Mollison brought permaculture to the United States through the formation of the Permaculture Institute of North America. The movement also spread to England and Europe and is now global. By 2002, it was estimated that five hundred to one thousand teachers had trained 100,000 people worldwide in permaculture through the design course. An online database (permacultureglobal.org) started by David Holmgren currently lists over two thousand active permaculture projects, among them Quail Springs.

Five years after founding Wilderness Youth Project, Warren and Cyndi's non-profit organization bought Black's Ranch. They laid out an ambitious two hundred year vision for the land. They began with a definition of sustainability: "A sustainable system must produce more energy than it consumes, enough in surplus to maintain and replace that system's elements over each element's lifetime." Warren and Cyndi saw themselves and their first collaborators on the land as a "pioneer species" in a long succession process that would culminate with a fully restored watershed ecosystem supporting a village that would serve as a model teaching vehicle drawing from a long lineage of experience on the land. They identified the key milestones that lay along the path of succession in categories that included ecological restoration, agriculture, housing, education, finances, and relationship building with the community. Some milestones have been reached on time, some delayed, some abandoned as unworkable, still others modified according to feedback from the land and the community. The vision is a work in progress.

A dramatic example of feedback from the land came in October 2010 when heavy rainfall over two days triggered a flood that sent a wall of water nearly 1,000 feet wide coursing across the farm. The flood washed away a garden, a pond, and the water harvesting structures that had been built to keep water from the springs on the landscape. Tractors, irrigation systems, myriad plantings, and fencing were destroyed. The three hundred year flood event wiped out nearly six years of work building soil and laying agricultural infrastructure. The disaster forced the farm's designers to rethink their water management strategies and gave everyone a lesson in the challenges of sustainability in our time of extreme weather events resulting from climate change. Recovery from the damage required several years of work. Another heavy rainstorm event in July 2015 damaged only the water recovery system for the springs, and it was functioning again after two days of repairs.

In 2008 Warren and Cyndi began a dialogue with a friend about operating a for-profit permaculture farm located closer to the urban centers of Ventura and Santa Barbara, where products of the farm could be sold. They began a conversation with this friend, who was also a potential investor who wished to divest some of her assets from "securities" into "natural capital." In 2012 they partnered in the creation of Regenerative Earth Farms LLC and purchased for $2 million a working forty-nine-acre farm planted with twenty-two acres of organic Haas avocados, two acres of persimmons, and one acre of apples, all producing positive cash flow. Additionally, the farm had three acres of bottomland suitable for annual crops, a market garden, cable houses, and an herb garden. There was also a dilapidated creamery, two conventionally powered residences, and room for other useful structures. The farm is located in the Casitas Valley, six miles inland from the Pacific Ocean, just east of Carpinteria.

Warren and Cyndi joined with members of their family to live together on the farm in fulfillment of what Cyndi describes as "the family's longing desire to be in close relation to our aging parents, future generations (i.e., grandbabies!), and in a land where we could truly honor and share in the unfolding stories and songs of life and death together." The passing of Warren's father in 2010 was an important catalyst for this "coming together."

With the generous help of family and friends, a central kitchen was built, pigs and chickens were added to the mix, the existing creamery was rebuilt and upgraded, and a roadside farmstand was opened on Highway 150 that sells meat from the pigs, organic produce from the farm, artisan cheeses made in the creamery, craft items, and more. The farm also sells its products at local farmers' markets, grocers, and restaurants.

Additionally, Warren conducts month-long Permaculture Design Courses, as well as one-day workshops on permaculture topics and charcuterie techniques. He also consults internationally on permaculture projects and advises local farmers on sustainable agriculture practices and land stewardship. Cyndi helps to co-manage the farm, assists in the care and tending of farm animals, operates the roadside farmstand, and fosters balance in the relationships with the wild and all who live and pass through the farm. She, along with others, serves as a host with Warren in the Permaculture Design Course.

———•———

On the second day of my visit to Quail Springs during the summer of 2015, I joined Brenton Kelly, the farm's watershed steward, on a goat walk. Twice a day, the small herd of goats is walked across the landscape to forage on the native plants that grow in abundance on the floor of the canyon. Goats are known for eating almost anything, but they particularly favor delicacies like buckwheat and elderberry.

Kelly is a giant of a man, seven feet tall, thin, and straight as the poplars that shade the farm's food forest. While the goats shuffled eagerly in their pen, Brenton picked up a long poplar branch that had been shaved clean of its bark by the goats, snapped it in two across his knee as though it were a match stick, and began to whittle one end into a point. He explained that walking with the staff made it easier to guide the goats because it made him look like a three-legged animal. Goats, he said, have little respect for bipeds. Carrying two staffs would make him even more welcomed by the herd. I asked if I could carry a staff, too, and he obligingly handed me the other half of the limb.

He opened the gate to the pen, and the goats trotted out in a bunch. Some wore bells around their necks that clanked melodiously in tempo with the patter of their hooves on the dirt road. Waiting for them patiently was Oakley, a massive white Great Pyrenees dog who serves as their chaperone, giving them the security of knowing that no predator would dare approach while they browse.

As the goats strung out along the road, Brenton pointed to three large females wearing bells. They ambled along unhurriedly at the back of the herd. "Leading from behind," Brenton winked. "They control where the herd goes. The one in front is not the leader. She's just curious. This one," he said, pointing to a small female with a tawny hide who was straying off the path by herself into the brush, "doesn't like to follow. She wears a bell with a distinctive ring so I can keep track of her."

With Oakley patrolling the perimeter of our walk, the goats fanned out across the landscape, feeding at will. Brenton remarked that he alternates north and south walks across the property to avoid overgrazing any one area. There's plenty of forage on the uncultivated 447 acres to feed a herd this size indefinitely, assuming the land is well watered.

As the watershed steward, Brenton is responsible for making sure that it is. The goats' wandering had brought us to the slope above the farm's center, where five large storage tanks held the water being harvested from the spring. Brenton climbed a ladder and peered down into one of them, noting with satisfaction that it was three-quarters full. The tanks can hold 40,000 gallons of water, enough to supply the farm's operations for two weeks. On average, over a year, the farm uses three thousand gallons per day, though consumption can rise to as much as seven thousand gallons per day, an amount that equals the daily harvest from the spring.

We were slowly following the goats through the sagebrush towards the east end of the property. I was hoping to see the springs and the catchment basin where the pooled water is diverted into pipes. But the herd had veered off to the south side of the road and crossed the stream. We descended the steep bank, and Brenton showed me how he had contoured the streambed to make the water flow more slowly across the farm, meandering the way a snake slithers. He pointed out the dampness in the banks, a sign that the riparian zone was holding the water. Cottonwood trees were flourishing along the banks, giving shade and holding the soil.

We walked back to the farm's core. The goats' bellies bulged from their foraging. As they approached their waiting pen, one of them brushed softly against my leg, and I patted her. Inside the pen, they lined up at the water trough to drink, then settled down on their haunches, chewing their cuds.

Brenton led me up to the cob house he shares with his wife Jan. It sits on a level shelf above the goat pen, overlooking the food forest. We entered through a beautiful wooden door with a stained-glass window. The door, Brenton told me, came from a house in Mendocino, California and had been resized to accommodate his height. The interior was cool and spacious, though it contains only six hundred and fifty square feet, enough for a large bed, a sitting area facing a small fireplace, a desk and chair tucked under a loft sleeping platform used by Brenton's daughter when she visits.

Brenton briefly reviewed issues that Quail Springs has faced with the County of Ventura, whose building codes were not written with cob houses in mind. Brenton's dwelling looks more like a sculpture than a conventional house. The only right angles you can find are in the doorway. Otherwise, the structure is a continuous flow of soft lines. Quail Springs has evaded the strictures of the code by having its natural buildings classified as livestock shelters. "Jan and I are considered goats," Brenton chuckled. He said county officials are cooperating with them to enable "green" buildings like his home to be built. Nearby stands another cob house, small but equally beautiful, that is used primarily as a demonstration model. It was built by students who had enrolled in the natural building program at the farm. The county's building director recognizes that although cob houses are made from simple, primitive materials, they require very little energy consumption to build and inhabit, and are extremely eco-friendly. "The technology is a little bit ahead of the regulatory curve," he admits.

———•———

Two stresses on industrial civilization are now converging in rapidly moving and related trends that threaten the future of society as we know it. One stress is the phenomenon of peak oil, the tipping point beyond which production of the non-renewable fossil fuels that power industry and enable our consumer lifestyle to go into irreversible decline. Estimates vary for the date at which peak oil occurs. Some analysts believe it has already passed; others predict a tipping point somewhere between 2030 and 2040. If energy from non-renewable resources declines faster than it can be replaced by alternative, renewable sources, our industrial and commercial systems will not be able to sustain the growth needed to support the planet's expanding human population. Degradation of the way of life in both highly developed and developing nations will surely follow, with developing nations suffering most heavily. Signs around the world abound that this process has already begun, especially the dislocation of populations in the less developed world and the Middle East.

The second stress is climate change, which the world's scientific community has unequivocally concluded is being caused by global warming traceable to greenhouse gas emissions from the burning of fossil fuels. Climate change is altering ecosystems across the planet, damaging habitat, and jeopardizing food supplies.

The more we burn fossil fuels, the faster we will move down the slope of descent from peak oil, and the more we will accelerate climate change. David Holmgren, one of the founders of permaculture, has outlined four possible scenarios for our energy future:

- Under the "techno-explosion" scenario, new, large, concentrated energy sources will come online, allowing us to continue on our path of material and economic growth in spite of constraints from the environment.
- The "techno-stability" scenario assumes that alternative, renewable energy sources will be sufficient to replace the power derived from declining fossil fuel sources and permit a sustainable leveling off of material well being at or near current levels.
- "Energy descent" predicts a reduction in economic activity, social and political complexity, and population as fossil fuels are depleted. Human society will move in the direction of preindustrial forms, powered by advanced technologies less rich in energy than fossil fuels, and by biological sources such as animal energy.
- "Collapse" occurs when fossil fuel depletion and radical climate change combine to bring about a disintegration of the natural and human systems that maintain and support industrial society.

Holmgren believes that the "energy descent" scenario is the most likely to occur and that it could occur in four variations, depending on the rate of fossil fuel depletion and the rate and severity of climate change. Each variant has consequences for social and political institutions, human settlements, and, most importantly, food supplies. The most benign variant that allows a gradual process of adaptation results from slow energy descent and mild climate change. Other variants are more ominous.

Faced with these futures, permaculture offers us a hopeful, positive response. Its greatest value is its ethical framework, which asks us to live more wisely, more compassionately, within the limits that nature imposes and in harmony with the earth that is our home. Its principles show us how. I have seen them in operation at Quail Springs and Casitas Valley Farm and can testify that they work. Warren and Cyndi Brush, and thousands more like them across the planet, are leading us forward by reminding us of our deepest roots in the earth.

Sources

Introduction

McGiffert, Michael. *The Character of Americans: A Book of Readings*. Homewood, Illinois: The Dorsey Press, 1970.

Rapson, Richard, ed. *Individualism and Conformity in the American Character*. Boston: D. C. Heath and Company, 1967.

Young, Ralph. *Dissent in America: Voices that Shaped a Nation*. New York, Pearson Longman, 2008.

———. *Dissent: The History of an American Idea*. New York, London: New York University Press, 2015.

Chapter 1: Roger Williams

Barry, John. *Roger Williams and the Creation of the American Soul*. New York: Viking, 2012.

Brockunier, Samuel Hugh. *The Irrepressible Democrat Roger Williams*. New York: The Ronald Press Company, 1940.

Caldwell, Samuel L., ed. *The Complete Writings of Roger Williams*. Vols. 3 & 4. New York: Russell & Russell, 1963.

Chadwick, Owen. *The Reformation*. Grand Rapids: Eerdmans, 1964. Print Pelican History of the Church; v.3.

Grimm, Harold John. *The Reformation Era, 1500-1650*. 2d ed. New York: Macmillan, 1973. Print.

Johnson, Claudia Durst. *Daily Life in Colonial New England*. Westport, CT: Greenwood Press, 2002.

LaFantasie, Glenn W., ed. *The Correspondence of Roger Williams*. 2 vols. Providence, RI: Brown University Press, 1988.

Morison, Samuel Eliot. *The Oxford History of the American People*. New York: Oxford University Press, 1965.

Parrington, Vernon. *Main Currents in American Thought*. Vol. 1. *The Colonial Mind*. New York: Harcourt, Brace, and Company, 1930.

Selinger, Suzanne. *Calvin Against Himself: an inquiry in intellectual history*. Hamden, CT: Archon Books, 1984.

Smith, James Morton, ed. *Seventeenth-Century America; essays in colonial history*. Chapel Hill: University of North Carolina Press, 1959.

Straus, Oscar. *Roger Williams: The Pioneer of Religious Liberty*. New York: The Century Co., 1894.

Vaughan, Alden and Bremer, Francis, eds. *Puritan New England: essays on religion, society, and culture*. New York: St. Martin's Press, 1977.

Wills, Garry. *Head and Heart: American Christianities*. New York: Penguin Press, 2007.

Winship, Michael. *The Times and Trials of Anne Hutchinson: Puritans Divided*. Lawrence, KS: University Press of Kansas, 2005.

Chapter 2: Anne Bradstreet

Gordon, Charlotte. *Mistress Bradstreet*. New York, Boston: Little, Brown, and Co., 2005.

Hensley, Jeannine, ed. *The Works of Anne Bradstreet*. Cambridge, MA: Harvard University Press, 2010.

Kellogg, D.B. *Anne Bradstreet*. Nashville: Thomas Nelson, 2010

Morgan, Edmund S. *The Puritan Family*. Boston: Trustees of the Public Library, 1944.

Porterfield, Amanda. *Female Piety in Puritan New England*. New York, Oxford: Oxford University Press, 1992.

Stanford, Ann. *Anne Bradstreet: The Worldly Puritan*. New York: Burt Franklin & Co., 1974.

Ulrich, Laurel Thatcher. *Good Wives: Image and Reality in the Lives of Women in Northern New England 1650-1750*. New York: Alfred A. Knopf, 1982.

Chapter 3: Thomas Paine

Foner, Eric. *Tom Paine and Revolutionary America*. New York: Oxford University Press, 2005.

Foner, Philip S. *The Complete Writings of Thomas Paine*. New York: Citadel Press, 1945.

Keane, John. *Tom Paine. A Political Life*. Boston: Little, Brown and Company, 1995.

Morison, Samuel Eliot. *The Oxford History of the American People*. New York: Oxford University Press, 1965.

Wilson, Jerome D. and Ricketson, William F. *Thomas Paine*. Boston: G.K. Hall & Co., 1978.

Chapter 4: Josiah Gregg

Bolton, Herbert Eugene, and Thomas Maitland Russell. *The Colonization of North America, 1492-1783*. New York: The Macmillan Co., 1930.

Fernandez-Shaw, Carlos M. *The Hispanic Presence in North America From 1492 To Today*. New York, Oxford: Facts on File, 1987

Fulton, Maurice, ed. *Diary and Letters of Josiah Gregg*. Southwestern Enterprises. Norman: University of Oklahoma Press, 1941.

Gibson, Arrell Morgan. *The American Indian—Prehistory to the Present*. Lexington, MA; Toronto: D.C. Heath and Company, 1980.

Gregg, Josiah. *Commerce of the Prairies*. Ed. Max L. Moorhead. Norman: University of Oklahoma Press, 1954.

Horgan, Paul. *Josiah Gregg and His Vision of the Early West*. New York: Farrar Straus Giroux, 1941.

Morison, Samuel Eliot. *The Oxford History of the American People*. New York: Oxford University Press, 1965

Natella, Arthur A. *The Spanish in America, 1513-1974. A Chronology and Fact Book*. New York: Oceana Publications, 1975.

Nugent, Walter. *Habits of Empire*. New York: Alfred A. Knopf, 2008.

Van Every, Dale. *The Final Challenge: The American Frontier 1804-1845*. New York: Quill/William Morrow, 1964.

Chapter 5: William and Ellen Craft

Blassingame, John W. *The Slave Community: Plantation Life in the Antebellum South*. New York: Oxford University Press, 1972.

Craft, William. *Running a Thousand Miles For Freedom*. New York: Arno Press and The New York Times, 1969.

Drescher, Seymour. *Abolition: A History of Slavery and Anti-Slavery*. New York: Cambridge University Press, 2009.

Fishel Leslie and Quarles, Benjamin. *The Black American: A Brief Documentary History*. Glenview, IL: Scott, Foresman and Company, 1976.

Franklin, John Hope. *Runaway Slaves: Rebels on the Plantation*. New York, Oxford: Oxford University Press, 1999.

Fogel, Robert William. *Without Consent or Contract: The Rise and Fall of American Slavery*. New York, London: W.W. Norton & Company, 1989.

Fradin, Judith Bloom and Fradin, Dennis Brindel. *5,000 Miles to Freedom. Ellen and William Craft's Flight From Slavery*. Washington, D.C.: National Geographic, 2006.

Grant, Donald. *The Way It Was in the South: The Black Experience in Georgia*. New York: Birch Lane Press, 1993.

Jefferson, Paul, ed. *The Travels of William Wells Brown*. New York: Markus Wiener Publishing, Inc., 1991.

Litwack, Leon. *North of Slavery: The Negro in the Free States, 1790-1860*. Chicago, University of Chicago Press, 1961.

Morison, Samuel Eliot. *The Oxford History of the American People*. New York: Oxford University Press, 1965.

Oakes, James. *The Ruling Race: A History of American Slaveholders*. New York: Alfred A. Knopf, 1982.

Phillips, William D., Jr. *Slavery from Roman Times To the Early Transatlantic Trade*. Minneapolis: University of Minnesota Press, 1985.

Sterling, Dorothy. *Black Foremothers*. New York: McGraw-Hill, 1979.

Chapter 6: Thorstein Veblen

Beatty, Jack. *Age of Betrayal: The Triumph of Money in America, 1865-1900*. New York: Alfred A. Knopf, 2007.

Diggins, John Patrick. *Thorstein Veblen—Theorist of the Leisure Class*. Princeton, New Jersey: Princeton University Press, 1999.

Dorfman, Joseph. *Thorstein Veblen and His America*. New York: A.M. Kelley, 1961.

Edwards, Rebecca. *New Spirits: Americans in the Gilded Age, 1865-1905*. New York; Oxford: Oxford University Press, 2006.

Hofstadter, Richard. *The Age of Reform. From Bryan to FDR*. New York: Alfred A. Knopf, 1981.

Horowitz, Irving Louis, ed. *Veblen's Century. A Collective Portrait*. New Brunswick and London: Transaction Publishers, 2002.

Jorgensen, Elizabeth and Jorgensen, Henry. *Thorstein Veblen: Victorian Firebrand*. Armonk, New York; London: M.E. Sharpe, 1999.

Lerner, Max, ed. *The Portable Veblen*. New York: The Viking Press, 1948.

Morison, Samuel Eliot. *The Oxford History of the American People*. New York: Oxford University Press, 1965.

Rees, Jonathan. *Industrialization and the Transformation of American Life*. Armonk, New York; London: M.E. Sharpe, 2013.

Chapter 7: Thomas Merton

Arendt, Hannah. *The Human Condition*. Chicago & London: University of Chicago Press, 1958.

Cunningham, Lawrence, ed. *Thomas Merton: Spiritual Master*. New York: Paulist Press, 1992.

Furlong, Monica. *Merton: A Biography*. San Francisco: Harper & Row, 1980.

Heilbroner, Robert. *The Future as History*. New York: Harper & Row, 1959.

Marcuse, Herbert. *One Dimensional Man*. Boston: Beacon Press, 1964.

McDonnell, Thomas P., ed. *A Thomas Merton Reader*. New York: Harcourt, Brace & World, Inc., 1961

Merton, Thomas. *The Seven Storey Mountain*. New York: Harcourt, Brace & Company, 1948.

Mott, Michael. *The Seven Mountains of Thomas Merton*. Boston: Houghton Mifflin, 1984.

Ruprecht, Louis A. "The Gift of Gay." *USC Annenberg Religion Dispatches*, April 17, 2012.

Shannon, William. *Silent Lamp: The Thomas Merton Story*. New York: Crossroad, 1992.

Suzuki, Daisetz Teitaro. *An Introduction to Zen Buddhism*. New York: Philosophical Library, 1949.

Wilkes, Paul, ed. *Merton By Those Who Knew Him Best*. San Francisco: Harper & Row, 1984.

Chapter 8: Brummett Echohawk

Bernstein. Alison R. *American Indians and World War II*. Norman, Oklahoma and London: University of Oklahoma Press, 1991.

Bishop, Leo V., Glasgow, Frank J., and Fisher, George A. *The Fighting Forty-Fifth: The Combat Report of an Infantry Division*. Baton Rouge, Louisiana: Army and Navy Publishing Company, 1946.

Echohawk, Brummett. "The Pawnee Story." *Westerners Brand Book*. May 1957: 17-19, 22-23. Print.

Hagen, William T. *American Indians*. Chicago: University of Chicago Press, 1979.

Morison, Samuel Eliot. *The Oxford History of the American People*. New York: Oxford University Press, 1965.

Munsell, Warren. *The Story of a Regiment: A History of the 179th Regimental Combat Team*. Warren P. Munsell, Jr., 1948.

Oswalt, Wendell and Neely, Sharlotte. *This Land Was Theirs: A Study of North American Indians*. London, Toronto: Mayfield Publishing Company, 1996.

Parks, Douglas R. "Pawnee." *North American Indians*. Volume 13, Part 1: Plains. Edited by Raymond De Mallie. Washington, DC: Smithsonian Institution, 2001.

Whitlock, Flint. *The Rock of Anzio. From Sicily to Dachau: A History of the 45th Infantry Division*. Westview Press, A Member of the Perseus Books Group, 1998.

Youngbull, Kristin. "Brummett Echohawk: *Chaticks-si-chaticks*." Diss. Arizona State University, 2012.

Chapter 9: Judith Baca

Acuña, Rodolfo. *Anything But Mexican: Chicanos in Contemporary Los Angeles*. New York & London: Verso, 1996.

Baca, Judith F. "The Human Story at the Intersection of Ethics, Aesthetics, and Social Justice." *Journal of Moral Education*, Vol. 34, No. 2 (June 2005).

Hammond, Harmony. "Judith F. Baca" in *Lesbian Art in America: A Contemporary History*. New York: Rizzoli International Publications, 2000.

Mesa-Bains, Amalia. "Oral History Interviews with Judith Baca." *Archives of American Art, Smithsonian Institution* (August 1986).

Olmstead, Mary. *Judy Baca*. Chicago: Raintree, 2005.

Rios-Bustamente, Antonio, and Castillo, Pedro. *An Illustrated History of Mexican Los Angeles 1781-1985*. Los Angeles: University of California, Chicano Studies Research Center Publications, 1986.

Rochfort, Desmond. *Mexican Muralists*. San Francisco: Chronicle Books, 1993.

Social and Public Art Resource Center. http://www.sparcinla.org

Starr, Kevin. *California: A History*. New York: Random House, 2007.

Stein, Philip. *The Mexican Murals*. Mexico, D.F.: Eclitur, 1984.

Chapter 10: Warren Brush and Cynthia Harvan-Brush

Allbright, Robert. *Cuyama Valley Yesterday and Today.* [Ventura, CA]: R & A Publishing Company, 1989.

Bell, Graham. *The Permaculture Way: Practical Steps to Create a Self-Sustaining World.* White River Junction, VT: Chelsea Green Publishing, 2005.

Broyles-Gonzalez, Yolanda and Khus, Pilulaw. *Earth Wisdom: A California Chumash Woman.* Tucson: University of Arizona Press, 2011.

Brush, Warren and Harvan-Brush, Cynthia. Interview by Arthur Hoyle. Ventura, California. July 6, 2015; August 3, 2015.

Cooper, Lara. "Heavy Rains Wash Away Years of Work at Quail Springs," *Noozhawk* (October 6, 2010).

Fukuoka, Masanobu. *Sowing Seeds in the Desert: Natural Farming, Global Restoration, and Ultimate Food Security.* White River Junction, VT: Chelsea Green Publishing, 2012.

Gamble, Lynn H. *The Chumash World at European Contact: Power, Trade, and Feasting Among Complex Hunter-Gatherers.* Berkeley, Los Angeles, London: University of California Press, 2008.

Gore, Albert, Jr. *The Future: Six Drivers of Global Change.* New York: Random House, 2013.

Greer, John Michael. *The Ecotechnic Future: Envisioning a Post-Peak Future.* Gabriola Island, BC: New Society Publishers, 2009.

Holmgren, David. *Future Scenarios: How Communities Can Adapt to Peak Oil and Climate Change.* White River Junction, VT: Chelsea Green Publishing, 2009.

Intergovernmental Panel on Climate Change. *Climate Change 2014. Synthesis Report. Summary for Policy Makers.* http://www.ipcc.ch

Jaffe, Joss. "Quail Springs: An Experiment in Permaculture Design." MA Thesis, Landscape Architecture. University of Arizona, 2007.

Kelly, Brenton. Interview by Arthur Hoyle. Ventucopa, California. July 26, 2015.

Kettmann, Matt. "Cuyama Valley Drying Up," *Santa Barbara Independent* (August 21, 2014)

————. "Getting Grief for Going Green," *Santa Barbara Independent* (September 10, 2009).

Kolbert, Elizabeth. *The Sixth Extinction: An Unnatural History.* New York: Henry Holt and Company, 2014.

McBay, Aric and Keith, Lierre. *Deep Green Resistance.* New York: Seven Stories Press, 2011.

Mollison, Bill. *Introduction to Permaculture.* Tyalgum, Australia: Tagari Publications, 1991.

————. *Permaculture: A Designers Manual.* Tyalgum, Australia: Tagari Publications, 1988.

Ray, Paul and Anderson, Sherry Ruth. *Cultural Creatives: How 50 Million People are Changing the World.* New York: Three Rivers Press, 2000.

Robinson, Richard Gotch. *Ventura County Beginnings*. [Ventura, CA]: The Last Teller Press, 2011.

Scott, Robert. "A Critical Review of Permaculture in the United States." http://www. robscott. net (January 1, 2010).

Schoenherr, Allan A. *A Natural History of California*. Berkeley, CA: University of California Press, 1992.

Smith, Jan. Interview by Arthur Hoyle. Ventucopa, California. July 26, 2015.

United States Environmental Protection Agency. *Climate Change*. http://www.epa.gov

Triem, Judith. *Ventura County: Land of Good Fortune*. Northridge, CA: Windsor Publications, Inc., 1985.

Van Dyke, Theodore S. *Southern California: Its Valleys, Hills, and Streams; Its Animals, Birds and Fishes; Its Gardens, Farms, and Climate*. New York: Fords, Howard & Hulbert, 1886.

Woodworth, Paddy. *Our Once and Future Planet: Restoring the World in the Climate Change Century*. Chicago: University of Chicago Press, 2013.

Index

About the Author

Arthur Hoyle is a writer, educator, and independent filmmaker. His documentary films have won numerous awards and have aired on PBS, and he received a media grant from the National Endowment for the Humanities. Before becoming an author, he produced corporate communications materials in print and video for a broad array of clients. He received Bachelors and Masters Degrees in English from the University of California, Los Angeles, and taught English, coached tennis, and served as an administrator in independent schools. He currently volunteers as a naturalist in the

Photo by Peter Register.

Santa Monica Mountains National Recreation Area, leading interpretive walks on Chumash Indian culture. His biography of Henry Miller, *The Unknown Henry Miller: A Seeker in Big Sur*, was published in March 2014 by Skyhorse/Arcade. He has also published essays in *Huffington Post*, *Empty Mirror*, *Across the Margin*, *Counterpunch*, and *AIOTB: As It Ought To Be*. He lives in Pacific Palisades, California.

Made in the USA
Columbia, SC
28 March 2020